Embo(

OSIRIS

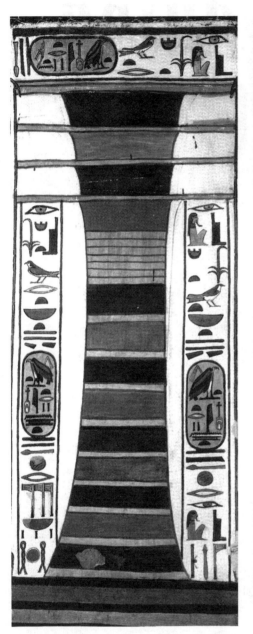

Djed Pillar and Osiris.

Embodying OSIRIS

THE SECRETS OF ALCHEMICAL TRANSFORMATION

Thom F. Cavalli, PhD

Theosophical Publishing House
Wheaton, Illinois * Chennai, India

First Quest Edition 2010

Quest Books
Theosophical Publishing House
P. O. Box 270
Wheaton, IL 60187-0270

www.questbooks.net

Cover image: Mural painting of Osiris. Burial chamber from 19th dynasty. Copyright © DeA Picture Library/Art Resource, NY.
Cover design by Margarita Reyfman.

Library of Congress Cataloging-in-Publication Data

Cavalli, Thom F. (Thom Frank).
Embodying Osiris: the secrets of alchemical transformation / Thom F. Cavalli.—1st Quest ed.
    p.   cm.
Includes bibliographical references and index.

ISBN 978-0-8356-0880-0

1. Osiris (Egyptian deity)   2. Alchemy—Psychological aspects.   3. Jungian psychology.
I. Title.
BL2450.O7C39 2010
299'.312113—dc22   2010017986

5   4   3   2   1   *   10   11   12   13   14

Printed in the United States of America

To my beloved sister and brother, Dyan and Robert

The decisive question for man is: Is he related to something infinite or not? . . . In the final analysis, we count for something only because of the essential we embody, and if we do not embody that, life is wasted.

—Carl Gustav Jung

Life's raison d'être *is to become conscious of oneself; then the* aim of life *is cosmic consciousness, the consciousness of the All, beyond transient and mortal contingencies. To accept and to attempt to fathom this, the teaching of all revealed religions, is worth living for.*

—R. A. Schwaller de Lubicz

CONTENTS

ILLUSTRATIONS

PRONUNCIATION KEY FOR MAJOR EGYPTIAN GODS AND PHARAOHS

GODS

Abubis	[uh-**noo**-bis]
Apopis	[uh-**poh**-is]
Aten	[**ah**tn]
Atum	[**ah**-tuh m]
Hathor	[**hath**-awr]
Horus	[**hawr**-uh s, **hohr**-uhs]
Isis	[**ahy**-sis]
Nephthys	[**nef**-thees]
Nun	[noon]
Nut	[noot]
Osiris	[oh-**sahy**-ris]
Ptah	[ptah]
Ra	[rah, ray]
Sekhmet	[**sek**-met]
Seth	[seth]
Tefnut	[**tef**-noot]
Thoth	[thohth, toht, thahth]

Note: Goddesses' names always end in *–et*. Most names, however, have been changed from the original language (Coptic, Greek, Latin, etc.) and therefore do not follow this rule. Isis's name, for example, was originally *Aset*, Hathor was *Het*, and Neith was *Net*.

PHARAOHS

Akhenaten	[ak-nat-n, a-ke-na-ten]
Hatshepsut	[hat-**shep**-set]
Imhotep	[im-hoh-tep]
Ptolemy	[tol-uh-mee]
Ramses	[ram-seez]
Tutankhamun	[toot-eng-**kah**-muh n]

The above pronunciation key is only meant as a guide to enliven the reader's experience. We do not know how these names were actually pronounced—they changed over time and place. Pronunciations are different according to each country's language. At best, this is how people in the English-speaking world pronounce these names today.

FOREWORD

We are separated from those who came before us not only by time but by sensibility. The ancient Romans are reasonably close; we can gaze at their marble busts and see them almost as people we know. The ancient Greeks and Hebrews are a step further removed, although we can still recognize in them the lineaments of our cultural ancestors. But when we come to Egypt, we hit a wall. The mind of every literate person is populated with images of Egypt—pyramids, mummies, bird-headed gods, ladies with eyelids green from ground malachite—and scholars have probed into the life of that nation with every tool of ingenuity. We know which Pharaoh ascended the throne in which year; we know what the hieroglyphs say and even how much beer the Egyptians drank. But for all this, their world, haunting, mysterious, ever-beckoning but ever-receding, holds us at a distance. We approach it as we might approach the sun setting in a Saharan landscape—we appear to come closer, but we never do.

One of the strangest and most distinctive features of Egyptian art reinforces this impression. Their paintings depict the faces of figures in profile, while the eyes remain frontal. We see only one side of the face and one eye—but that eye appears to be gazing at the viewer. Thus it is with Egypt as a whole: it confronts us directly with its single eye (an ancient symbol of spiritual perception), but half its face is always averted. The ceaseless flow of books, excavations, museum exhibits, and bizarre theories of "alternative history" constantly promises to reveal this hidden side of the face of Egypt, but somehow it never does.

Thom Cavalli's *Embodying Osiris* highlights another way of looking at the ancient Egyptians. It takes their central myth—the death and resurrection of Osiris—as an illustration of certain processes that occur both in the universe and in the human psyche. As Cavalli suggests, it may be more accurate to see the Egyptian gods not so much as divine personages ruling over certain isolated spheres of reality, as the Greeks and Romans of late antiquity did (so that Mars presides over war somewhat like a secretary of defense), but as the embodiments of certain fundamental processes.

To understand this view, we might turn to a work that is as old as the myths of Egypt. The Indian *Rig Veda* (much of which was composed, probably, in the second millennium BC) includes a hymn to a storm god named Vata. Part of it says, "Moving along his paths in the middle realm of space, he does not rest even for a single day. Friend of the waters, first-born keeper of the Law, where was he born? What was he created from? Breath of the gods, embryo of the universe, this god wanders wherever he pleases. His sounds are heard, but his form is not seen. Let us worship the gale with oblation.[1]

As these lines imply, Vata is not the god of the storm; he *is* the storm. He does not exist apart from his manifestations in nature; he is identical with them. In a way, such a view of the universe comes close to the contemporary scientific outlook. The ancient view differs in this respect only: it sees these events—storm and wind and sun—not as impersonal forces but as personal beings that can be addressed and propitiated and appeased. This, we could say, is the basis of all paganism.

But the gods of the Osiris myth are not quite in this category; rather, their nature and power go further and deeper still. One man who understood this dynamic was Plutarch. Best known as a biographer, Plutarch, who lived in the first century AD, was an initiate into the ancient mysteries; indeed, he spent the last thirty years of his life as a priest at Delphi. His treatise *On Isis and Osiris* gives the most complete version of a myth that is known only in fragments from Egyptian sources. In this work he considers, and dismisses, the possibilities that Isis and Osiris are merely mythologized depictions of the moon and sun, as well as deriding the "dull crowd" who associate these gods "either with changes of the atmosphere according to the season, or with the generation of the corn and sowings and ploughings, and in saying that Osiris is buried when the sown corn is hidden by the earth, and comes to life and shows himself again when it begins to sprout."[2]

Plutarch would have had little use for Sir James Frazer, whose classic study *The Golden Bough* makes exactly this equation: "In one of his aspects the god was a personification of the corn, which may be said to die and come to life every year."[3] Frazer adds that Osiris in his other aspects was a tree spirit and a fertility god. Frazer, a monumentally erudite classicist, was familiar with Plutarch's text, which he quotes in his own writings, but he evidently did not take it seriously.

What did Plutarch himself think? Here is his view of Set, the villain of the Osiris drama, whom the Greeks called Typhon: "Neither drought nor wind nor sea nor darkness is the essential of Typhon, but the whole hurtful and destructive [element] which is in nature." That is, Set is not merely a destructive aspect of the wind or sea, but the principle of destruction and dissolution that operates at all levels of nature—and in the human psyche as well. Plutarch goes on to say: "Typhon is the passionate and titanic and reasonless and impulsive [aspect] of the Soul, while of its corporeal [side he is] the death-dealing and pestilent and disturbing, with unseasonable times and intemperate atmospheres and concealments of sun and moon."

As for Osiris: "In the Soul [of cosmos], then, Mind and Reason (*Logos*), the guide and lord of all the best in it, is Osiris; and so in earth and air and water and heaven and stars, that which is ordered and appointed and in health, is the efflux of Osiris, reflected in seasons and temperatures and periods."[4] Isis is "the feminine [principle] of Nature and that which is capable of receiving the whole of genesis," while Horus is the force of reintegration, "who has not destroyed Typhon utterly, but has brought over to his side his efficacy and strength."[5]

In short, there are principles of order and destruction in the universe. None of these has complete supremacy, but they vie and alternate like the yang and yin of the *I Ching*. They express themselves at all levels of reality—in seasons and storms as well as in the human psyche. It is as if one were to take the primary forces known to contemporary physics—gravity, electromagnetism, and so on—and regard them as personal entities that we can anger and appease. As the Vedic hymn suggests, we may not know where these forces came from, but we are foolish to ignore them. They exist within us, and, as C. G. Jung understood, they are expressed in dreams and archetypes.

Even so, alchemical imagery is much more than a projection of unconscious elements in the psyche; it depicts genuine substances and processes that can be found in the alchemist's laboratory. But alchemy also differs from conventional chemistry in acknowledging that these same processes operate in the mind and soul of the practitioner and that the alchemist must work on himself as he works on his material.

That few grasp these mysteries is a testimony not to their falsity but to their subtlety and grandeur. One of the few practicing alchemists I know is a former professor of chemistry who left his field of study when it began to bore him. After all, it is comparatively easy to perform an experiment in chemistry: you follow the instructions, and you get certain results. In alchemy, it is not so. Everything must conjoin for the work to succeed: the planets, the materials, and even the soul of the alchemist must be in proper alignment. No set of directions can map out this process entirely. This may be why the directions are so cryptic.

What this process entails, and how it transforms the individual, is the theme of this book. As Cavalli's magisterial survey of Egyptian art and myth suggests, it may have been the central theme of Egypt itself.

—Richard Smoley
May 2010

Richard Smoley's latest book is *The Dice Game of Shiva: How Consciousness Creates the Universe*. He is also the author of *Inner Christianity: A Guide to the Esoteric Tradition*; *Conscious Love: Insights from Mystical Christianity*; *The Essential Nostradamus*; *Forbidden Faith: The Secret History of Gnosticism*; and *Hidden Wisdom: A Guide to the Western Inner Traditions* (with Jay Kinney). Smoley is the former editor of *Gnosis: A Journal of the Western Inner Traditions*. Currently he is editor of *Quest: Journal of the Theosophical Society in America* and of Quest Books.

INTRODUCTION:
EQUAL TO GOD

*Egypt is an image of heaven, or to speak more exactly, in Egypt all the
operations of the powers which rule and are active in heaven have been
transferred to a lower place. Even more than that, if the whole truth be
told, our land is the temple of the entire cosmos.*

—Thoth, *Corpus Hermeticum*

The most difficult obstacle in unraveling the secrets of ancient
Egypt is acknowledging the possibility that we might never know
what these people were really thinking. In Jungian psychology,
the unknown is relegated to the boundless world of the unconscious.
What little we know of this world is that it is the realm of dreams, archetypes, and myths. Certainly, the greater part of the unconscious is not
known and will remain forever beyond our grasp. But somewhere before
we reach this outer dimension is a mysterious place that lies just beyond
the threshold of our ordinary perception. We can, with some conditions,
apprehend this numinous territory. The secret of gaining access to this
place has to do with the way we view the unconscious and, for our present purpose, ancient Egypt.

Many people today struggle with the whole notion of the unconscious. Some are curious while others wrestle with ways to make sense

of it. Most people either give it no mind or do not believe it exists in any significant way. The unconscious world wasn't a problem in ancient Egypt. For these people, it was an explicit part of everyday life. Their gods were very much alive for them, and magic was widespread. Evidence of the unconscious is especially apparent in their cosmology and funerary rites. For example, an important step in the mummification process was the Opening of the Mouth ritual. In order for the spirit of the dead to function in the afterworld, the senses of the deceased body had to be reanimated. This ritual involved specific operations that enabled the spirit to see, hear, speak, and navigate through the underworld until it ascended into the heavens.

With some modification we can apply a similar approach to gaining access to the psychic land of mystery. Note that I equate the Egyptian's concrete conception of the underworld with our modern notion of the unconscious. In this way we will unveil secrets of the ancient past. More importantly, this approach offers an entirely different view of death and rebirth, one that is especially important to anyone interested in exploring the development of human consciousness. Specifically, the ancient world teaches us how to view death as a critical stage in an ongoing process of individuation that does not end with physical life.

What little we know of the unconscious shows us it not only contains vast amounts of information but also has a peculiar intelligence that reveals more of human nature than today's science might glean from rocks and artifacts. Modern science, bound by rational methods of inquiry, cannot fully account for the unconscious, which includes irrational content and is far more expansive than reason alone can grasp. The whole of humankind rests on pillars of a collective unconscious that spans all time—it is transpersonal. Such intelligence is not directly visible. We look at remnants of ancient Egypt but cannot fathom a world so radically different from ours. Misguided notions and unanswered questions abound. For instance, we may have cracked the code of the hieroglyphs, but we have no idea how these words sound or if they were ever spoken. Great debate still surrounds Egyptian religion: Was it truly polytheistic? Did these people have mystical experiences, or was their religion entirely concerned with salvation after death?

Despite many years of intense study of ancient Egypt, mystery still pervades this magical place. We are so fascinated by what our eyes see that we seldom ponder the deeper, mystical meaning of past traditions. "We don't realize," writes philosopher Jeremy Naydler, "that we live in the presence of mystery and we don't realize it because we are so distracted, so fascinated, by the apparent 'out-thereness' of everything."[1] Those who manage to look "inside" seem to make a deliberate effort to conceal their insights, perhaps for good reason. Power was the chief reason for keeping esoteric knowledge secret. A pharaoh's power rested on his unique ability to commune with the gods. He kept sacred knowledge within the royal bloodlines and out of the hands of those who might misuse it. Tomb robbers were a constant threat. Then, there were others: politically motivated revisers of history and those who purported to speak or channel the voices of ancient deities. For all these reasons a true, mystical understanding of ancient Egypt is extremely difficult to achieve and perhaps not possible at all.

The truth of this ancient land is as complex and elusive as that inscrutable expression on the face of the Sphinx. This is the mystery one must accept as we begin our Jungian exploration of the Osiris myth. Of course, I will offer dozens of interpretations and amplifications, but none of these is intended to explain the mystery of this strange god and the exotic country of his origin. A mystery can only be known by "divine revelation," and that comes by way of grace. At best, we can prepare our minds to receive such a blessing.

Most people love a good mystery story. It keeps us guessing and wondering where the narrative will end—who will survive and who will die. Authors manipulate plots to keep us in suspense. Like magicians, they deftly suspend disbelief with literary device and poetic license. We will certainly find all this and more in the myth of Osiris. But what of the mystery that has no conclusion, one that keeps us endlessly fascinated and in full pursuit of the unknown? This mystery lives up to its definition in that it keeps our eyes closed and our lips sealed tight. Osiris, the god of the dead, certainly offers a mystery that brings us eerily close to death, the greatest mystery of all. Maybe the way to complete the journey of individuation begins by passing through these gates: mystery and death, two subjects that will engage us throughout this book.

While I am aware of many hundreds of gods—pagan, Hindu, and Christian—I have rarely experienced the kind of mystery embodied in the archetypal image of Osiris. The antiquity of his myth transports us back in time to ingenious people who built the physical and psychic pillars on which the contemporary world rests. We are all familiar with their physical accomplishments, but to know Osiris is to discover the secrets behind his myth—movements that gave rise to the modern human psyche. Unlike the objective study of physical evolution, understanding the nature of psyche requires personal involvement. We must equip ourselves with imagination and "empathic engagement"[2] in order to reveal truths that lie hidden within ancient formulae, hieroglyphic texts, and cryptic images. We must embody this god, not just study him. By embodying Osiris we experience the kinetics of change. Indeed, Osiris is the god of being and becoming.

To master these secrets means to become like a god. A third-century text, the *Corpus Hermeticum*, states, "If you don't make yourself equal to God, you can't perceive God; for like is known by like. Leap free of everything that is physical, and grow as vast as that immeasurable vastness; step beyond all time and become eternal; then you will perceive God."[3]

This passage may sound like heresy to some, but it is not intended to offend. Rather, the purpose of the alchemists was to illuminate the power of creation each of us possesses. It is heresy only to those who reject mystery, can't tolerate paradox, and hold tightly to a strictly rational view of reality. The task before us is not to challenge God but to cultivate an inner sense of divinity that adds mystery to all human life. For this reason I will draw from the alchemists since they, unlike most modern scientists, never split psyche and soma; spirit resides in matter, God is within the province of human experience.

To define Osiris in any rational way is virtually impossible since the essence of his spirit is mercurial, numinous, and deeply mystical. While I will describe him in great detail, the mystery of his basic nature cannot be understood any more than we might expect to explain love. This inability is of course vexing to any author who wants to define his subject with accuracy and completeness. Such a claim I cannot make. I offer bits of myth, cosmology, and history that only hint at the mystery we call Osiris and point to important ways he touches our lives.

As with all gods, Osiris exists in the unconscious, and it is our job to resurrect him. In doing so we gain a depth of understanding that enriches our quality of life. Through deep understanding we learn that death is not to be feared. Instead, death is a teacher that shows us how creation comes by way of loss and regeneration. Physical death is a natural ending of material existence, but if we go no further than this objective explanation of loss, we lose all sense of the mystery that results from surrendering our physical life to a greater reality.

Mystery brings us to the limit of the known world. The philosopher Henry Corbin referred to this dimension as the "imaginal world." We naturally avoid this world. It has a disquieting effect on our sensibilities. The mind and senses are founded on the certainty that come with cognition and sensory experience. An imaginal view of life requires us to apprehend unseen realities. Imagination, wonder, intuition, curiosity, and mystery describe this numinous territory. On the one hand, we abhor the ruthlessness of a world that defies our most cherished faculty, rationality. It strips us of all attempts to organize data. Without this organizing principle, we do not have the means to form comforting concepts like wholeness, closure, and unity. Paradoxically, it is just such concepts that at times are the very impediment to divine knowledge. "Mysteries," says Egyptologist Bojana Mojsov, "were wordless sermons . . . meant to imply the profoundest revelation of the truth that was all embracing and the source of all teaching."[4]

Egypt is an exceptional example of the imaginal world. Other than scholars, most people view ancient Egypt more as a fantasy than as a place that actually existed. The mystery of this world is heightened by the fact that there is no Homer to sing the praises of this ancient land or even Hesiod to frame the Egyptian mystery in a complete, cohesive narrative. (Plutarch comes closest to stringing together spells and exaltations to form a myth of Osiris.) The Egyptians left us no formal philosophical system, concise literary tradition, or consistent theological canon. No Vedic texts, Bible, or Koran exist to help us understand Osiris and his strange world.[5] At best, the Egyptians left us many sacred texts that confound the rational mind. The Pyramid Texts, from which much of the Osiris myth is drawn, are, according to the famed Keeper of the British Museum E. A. Wallis Budge, an "agglomeration of beliefs, legends, and speculations concerning the Other World, which defy systematic arrangement and logical classification."[6]

Unlike other major religions that depict a single, concise creation story, Egyptian religion gave us four, one for each of its major theological centers, Hermopolis, Memphis, Heliopolis, and Thebes. Instead of a book that clearly delineates a path to salvation, we are left with papyri containing magical spells and mythological maps of the underworld. Their language is obscure and elusive, involving three methods of interpretation, with words written in every direction. It isn't simply the corrosive effects of time that prevent us from understanding ancient Egyptian culture. Even if there were an original intact volume on Osiris, we would still be faced with the greatest impediments of all— our rational view of life and a short memory.

We come to a point at which memory ends and imagination takes precedence. Most of us cannot recall events before age three. With some effort we might be able to identify the first memory that dispersed the clouds of unconsciousness and enabled us to become conscious, sentient, and somewhat independent beings. But, beyond this isolated moment in time, we more typically rely on the recollections of others, be they orally communicated to us or, in the case of history, handed down through the filters of cultural revision, literary style, and religious bias. In every instance, interpretation stands in the way of actual experience. Interpretations alone get us no closer to embodying the consciousness of a poet, much less an Egyptian priest. I believe we do far better to employ our creative faculties to take the so-called facts of history and recreate them as best we can in our mind. With every interpretation I offer, it is imperative that something deeper in our psyche be aroused if we are to bring to life Osiris and the chthonic regions of his world.

Imagination allows us to experience Egypt and its gods as states of mind and psychic functions rather than as well-developed gods whose identities were defined by more recent cultures. While the world is first created in our mind by images and then processed by the imagination, yet another point exists at which even images fail and perception is no longer useful. With ancient Egypt we enter this world of mystery that can best be apprehended by the unconscious mind. We descend back in time from memory to imagination and finally arrive at the hinterlands of mystery. They are a dark place where only mystics and the curious dare enter, for as we distance ourselves from memory, we drift farther and farther from familiar shores. Ancient Egypt is located somewhere between imagination and mystery, the psychic place where inchoate images have little to offer the rational mind and mystery points to a bizarre realm of existence.

"The important thing," said Albert Einstein, "is not to stop questioning. Curiosity has its own reason for existing. One cannot help but be in awe when he contemplates the mysteries of eternity, of life, of the marvelous structure of reality. It is enough if one tries merely to comprehend a little of this mystery every day. Never lose a holy curiosity."[7] In this spirit, the present book is a guidebook intended to revitalize this holy curiosity that was so prevalent among people who lived among animal-headed gods and fierce demons. Although I offer abundant data about Osiris and ancient Egypt, this book is not meant to give a history lesson or educate us on the ways of the ancient life.

Much of what is popularly known of ancient Egypt is based on Greek historians like Plutarch and Herodotus. While I will at times refer to their writings, my first preference will be the original Egyptian texts. Additionally, it is important to consider an endless number of people who either through error or enthusiasm added to the Osiris myth. In point of fact, most of the historical record of Egypt comes to us from the Greeks. Yet, there are significant differences between the two cultures. While, for example, Greek gods were immortal, the Egyptian gods and everything else that existed under the desert sun were not meant to live for eternity. Alas, even the great Egypt, in the end, disintegrates.

Another important difference lies in the fact that, unlike in ancient Greece, initiation into the mysteries was not taught in Egyptian schools. Rather, the way of transcendence came by self-discovery, spurred on by an insatiable need to find one's place among the stars. What I intend to show is the genius of the Egyptians' brilliant insights into the nuances of natural energy and how these energies manifest in divine and human form. Further, we will grasp the subtle way that energy changes form, moving toward ever-greater states of being.

This work is subtle, requiring long pauses, daydreaming, and laying aside the ordinary ways we think about things. No words can capture what people of ancient Egypt were actually thinking. No amount of archeological study can tell us the psychology behind mummy masks, false doors, and the embalmer's art. About the best we can do is rely on the myths "they used . . . to convey their insights into the workings of nature and the ultimately indescribable realities of the soul."[8] Of course, beyond any description of this amazing land is a world completely alien to ours, and yet, as we shall see, Egypt possesses a wisdom that is timeless and infinitely helpful in enriching our lives. I say this in light of those philosophers, scientists, and scholars, including Plato, Democritus, and Pythagoras, who knew what treasures Egypt possessed and devoted many years to learning their sacred science.

CHANGING YOUR MIND

It is not possible to understand deeply, much less embody, the soul of Osiris without making some significant change in the way we ordinarily think. In *The Ordinal of Alchemy*, the fifteenth-century alchemist Thomas Norton told his students that the "mind [*mens*] should be in perfect harmony with the work."[9] Without attuning our mind to the psychological milieu of a myth, we should expect to understand only its objective meaning. In order to experience a myth, we must not only read it but with our imagination penetrate the many barriers separating us from its reality. We need to inject ourselves into the beliefs, mores, and living circumstances that allow the myth to come alive. In the myth of Osiris, we will want to know how early Egyptians conceived their world and arrived at thoughts that lead to creating a culture so radically different from our own. We will want to go back to their earliest cosmology in order to learn about the conditions that gave birth to one of the most mysterious Egyptian deities. Just as the Egyptians regarded words as having a living presence, Osiris's myth comes alive for us by following Norton's instruction. Surrendering ourselves to a god who knows the secrets of life and death further heightens this experience. His birth, dismemberment, death, and resurrection model the alchemical methods involved in transforming living spirit into physical matter. In this introduction, I propose five changes that will adjust our way of thinking so that we might learn the secrets of ancient Egyptian wisdom.

I start with the mode of thinking that dominates the Western mind—rationality. We take it for granted that rationality has a value greater than any other type of cognitive style that preceded it. And yet, when we consider the great achievements of the ancient world, the question is left open as to whether rational thinking offers any real advantages over prerational thought. For one thing, a good deal of imagination has been lost as a result of the emphasis given to rationality. Here I am using an old definition of imagination that includes intuitive thinking, wonder, memory, reflection, reverie, deep introspection, and meditation. This faculty has been virtually lost in modern times, yet it dominated the thinking of our Egyptian ancestors. The value of prerational cognition cannot be underestimated. Einstein recognized its worth. "Imagination," he said, "is more important than knowledge . . . the only real valuable thing is intuition."[10]

Imagination and memory are critical faculties required to comprehend a myth fully, and, for our purpose, to conceive what life might have been like in Egypt thousands of years ago. Take for example the archaic way the Egyptians venerated their gods and the dead. Placing foods at an offering table in front of statues and beside coffins was common practice. To our mind, neither gods nor dead people eat food; it simply lies there until it rots and eventually disintegrates. Even the rational mind can accept that the food is an offering, but that kind of thinking does not go far enough to appreciate the deeper meaning.

Obviously, gods and dead people do not eat like living beings. Offered foods "would not actually be consumed in our sense of the word; the god in his *naos* [temple] satisfied himself without leaving visible traces of his appetite."[11] Instead, the spoiled and decayed food that eventually wasted away was precisely the means by which these spirits consumed their sacred meal. These same processes, *putrefactio* and *mortificatio*, are operations used in the alchemical laboratory and even have their corollaries in modern chemistry. But without attuning our mind to the Egyptian psyche, we would dismiss these rituals as the product of primitive and superstitious thinking. Without applying our deeper imagination to such phenomena, we run the risk of wrongly concluding that prehistoric peoples, lacking modern reason, were unintelligent. Peter Kingsley, professor of humanities at Simon Fraser University, points out, "We've actually succeeded in creating the illusion that we're wiser than people used to be."[12] As a psychologist, I would add that the concept of intelligence remains poorly defined, and knowledge is certainly no substitute for wisdom. One is not reduced to idiocy or insanity without rational thought.

Thus, the first change necessary for putting our mind in harmony with the present task is to give priority to an imaginative, intuitive way of thinking. This step will spare us from making unsound judgments, deriving spurious conclusions, and, worse, propounding untruths that perpetuate ridiculous notions of ancient myths. Seth is no more the devil than Pan; neither the *duat* (the Egyptian underworld) nor Hades is the hell pictured in Christian mythology. More importantly, I believe we will better understand why the Egyptians' style of thinking was concrete and based on immediate, tangible experience. Despite the appearance of bizarre imagery in Egyptian art and writing, their imagination was founded on the down-to-earth reality of living in a harsh desert land. These must have been people whose nonrational functions, sensate and intuitive, were highly developed.[13] If we avoid assigning a negative value to concrete thinking, considering it childish or disturbed, then we begin to appreciate the beauty and profound simplicity of their world. Many of their symbols sprang from an ecology that juxtaposed white hot landmasses and the brilliant blue waters of the Nile.

A second modification concerns the nature of concrete thinking that characterizes the ancient Egyptian psyche. According to many noted Egyptologists, the cognitive mind during most of ancient Egyptian rule precluded sophisticated operations like abstract thinking and philosophical thought. This form of thinking has been described as anterational, mythical, and prelogical. For psychologist Julian Jaynes, the matter is quite clear: "It is generally agreed that the ancient Egyptian language . . . was concrete from first to last. To maintain that it is expressing abstract thoughts would seem to me an intrusion of the modern idea that men have always been the same."[14] If the Egyptians were incapable of expressing complex abstract thoughts, then it may be argued that these people were incapable of having mystical experience, a view held by many prominent Egyptologists. In his book *Shamanic Wisdom in the Pyramid Texts*, Naydler put forth a well-researched argument to refute this contention: "Despite being for the most part invisible, the transcendent reality that we refer to in shorthand as the spirit world was, for the Egyptians, a very full world. It was a multilayered and infinitely complex world that the human spirit must negotiate, gain knowledge of and power over, in order to attain full human-divine stature."[15] What Naydler shows in an exhaustive analysis of the Pyramid Texts is that the Egyptians' cosmology was highly complex and imaginative, relying on concrete observations and intuitive thought rather than intellectual abstraction.

Evidence that the Egyptians were concrete *and* imaginative is found in their art and architecture. Lacking any formal philosophical system, they created an elaborate mythology and cosmology. While philosophy is based primarily on cognitive, analytic process, mythology relies on intuitive thought. This penchant toward concrete reality allowed the Egyptians to realize their dreams, which shows itself in a number of ways. They placed enormous importance on material objects, especially all things related to funerary preparation and rituals. Pyramids and burial sites were crammed with common objects that would be useful in the next world. The corpse was particularly important to the critical transformations that were necessary for the spiritualization of the body and its entrance into the afterlife. "There was," says Jungian analyst Marie-Louise von Franz, "a belief in immortality . . . attained through *chemical treatment of the corpse*—an incredible, primitive-magic concretism!" Referring to papyri that give instructions in the precise method of embalming, she concludes, "Everything was done concretely, in such a way as to make the human being actually chemically immortal."[16]

Even in the Field of Offerings, the place where the souls of the dead come to rest, there were no lofty visions, but rather a simple image of the earthly life they so treasured. In all these examples, the emphasis is clearly on the physical, immediate, and concrete way of thinking about life in this world and, by remembering earthly life, recreating it in the next. In other words, the love Egyptians had for their beloved country was so deep and abiding that they literally wanted to take this life with them into eternity. Such a heartfelt belief represents the ultimate resistance to change, the height of concrete thought, and the one truth that even death cannot alter.

We come now to the third needed change in our thinking: understanding how the Egyptians perceived time. For the Westerner, time is sequential; past, present, and future form the structure of our temporal space. Only in dreams does time lose its ordinary definition. Nightly, we experience a more fluid dimension of time in which multiple events often occur without any regard for a causal sequence. The artwork of Chagall and Dali capture this timeless dream world where people float above the earth and clocks melt. Increasingly, science, especially relativity and quantum physics, demonstrates the elasticity of time. We can, in fact, go back to the future and find a more subjective perception of time in Egyptian culture. Our 365-day calendar, for example, is derived from the Egyptians, whose counting of years was based on subjective observations like the pharaoh's reign, the Nile's behavior, and astrological considerations, rather than more objective calendrical measures of time.[17]

An interesting anecdote drawn from C. G. Jung's visit to Egypt shows how differently an Egyptian, even today, views time. While traveling throughout northern Africa, Jung visited Cairo. Observing the squalor of the city, he asked his cabdriver, "Why is so much importance put on building monuments to the dead while the living are left to suffer under these terrible conditions?" The driver, nonplussed by this Westerner's reaction, pointed out that the pyramids were built for eternity, while the city was little more than a temporary outpost. Again we see the seamless way Egyptians manage to live with one foot in the finite world of temporal reality while the other foot is planted in eternity. For them, the former existed "on top of the earth" and the latter "below the horizon." In this concrete manner there was no rational conflict in simultaneously maintaining different orders of time.

I mention Jung particularly since we will be using his psychology to explain what we find in the symbolic images embedded throughout the Osiris myth. While I will describe his psychology in more detail as we proceed, for now I introduce his concept of synchronicity since it comes closer to the Egyptian's perception of time than our own. He defines synchronicity as "a coincidence in time of two or more causally unrelated events which have the same or a similar meaning."[18]

In my previous book, *Alchemical Psychology*, I listed six characteristics that form a common thread running throughout the many forms of alchemy.[19] One of them is the frequent occurrence of synchronistic events. Even writing on the present subject invites this kind of shift in time. On the morning when I was to give a lecture at the International Alchemy Conference, my wife and I stopped to have coffee. As we sat down, we couldn't avoid noticing on the wall the phrase "Hopping out of bed and thinking about the one thing." In alchemy, the One Thing is synonymous with the philosopher's stone, the object of every alchemist's goal. Of course, I realize the "one thing" on the wall referred to a cup of coffee, but for me it was a synchronistic event that was a nod from the divine, a small blessing that my talk was in harmony with the work.

Reason alone can't explain the mysteries of either Egyptian myth or Egyptian alchemy since neither adheres to a linear sequence of events. In an oft-told incident, a young woman was telling Jung of a dream in which she had received a golden scarab, an Egyptian symbol of rebirth. As she spoke, a common rose chafer, "the nearest analogy to a golden scarab that one finds in our latitudes," flew in through his office window.[20] The synchronicity of this event was a surprise even for the man who coined the term.

The early science of Egypt included both institutional and individual magic. In the world of magic, time and space are juggled like balls in a circus act, each alternately disappearing into thin air. Even reading books on ancient Egypt defies any hope of rational understanding; nearly every book I used in my research on Egypt gave different facts, interpretations, and explanations. One must approach this subject not only with an open mind but also with full acceptance that acausality offers a more plausible approach than reason alone can provide. Using our intuition, we are closer to understanding the nature of psyche with all its contradictions and paradoxes than to some "objective" truth. While Osiris refuses to be pinned down, so do all the great mysteries of life.

The fourth change in our thinking that will help us understand and even embody the mind of this god is suspension of some ordinary rules of morality. The Osiris myth is not for the lighthearted; it involves incest, murder, dismemberment, and necrophilia, all things we regard as repugnant and not befitting the behavior of humans, much less gods. Yet, given that this myth was first written sometime around 2300 BC, we must bear in mind that its contents relate to the earliest impulses that gave rise to civilization and the initial "construction" of the human psyche. Creation, in its earliest stages, is messy business. The story of the seven days of creation so nicely told in the book of Genesis is beautiful, but by the time of its writing the Osiris myth was already at least a thousand years old. While the Old Testament is saddled with abundant moral strictures, the far older Pyramid Texts in which the Osiris myth is first mentioned, dating back two millennia before the Bible, make no mention of moral rules or any formal court of law. In fact, there were no lawyers in early Egypt. One either represented oneself before the pharaoh or appointed a *ba* soul for his or her defense.[21]

Morality has put a supercilious, pleasant face on death. Medicines shield us from the daunting realization that death is final. In defense against this fear, we've managed in any number of ways to idealize death. Unlike the Egyptians, we don't desiccate dead bodies or pour their "wet organs" into jars. We are far from the reality of death—its grittiness, guts, and gore.

More than death, the Egyptians feared missing their chance to resurrect into eternal life. Their desire wasn't to obfuscate the death process; certainly one cannot look at the golden sarcophagi, towering pyramids, and elaborate temples without gasping at the sheer beauty and considerable thought that went into their funerary preparations. Their eyes were fixed on eternity, not temporal life. Birth is the process that conveys us into this life, and death is the prelude to spiritual existence. In the Egyptian view, one doesn't leave this world but rather becomes one with it; the deceased "becomes earth." Death was viewed simultaneously as the next stage of life and a realm (the *duat*) that interpenetrated and even nurtured the living.

"The Egyptian understanding of the realm of the dead," according to Naydler, "was that it was the source of the fertility of the land, the growth of crops, and the increase of herds. And the dead were not just passive in this realm but were felt to have a special role as the guardians of the forces of life, and hence the well-being of the whole land of Egypt."[22] In their view, *life sprang from death!* Death is a temporary stage in the larger scheme of existence. However, there is always the danger of falling into nonexistence, a state different from but very close to the realm of death. Thus, in addition to the elaborate funerary preparations taken to prevent one from being totally annihilated, other precautions were required. In addition to venerating the gods and the souls of the deceased, people still needed to remain loyal to the pharaoh, behave ethically toward their neighbors, and exhibit a special talent in their work. These behaviors weren't meant to accomplish a moral end but rather reflected the fear of perishing from existence.

The distinction between moral and ethical behavior is not clear-cut. For our purpose, morality describes an individual's sense of right and wrong; ethics, on the other hand, are more broadly defined to include a set of principles that applies to the populace at large. Although ancient Egyptians had no ethical philosophy, we will discover in their concept of Ma'at an ethical principle that existed throughout dynastic history. A person acts morally in order to serve his or her idea of right action, whereas ethical behavior takes into consideration how one's behavior affects another person. Morality appeals to those of a religious persuasion; ethics has no connection with any religion.

The final adjustment in thinking that will help us subjectively engage with the Egyptian experience and the role played by Osiris is reducing the importance given to the concept of the individual, which may seem at odds with what I have said about the ambition driving every Egyptian to particularize himself or herself. On this point, Egyptian society is in sharp contrast to our own in the West. Whereas the accent in Western countries is on the individual first and the collective second, the opposite was true in Egypt, where there were three levels of organization: the people, the pharaoh, and the gods. The people served the pharaoh, and the pharaoh was the intermediary between the worlds above and the worlds below.

Group identity was necessary to carry out the wishes of the pharaoh. Tens of thousands of men working in hundreds of teams accomplished astounding feats, the pyramids being one example of what could be done with this kind of social organization. Within each gang, one's talents placed him in a special position; painters, carvers, engineers, and scribes were all needed in these massive undertakings. Likewise, social organization was required to defend the country against outside invaders. Battle victories are displayed on the outer pylons of temples throughout the country. While the pharaoh led his armies in battle, individual specialization dictated how each man would serve his king. These activities often involved many generations and required families to be committed to passing responsibilities from one generation to the next. Building a moderate-sized pyramid could take more than twenty years. Collective consciousness was thereby inbred into the Egyptian society and reflected in its culture and traditions.

Collective consciousness also manifested in sacred festivals. In the next chapter I will describe the Heb Sed festival, which was especially important to the rejuvenation of the pharaoh and all that he represented. Another festival, celebrated each year at Abydos, gave tribute to the Osiris myth. For seven days mystical rites and secret ceremonies were performed reenacting the Passion of Osiris. Bojana Mojsov describes the significance of this sacred event:

> Pilgrims from all walks of life came to Abydos for the occasion. Visitors
> were offered accommodation and food, magical papyri, lanterns, statuettes,
> and amulets to be dedicated at the holy sites. Vestments and flowers were

18

laid in the ancient cemetery. Osiris' tomb in Abydos came to be known as Hemhemet—"great in fame." The festival took place from the twenty-third to the thirtieth of the month of Khoiak (November). . . . . Abydos became to the Egyptians what Jerusalem is to Christians and Mecca to Moslems. Every year, pilgrims from all over Egypt would gather to seek and find the body of Osiris. It was a drama out of doors, a collective celebration of the god's resurrection.[23]

On a sunny Christmas day I visited the Osirion, the legendary place where Osiris's severed head was supposedly buried. This is the *temenos*, the sacred ground where pilgrims came from everywhere in Egypt to pay homage to their beloved Osiris. Here the great festival was staged and the old kings buried. The experience jolted me out of time and place, out of my ordinary Western way of thinking about this god and this strange place. It showed me how we must proceed in order to experience this extraordinary myth of Osiris.

To summarize, I propose five changes that will help us empathetically engage this material and the psychological complex that Osiris represents:

- Intuitive thinking takes precedence over rationality.
- Concrete thinking takes precedence over abstract thinking.
- Synchronicity takes precedence over linear temporality.
- Ethical behavior takes precedence over moral behavior.
- Collective individuation takes precedence over personal individuation.

While it is easy enough to suggest these changes, I realize that such "adjustments" require enormous effort. These five factors are critical determinants in our orientation to life and may be impossible to alter. Nonetheless, I hold to the idea that when life first comes to us through psychic images, we have the ability to alter this stream of images by filtering it through our imagination. The vagaries of Egypt will certainly put us to the test. The Egyptian orientation is in many ways inverse to our own. But however bizarre the imagery of the myth, we can still relate to the basic desires and feelings of each character. Instead of judging and evaluating the myth, we would do far better to give our imagination full reign as we analyze the myth scene by scene and at the conclusion take a more pragmatic look at what it means to embody a god.

COMING UP

With these changes in mind, we begin our psychological treatment of the Osiris myth. To start, I should point out that this ancient civilization wasn't called Egypt: that name derived from the Greek *aigyptos*, a word tracing its origin to *hekaptah*, "the domain of the *ka* of Ptah." *Heka* refers to magic, *ka* to the living soul, and Ptah to the divine creator god, patron of Memphis and model for *Homo Faber*. Nor was Osiris his original name. He was known by many names, two among the oldest being *Afar* or *Usir*, "Mighty One," and *Khenti Amentiu*, "Foremost of the Westerners." The western direction is, of course, the place of the setting sun. The Egyptians believed that the sun died each evening in the west and was carried through the treacherous underworld, the *duat*, in a solar boat by Osiris. If successful, Osiris delivered the sun—reborn—in the east each morning. As we will see in many more Egyptian words, each syllable contains a story, one that is lost without excavating the original meanings.

In the next chapter, I present a psychological précis of ancient Egypt, its ecology and history, myths and folklore, government and traditions, and other details describing the magical world that gave rise to Osiris. Although historical accounts differ widely, there is no doubting that

Osiris is a god of life and death. We will see him emerge from the land and sea and return again to the underworld after bringing civilization to the people. Were Osiris an actual king, he would undoubtedly have been familiar with alchemy. His life itself represents the major alchemical stages, the *nigredo*, the *albedo*, and the *rubedo*. In the nigredo, Osiris is unconscious, hardly differentiated from nature; in the albedo, he is purified by Anubis and readied for his resurrection into the underworld; in the rubedo, Osiris is awakened as he brings light to the world of the dead and, by analogy, the human unconscious.

Once we get a taste for the magical world of Egypt, we will be ready to enter the fantastic world that describes the origins of Osiris's birth and genealogy. This task is not simple, given that ancient Egypt had four major spiritual centers, each having its own set of gods and creation myths. By far the most popular of these is the Hermopolitan myth that derives from the Archaic period (3100–2700 BC), which describes Osiris' ancestry and the "group of eight," the gods who created human beings. Egyptologists in general draw no connection between these four myths. But R. A. Schwaller de Lubicz, an Alsatian mathematician, alchemist, and Egyptologist who emphasized symbolic interpretation, discerned continuity between the stories. Although chiefly ignored by others in his field, he showed that these myths were integrally and organically part of one complex cosmology. Others, like John Anthony West and Rosemary Clark, elaborated his concept. "De Lubicz," says Clark, "believed that the teachings of these schools were not only creation myths, but an esoteric code of cultural unfoldment taught by the temple elite. As such, the different pantheons represent cycles or resonances of the civilization itself whose characteristics are embodied in the art, architecture, and literature of the time in which they came to prominence."[24] While describing each of these four mythologies and how they are different aspects of one core myth is beyond the scope of this book, we will hold to the Symbolist school in analyzing the Osiris myth.

For our purpose, I have integrated the salient points of these my-thologies, drawing also from the historical record and even folklore, to re-create an Osiris myth that embodies the essential spirit of this god. This approach is in keeping with the Egyptian tradition, since there is no one comprehensive telling of this tale.

In chapter 3 we begin with the genesis of the world that by the fourth generation yields the family of gods most familiar to us: Atum, Shu and Tefnut, Geb and Nut, Osiris and Isis, Seth and Nephthys. The next eight chapters tell the great myth of Osiris. Throughout, I emphasize certain symbols that contain alchemical secrets—the myth is littered with them. But the central symbol that will command our attention is Osiris's dismemberment and his re-memberment. I believe these awful and awesome acts contain a secret formula that appears to represent the true mythic beginning of alchemy.

When I first realized this myth was really about the origins of the psyche and the unconscious genesis of alchemy, I felt as if I'd discov-ered the Rosetta stone.[25] I will elaborate the importance of this finding as we see alchemy rise from the shadows of the myth. I can only say for now that a gold mine of secrets is waiting to be revealed, not only for those who practice alchemy, but also for all who seriously seek to have a deeper understanding of their personal and spiritual development. These secrets unleash powers that come with attaining higher states of consciousness.

In the final chapter, we will discuss what it means to embody a god or, as the Egyptians would say, "become Osiris." To do so requires an empathic engagement of the god on an imaginal and physical level. In many of the clinical examples given throughout the book, we will focus on the central image of Osiris's dismemberment and reconstitution and how these actions appear in life and dreams as part of a healing indi-viduation process. In this chapter we will gather together the pieces of our investigation in order to draw conclusions. The principle questions asked are: How do we embody Osiris? What does the myth have to say on the individual, collective, and mystical levels?

Dismemberment as a psychological operation is part of the individuation process. It is critical to the evolution and personal development of the individual psyche. We often suffer this process blindly in the form of depression, derealization, and, in its worst form, a break with reality. The intent of this book is to help us understand the necessity of this process and other operations exemplified by Osiris; by making them conscious we move toward wholeness. Embodying Osiris is a means of reconstituting his spirit, providing a "body" of experience to show what he represents: the promise of regeneration and resurrection to a higher, more integrated plane of reality.

1

IN THE LAND OF HIS BIRTH

In reality a darkness altogether different from natural night broods over the land. It is the psychic primal night which is the same today as it has been for countless millions of years. The longing for light is the longing for consciousness.

—C. G. Jung, *Memories, Dreams, Reflections*

Only in relatively recent times has the West embraced the Eastern traditions and recognized their immense contributions to world consciousness. The West has yet to discover wisdom that stems from other, equally old civilizations. The question of which society represents the earliest civilization remains unanswered, in part because archeologists continue to dig up remnants of ancient towns and settlements. What is apparent is that human consciousness awoke from its two hundred thousand–year slumber, and great civilizations sprang up in Mesopotamia, the Indus Valley, Anatolia, China, and Central America at about the time that Egypt blossomed as a dominant culture around 3000 BC.[1] Each made significant, unique contributions to the development of consciousness. While archeologists continue to dig, depth psychologists are also unearthing ancient wisdom from their study of these early societies.

In this book we will turn to the myth of Osiris to acquire remarkable insights from the people of ancient Egypt. While it is certainly true that

every new excavated mummy has a story to tell, every fresh reread-
ing of this amazing myth reveals deeper and more profound mysteries.
Clearly, Egypt stood at the threshold of collective consciousness, when
the world first opened its eyes and discovered order in the infinitude of
stars and endless miles of sand. The Egyptians saw the beauty of *their*
earth, the auspicious arrangement of stars and planets as well as the
sacred place held by humans in the universe.

The period in question dates back to 2300 BC.[2] Popular interest in this
time period is severely limited to a shallow fascination with mummies
and pyramids. Museums still draw record crowds whenever mummies
are on exhibit, and people travel to Egypt to stand in awe before the
pyramids, not really knowing much about the pharaohs who built them
or the gods that occupy them. To fully embody our understanding of
ancient Egypt requires that we not simply retell the old myths; especially with Osiris, whose spirit pervaded the dynastic kingdom from
beginning to end, we need to describe his story within its geographical,
historical, mythological, and philosophical settings.

The preponderance of evidence points to Africa as the land where
human life began and one of the most enduring civilizations took root
in a formidable environment. Exactly how this genesis from tribal kingdoms to pharaonic dynasties occurred is not known, but of all the African nations, Egypt managed to remain intact for three thousand years
before being overtaken by foreign powers. Imagine for a moment the
date of origin of any country existing today: project that date forward
three thousand years and you get some sense of the weight of Egypt's
history. Both time and space make Egypt unique. Even today Egypt is
somewhat of a geographical anomaly. Located on the African subcontinent and juxtaposed to the Middle East, it borrows a great deal from
both regions while maintaining its own unique identity; culturally, it
is neither African nor Middle Eastern. At the same time, it formed a
natural land bridge between these diverse regions. While many factors

account for Egypt's incredible legacy, it was the land itself that allowed Egypt to rule the Middle East for a remarkably long time. In all, thirty-one consecutive dynasties under Egyptian rule weathered ecological challenges, civil strife, and countless attacks from their infamous nine enemies.[3] The land gave rise to Egypt's cosmology, governmental structure, religion, and public works.

Before Egypt had unified its "Two Lands," the northeast corner of Africa, including what is now Sudan, Somalia, and the Eritrean coast of Ethiopia, was believed to be the mystical land of Punt. It was also called God's Land because it provided much of the supplies used in Egyptian temples. Incense, fragrant woods, animal skins, and possibly even the pygmy god Bes were imported from Punt. The region was also known as the pleasure garden of Amun. Although we know of several major expeditions undertaken by pharaohs to this wondrous land, its exact location remains unknown.

Egypt's immediate neighbor to the south, Nubia, was also very important because of its vast supplies of hardwood and gold, resources scarce in Egypt. Nubia supplied the gold used for making fine jewelry, the pharaoh's regalia, and funerary objects. The Egyptians regarded gold as the skin of the sun. Relations between the two countries alternated between fighting as allies and fighting each other; in the end, Nubia ruled Egypt for a relatively short time. Ironically, the idea of a king as pharaoh likely emerged from the Nubian tribal kingdoms. And the seminal concept of Osiris may well have originated in Nubia's misty past.

Prior to unification, Egypt was divided into two lands: Upper Egypt in the south spilled over into Nubia, and Lower Egypt began at Aswan and extended northward to the Mediterranean (the Green Sea). The country was first unified around 3000 BC under the rule of Narmer; Egypt subsequently split apart and through ingenious politico-spiritual machinations was brought back together. However, war and political means were not sufficient to coalesce the country into a stable, unified nation. "New epics," writes Mojsov, "had to be invented to help transform the prehistoric tribal society into a single state. Tribal myths had to be transfigured into a Great State Myth."[4]

These myths describe a divine king who eventually was seen as either the son of a god or god himself. The gender of kings was decidedly masculine, since the source of power appeared to flow from three principle masculine deities—Amun, Ra, Ptah. Even Hatshepsut, one of the mightiest women to rule Egypt, proclaimed herself king, not queen; like her male predecessors, she strapped on the false beard that signified royal authority, and at her death she had herself buried in the Valley of the Kings in Thebes. The first large-scale expedition to Punt is depicted on the walls of her mortuary temple in the west bank.

Originally, Egypt was called Kemet, meaning "the Black Land." The current name was not used until the Greek occupation thousands of years later. By then rituals had evolved into state-sanctioned myths, and eventually the outlines of Egyptian religion took on a fairly permanent form. Thinis was founded as the first capital, followed by Memphis, which is strategically located at the Nile's delta in the north. The patron god of Memphis was Ptah, the supreme maker of all things and protector of artisans and craftsmen—a true alchemical god. Here we see the importance placed on the concrete tasks of building, painting, and stonecutting. The Masons anchor their history in early guilds that eventually emerged from these ancient arts.

"The religious centers," explains Egyptologist John Anthony West, "at Heliopolis, Memphis, Thebes and Hermopolis did not represent separate and vying cults, or a political and social federation. Rather, each reveals one of the principle phases or aspects of genesis."[5] Recalling the Symbolist theories of de Lubicz, West describes both Egypt and many of its temples as living entities. Thus, Heliopolis represents the "primordial creative act" that gave rise to the Ennead, or *Neteru*, which includes Osiris and the other gods so important to the Osiris myth. Memphis was dedicated to Ptah, "producer and animator of form." Thebes is especially important in de Lubicz's theory. He spent twelve years of intense study and data collection to prove that the Temple of Luxor (the modern-day name for Thebes) was "alive," complete with three axes that replicate the human form and a nervous system that runs throughout the entire structure. As humans are believed to draw together the above and the below, Thebes was thought to be the "reunion of that which had been separated." Finally, Hermopolis was the "creation of the manifested universe" through words, the province of magic, which was most powerfully ruled by the ibis-headed god Thoth.

Most of the early gods originated from direct observations of the surrounding ecology and only later acquired divine status. Initially, Osiris was an ordinary god of the dead, a nature spirit who had a special relationship to the Nile. The Egyptians lived close to the land and even closer to the river that made life possible. They weren't people who mastered the open seas; only on rare occasions did they sail into the Mediterranean or the Red Seas. The river Nile offered safety and abundance, and Osiris presided over its currents and the tides of life and death. Even today a large percentage of the population is crowded around its busy shores. Until the building of the Aswan High Dam some forty years ago, the Nile annually overflowed its banks with dependable efficacy, fertilizing the arid land and washing away harmful sediments. From the Nile issued the basic elements of civilization: farming, trade, religion, taxation, mathematics, language, building, and transportation. Herodotus, the fifth century–BC Greek historian, justifiably said, "Egypt was a gift of the Nile."

It is difficult to imagine how the Egyptians survived under such harsh desert conditions where temperatures rose to 120 degrees and the hot winds were like blast furnaces. Clearly, without the Nile River there simply wouldn't be an Egypt. This sacred river, the longest in the world, covers a distance of 4,148 miles. Having no tributaries, it gently winds its way northward from Lake Victoria (the White Nile) in Uganda and Lake Tana (The Blue Nile) in Ethiopia, continuing in a northerly direction to the Delta, where it branches out like a tree and eventually empties its waters into the Mediterranean Sea.

Along with rich farm fields skirting the Nile's banks, most of the great monuments, temples, sanctuaries, and pyramids are situated within close reach of its waters. To behold the Nile is something special. Especially in the south, one can easily fall into a reverie recalling times when garlanded boats bearing golden statues of Hathor and Horus sailed up and down the river to bring these deities of love and strength into an embrace. Another glance back reveals supply boats carrying red granite from Aswan to Cairo to build the pyramids of Giza and a flotilla of military boats transporting huge armies to foreign lands. Even today, it is a wonder to see people from the world over journeying from Aswan to Luxor, a river course that has been a tourist attraction for hundreds of years. Given the right frame of mind, visitors can hear the voices of the gods. They are everywhere.

Nearly everything in Egypt is named after a god. The god of the Nile was Hapy, but Osiris was its spirit. Osiris symbolized the ebb and flow on which life depended. The annual inundation vitalized the land and made agriculture possible. Osiris taught the people how to farm their land.

Agriculture transformed Egypt economically, militarily, and spiritually. Law, trade, and mathematics were necessary as the society became increasingly reliant on its ecology to produce food. Ample evidence supports the view that, before Egypt became an agrarian society, people there practiced cannibalism for a variety of reasons. Survival alone did not account for this practice; they believed that consuming human flesh was a magical means of acquiring the strengths of their victims. The ultimate prize for accumulating enough power was immortality. With agriculture, new sources of food became available, and excess resources allowed for the creation of a code of law, order, and a standing army.

However, more than the introduction of agriculture was necessary to stop uncivilized activity. In fact, it took a god to bring civility to the land. The cult of Osiris forbade the eating of human flesh or at least prohibited the consumption of fellow Egyptians; eating raw meat and cannibalizing foreigners continued for some time. Cannibalism eventually ceased and transformed into a metaphor used at great length in the Cannibal Hymn. In this text, the pharaoh Unas "eats the magic" and "gulps down the spirits."[6]

The Nile's annual inundation made agriculture possible. The new year began when the Nile overflowed its banks in July, and the first season of the year was called Inundation. Emergence, the second season, followed when the crops were harvested, and finally, summer, "the Time When the Land Is Dry," arrived. Each of these three seasons had four thirty-day months. But because this 360-day calendar was not accurate, the Nile's inundation was increasingly late each year, a mistake that caused havoc for farmers. To correct the error, the pharaoh declared that five days would be added to the year, making for a 365-day year. To explain how the adjustment was made is simple enough, but since our purpose is to understand the Egyptian psyche, we will do better to recall the myth explaining how these five extra days were added to the calendar. In the next chapter, I tell how Thoth tricks Ra and exacts these extra days, during which time the gods of the Osiris myth come into existence.

As I mentioned earlier, Abydos is a very ancient city that unquestionably holds the most significant meaning for Osiris. His spirit is still very much alive at the Temple of Seti I in Abydos. At first sight, Osiris's temple is different. It doesn't have the usual imposing pylons (high-walled gates) that stand before most Egyptian temples. To get to Abydos one travels in a convoy for some six miles inland from the banks of the Nile. This desert city was the traditional cemetery of the old kings; the tomb of Narmer is among eleven royal tombs found there. Great feasts and ceremonies were held at Abydos for thousands of years. It was the cemetery for Thinis, capital of old Egypt. A funerary temple, begun by the pharaoh Seti I was built in Abydos—a great honor to a great warrior. The Temple of Seti I was built in front of statues—the "houses of the ka"—that originally served to keep the kings alive long after their physical death. Abydos was regarded as the transit point for the dead, where spirits returned for food, shelter, and contact with the living. It is also home to Rostau, the supposed entryway to the duat.

Once Osiris became a popular god, he replaced Ra, or perhaps merged with him, in the solar boat carrying the light of the sun (consciousness) through the duat. Over time Osiris's image changes from a cosmic deity who keeps chaos and the enemies of consciousness (Seth, Apopis) at bay to a god who is closer to the struggles and challenges faced by humans. In this latter role he is besieged by evil, teaches people how to farm, and holds court at the judgment of each person's soul. But what sets Osiris apart from every other Egyptian god is that he is the only god who suffers and dies. Here we must dispense with rationality, for reason alone dictates that a god is immortal. Again, we resort to mythic imagination to appreciate the meaning of Osiris's death. Surely we can sooner relate to a god who shares with us the most defining event of our life in the temporal world—death. But, more than dying, Osiris also resurrects, and in his resurrection we find hope that life does not end with the termination of physical existence. Thus, each person strove to "become Osiris," and in death the deceased married his or her name with that of the god.

Osiris represents a new order of gods, a consciousness just becoming self-aware and learning to manage the outer world. His interactions with humans are simple and somewhat childlike. It is easy at times to confuse him with nature, and, as we shall see, he comes from the Neteru, a term that may well have given rise to our word for nature. Only through his son Horus, who represents the next level of consciousness (ego), does Osiris understand the complexities of human motives. Osiris's innocence makes for a pliable image that pharaohs were certain to include in their pronouncements.

Figure 1.1. Ra in the Solar Boat.

The first god worshiped in Egypt was the star Sirius (Sopdet), which for seventy days each year sank below the horizon. Its reappearance more or less coincided with the Inundation, marking the beginning of the new year, the time when the fields once again sprang to life. The second god that gained widespread attention was the cow, symbol of the Great Goddess. Her horns adorn the headdress of Hathor. Adoration of the Great Mother was a means used by various pharaohs to attain divine status. By associating himself with the goddess, a pharaoh assumed her royal position and her power. Through sympathetic magic, the pharaoh absorbed the energy of her ka, the life-giving energy of all things natural and supernatural. He then took the name Kamutef, Bull of the Mother, and through her power he came to represent life itself. At the same time, every pharaoh paid homage to Osiris, since he too held great power as a fertility god. The divine Apis bull is an image of Osiris's ka.

Figure 1.2. Apis Bull.

The Apis bull was not just a divine image but also a very special animal whose markings indicated a royal lineage; it was kept in the king's stalls, where it was treated with the same reverence given a god in his "holy of holies." Only one Apis bull was kept at a time, and when it died it was mummified and buried at the Serapium in Saqqara just outside Cairo. Even the cow that produced the Apis bull, known as the Isis cow, was given special attention. Again, each pharaoh associated himself with the Apis bull and thereby strengthened his tie with Osiris, the Old Kingdom, and ancient tradition. In time the affinity between Osiris and the Apis bull led to the two merging into one god, Osirapis, and in Hellenistic times to the emergence of a new god, Serapis. Not only does this hybrid god merge the attributes of Osiris and the Apis bull, but because he appears at the time of the Greek occupation during the reign of the first Ptolemy, Serapis also acquired the qualities of powerful Greek gods. Still, Serapis retained the original source of power derived from Osiris: the secrets of fertility and the afterlife. He is the Egyptian god of dreams.

Through his association with the Apis bull, the pharaoh gained the strength needed for his ascension, an archetypal power that flows from the Great Mother. Yet, even with these forces, the pharaoh had to demonstrate his vigor as time took its toll. Public works and winning wars helped bolster the pharaoh's deified image, but it could never be taken for granted; it had to be periodically rejuvenated. Even the gods were not immune from the ravages of time or falling into disfavor with the people. On this point, Jungian analyst Theodor Abt reveals the psychological meaning behind this need to restore power: "The Ancient Egyptians believed that these gods and other beings of the Netherworld also die regularly and therefore have to be renewed in their image. It is a well-known psychological fact that the living entities of the collective unconscious, the archetypes, have a tendency to fade in their vigour and die away. They need a regular renewal by an ego-consciousness that enters the realm of the transpersonal unconscious. This enables the ego to reconnect with this archetypal reality."[7]

Even the great god Ra was vulnerable to the ravages of time and the disaffection of humans. An early myth tells how Ra became angry with humans because they suspected he was losing his power. Having entered the field of earthly time, no one, not even a god, is immune to the deterioration of physical and supernatural power. Consequently, the people began shifting their allegiance to Apopis, the serpent who represents all that is anathema to life and consciousness. After consulting other gods, Ra creates the lion-headed goddess Sekhmet, whom he orders to destroy humans. Her bloodthirsty appetite is insatiable.

When it appears that she will soon devour all humankind, Ra realizes that without humans there would be no one to worship him. Such a calamity has to be avoided, so Ra dispatches assistants to obtain large quantities of beer and red dye from Elephantine Island. The beer is dyed and poured on a field where Sekhmet is expected to be the next morning. Mistaking the beer for human blood, she drinks it until she falls into a drunken stupor. With her power weakened, Ra magically transforms her into Hathor, the mother goddess of love.

Life wasn't any easier for the pharaoh. In order for a pharaoh to affirm his continued vigor in advancing old age, he had to demonstrate physical prowess. Were a pharaoh fortunate enough to live thirty years into his reign, a physical trial was held at the Heb Sed festival, where the king's strength was put to the test to show the renewal of his power with the solar principle (Ra). On this special occasion, particular gods were paraded before the people. At the event, the king had to complete a course of very strenuous physical exercises, including running a track four times in each direction, to prove he still possessed the strength of a god, and in the process his spiritual powers were renewed. Then a statue of the pharaoh was buried, a ritual symbolizing his death and resurrection. The Heb Sed ceremony did more than rejuvenate the king—"It endowed the temple and the kingdom with perpetual renewal and eternal life."[8]

An important theme is touched on here: the contraction and expansion of consciousness. We find numerous examples of this process in Egypt's history. The ebb and flow of the Nile and its effect on the land, crops, and food; the rise and fall of dynasties; gods (Huh and Hauhet) who represent the principles of expansion and contraction; the waxing and waning of pharaonic power; the rising and setting of the sun, as well as the phases of the moon—all are examples of the many ways psychic energy behaves. Many more examples can be added to this list, but suffice it to say that the template for this dynamic give-and-take creates a tension of opposites essential for psychic functioning, a process that will become very apparent at critical moments in the Osiris myth. It seems quite possible that the alchemists intuited their famous recipe *solve et coagula* from this dynamic interplay of opposites. Osiris's death and resurrection is emblematic of this essential feature of consciousness, how it moves and transforms.

Confronted with many forces seeking to disrupt their way of life, Egyptians held tightly to their traditions, even when challenges came from the pharaoh himself. They fiercely opposed change, and when it was inevitable they persistently sought to return to their beginnings. To the best of their ability they strove to keep things constant; such stability reflects the unchanging permanence of the god. This ideal met its greatest challenge during the middle of the New Kingdom era with a radical disruption to the otherwise steadfast tradition of Egyptian religion and collective society.

First came the reign of Amenhoptep III, son of Hapu, and then the dramatic rule of Amenhoptep IV, better known as Akhenaten. Until the latter's reign, all pharaohs presided over Egypt as if it were a singular collective body. Like a school of fish, the Egyptian people followed the currents of myth and tradition presided over by the priests and pharaoh. On acceding to the throne, Akhenaten dismissed all previous gods and proclaimed Aten as the one supreme god who subsumed all others. Unlike Ra, who, as we have seen, entered the world and was affected by it, Aten represented a more concentrated, monotheistic, and abstract form of solar energy. He was not just the giver of life, but, as the physical substance of the sun, was essentially life itself.

This difference between Ra and Aten had an enormous effect on the human psyche. The individual no longer needed to look to any god other than Aten, the life-giving force of light. In this sense, Akhenaten released Egyptian citizens from the bonds of the collective and the concept of the individual emerged—one man, one god. For this reason the historian James Henry Breasted claimed that Akhenaten was the "world's first individual."[9]

Akhenaten moved the capital into the desert, where he reigned for sixteen years. He fathered a son, the famed Tutankhamun, by Kiya, a lesser royal wife. Upon Akhenaten's death, a military man named Ahi tutored the boy king. Some say that Ahi murdered Tutankhamun and assumed the throne.[10] Ahi put a quick end to the radical departure from Egyptian polytheistic religion and recanted the idea of a faith based on one god espoused by Akhenaten. The new city, Amarna (1352–1335 BC), was dismantled and the old traditions rapidly reinstalled. This reversal was a stunning example of a relatively brief period of expansion and contraction in Egyptian society. In the end, the Egyptians' resistance to change trumped the emergence of a new theology, one that ironically became the prototype for the monotheistic religions. I will have much more to say about this heretical king in the final chapter.

Another example of this same desire to keep things constant, permanent, and fixed is seen in the succession of kingly power. In most dynasties, the rules of succession had the throne passed on to designated heirs, priests, or military men. The critical criterion was having royal blood. For this reason, incest was commonly practiced in the palace. It was a means of protecting the royal bloodline and, in effect, staying in touch with the ancestors and through them with the original gods. A chain of associations drawn from alchemical symbolism shows that blood relates to the Red Sea, which in turn "refers to the *aqua permanens*, the universal solvent—that is, the liquid form of the Philosophers' Stone."[11] This healing stone, the *lapis*, which possessed unearthly powers to heal and transmute metals, represents in this case a current of unchanging power that enervated the kingdoms of some three hundred pharaohs for a period of 2,920 years. Many scholars believe that the Osiris myth is principally a story about a transition of power: a change in the traditional order of succession, which is challenged and overthrown. This interpretation will become especially clear in later chapters when Horus and Set confront each other in a court of law.

Stability involved maintaining a reverential connection with the gods and the dead, since both dwell close to the primal source of power. This source was variously imagined as Nun, Aten, and the duat. "Egypt," says John Anthony West, "held that man's purpose on earth was the return to the source. There were recognized in Egypt two roads to this same goal. One was known as the way of Osiris, which represented the cyclic nature of universal process; this was the way of successive reincarnations. The second road was the way of Horus, the direct path to resurrection that the individual might achieve within a single lifetime."[12]

Venerating the ancestors was an important way to maintain a vital link with Osiris and the realm of the dead. This practice in part explains the enormous importance placed on cemeteries. Egyptologist Rundle Clark explains:

> The ancestors, the custodians of the source of life, were the reservoir of power and vitality, the source whence flowed all the forces of vigor, sustenance and growth. Hence they were not only departed souls but remained active as the keepers of life and fortune. Whatever happened, whether for good or evil, ultimately derived from them. . . . Hence the place where the ancestors dwelt was the most holy spot in the world. From it flowed the well being of the group. Without the tomb or the cemetery, life on earth would be miserable, perhaps impossible.[13]

Keeping the royal blood in the family was critically important to preserve stability. It was no easy feat. A good part of Egypt's mystery includes murderous plots and assassinations of fathers and sons. At times the center of power collapsed, and civil war threatened; military responses restored unity. Thus we find, even in a cursory view of any list of pharaohs, a large number of military men. Clearly, most pharaohs did not live in an ivory tower where they spent their time in worship;

physical strength and courage as well as abilities to connect with the gods were essential. Maintenance of the bloodline kept power secured within a long tradition of pharaohs and their link with the ancestors and the gods.

We see the same drive toward centricity in the Egyptians' conceptualization of their gods. While the Western mind tends to think of Ra, Osiris, and Horus as separate gods, it is more accurate to understand them as different aspects of a single phenomenon. Divine trinities are commonly found in the Egyptian pantheon. In Jung's psychology, we find this same phenomenon in the psyche, where the Self reflects aspects of all archetypes. The alchemists called this concept the One and the Many. According to Jung, the Self is an archetype that "expresses the unity of the personality as a whole. . . . It is a *transcendental* concept."[14] The pharaoh was the closest physical example of a human being who represented the Self. As we examine some of the principle deities that play a role in the Osiris myth, we can identify their function in Egyptian religion and society.

Although no precise equivalencies exist between gods and archetypes, there certainly are apparent affinities worth mentioning. Ra represents the Self, the archetype of wholeness that includes everything conscious and unconscious. Isis, Hathor, and Sekhmet reveal different manifestations of the Great Mother. Seth is the shadow incarnate and Horus the ego that controls the conscious affairs of daily life. Osiris is a more personal archetypal figure. He acts as an intermediary between the divine Ra and the defender of earth, Horus. Thus, Osiris is best understood as a complex consisting of a cosmic deity, an earthly deity, and an underworld deity that still exists within the realm of psyche.[15] This understanding is important to bear in mind as we follow the evolution of Osiris through these three realms.

In his chthonic form, we meet Osiris following death in the netherworld, where he nourishes the earth, breathes life into the air, sets the Nile's tides, and ignites the fire of passion in the hearts of men and women. In the underworld Osiris ceremoniously presides over the judgment of the dead. As I mentioned earlier, the underworld is synonymous with the unconscious. Osiris, then, is the archetypal energy activating the unconscious so that it is not only a repository of memory, but also an incredible resource in everyday life. In other words, the unconscious is by nature a sort of death of consciousness—not its termination, but a creative force that rejuvenates the conscious mind. To help understand death in this way, it is helpful to distinguish the Egyptians' attitude toward death from our own.

Their view of life wasn't based on a time continuum culminating in death. "The Egyptians," according to the Henri Frankfort, director of the Warburg Institute, "considered death an interruption, not the end, of life—a change in a man's personality."[16] They did not focus on resurrection as a means of gaining salvation, but as a method of achieving unity of body, mind, and spirit. For them, death wasn't thought of as an endpoint, but rather as an integral part of one's existence and an inevitable stage one could pass through with all five senses intact. "The Egyptian cosmology," explains Mojsov, "was without an apocalypse, without the end of time. Time was not moving towards an eternal consummation. It simply *was*. It was cyclical and ever repeating. The cycles of decay and renewal occurred in indefinite time, so that, with respect to human observation, this world had neither a beginning nor an end. Eternity was outside time."[17]

While human existence is generally perceived as a fixed quantity of time, life beyond death is open-ended; immortality then becomes a viable possibility. The body dies, but the soul lives on. Since time isn't linear, transcendence isn't tied to the future; it is available *at any moment*. Neither is resurrection tied to the physical body; transcending the limitations of the physical body is also possible at any time. The pharaoh was the one who lived between the earthly and spiritual realms;

additionally, the pharaoh exemplified the rule of Ma'at, the archetypal goddess of order. In other words, the pharaoh exemplified the way by which order between worlds was kept intact. Ma'at, says Egyptologist Erik Hornung, "is the order, the just measure of things, that underlies the world. . . . This state is always being disturbed, and unremitting effort is necessary in order to recreate it in its original purity."[18]

In emulating the pharaoh, each citizen was in effect upholding the cosmic principles of order. None of this is to say that physical death could be avoided, as it is an essential part of the natural rhythm of life. Yet, while it is inevitable, the manner by which one makes the crossing into the netherworld depends on how one lives his or her life.

To be sure, despite the importance of upholding ethical principles in daily life as well as in the pharaoh's court, we must guard against idealizing Egypt. Abundant evidence from Deir el-Medina, where the Valley of the Kings is located, shows that ancient Egypt was not immune from crime. In addition to tomb robbing, documents provide ample evidence of violence, bribery, regicide, robbery, and possibly even human sacrifice occurring as early as the First and Second Dynasties. There was plenty to be weighed in the final judgment of the dead.

Before the soul is admitted to the Judgment Hall of Osiris, forty-three assessors examine it through a curious process known as the "negative confession." The Egyptians took great pains to avoid insulting the gods. In this confession, the soul replies to the questions put to it by responding in the negative. Doing so would avoid any appearance that the soul was placing itself above the level of a god, for to violate what only a god can do is in effect to say one is greater than that god. We can discern an implicit rule here: we may rise to the level of a god but not think for a moment we can transcend a god.[19] With this in mind, the deceased carefully worded their responses to the assessors. The phrase "I did not interfere with the Nile's inundation" honored Osiris, for he alone ruled over the Nile's movements. "I did not steal from my neighbor" and "I did not forget to venerate the gods" were typical answers given to the assessors.

Before ending this brief introduction, I come to one of the most vexing problems of Egyptian cosmology—the apparent contradiction between a conception of existence in which immortality is achievable and another in which everything, even gods, eventually die. Now we must employ one of the "adjustments" I mentioned earlier; namely, we cannot wholly approach this difficult subject with a strictly rational method. Just as I've suggested that Egyptian cosmology laid the groundwork for the psyche and, as we shall soon see, alchemy as well, it also shaped the embryonic beginnings of philosophy; thus, it is wiser to appreciate their cosmology as a fluid stream of noetic images rather than one that conforms to any formal philosophical system.

As Hornung points out in *Conceptions of God in Ancient Egypt*, death is not the same as nonexistence: "Like men, the gods die, but they are not dead. Their existence—and all existence—is not an unchanging endlessness, but rather constant renewal." But, renewal only takes place "outside the ordered world of creation."[20] I will describe in some detail how the Egyptians perceived the creation of the world in the next chapter, but for the moment we need to draft some conception of their cosmology in order to understand the meaning of the gods, especially Osiris. The Book of the Dead says, "This earth will return to the primeval water (Nun), to endless (flood) as in its first state. I [Atum] shall remain with Osiris after I have transformed myself into another snake [Apopis] which men do not know and the gods do not see."[21]

Gods are born and expire within the realm of existence but they, like humans, must step into the abyss of nonexistence in order to be renewed. In addition to being subject to the laws of the real world, gods have other specific limitations. With the exception of the gods of the earliest kingdom, the power of most gods was limited to particular places. These were local gods who presided over their sacred cities; thus, gods of one city might prove powerless in another place. Gods did not generally have absolute power, for it was in their nature to become highly differentiated. In fact, one measure of a god's power was his or her number of manifestations. Being a major god of the Old Kingdom, Osiris held enormous power, due in large part to his enduring resistance to change, even under very dire circumstances. I have already mentioned some of the complex manifestations that attest not only to his stability but to his universality.

With creation comes death and the "two things" (duality) that differentiate existence and nonexistence. Within the realm of the differentiated world, gods and humans, life and death, time and space are all created and eventually perish. The existent world, including the duat, is encircled and shadowed by nonexistence. We might say that imagination takes us to the brink of this world, and beyond it we know nothing. Gods help extend human life well past physical death and to the brink of the existent, created world, but not beyond it. The philosopher Naydler, author of three excellent books on ancient Egypt, explains: "None of the gods know it [the supracelestial world] because they belong in the world of the existent, and yet all the gods are ultimately manifestations of it. They do not know it because it is greater than them. It is the 'void' that is beyond distinctions of subject and object, and which has a central place in the teachings of Buddhism. In Christian theology, it is the GROUND of being, as distinct from any existent thing."[22]

Immortality exists within this world, and beyond it nothing can be said. Only silence remains. But, within the existent world, *nonexistence is everywhere*. It "stretches under every place." As Hornung says, the nonexistent is in "the ground water . . . [which] reminds them of the state before creation. . . . The yearly inundation brings the timeless non-existent back into the world of creation and 'the earth is Nun.' . . . Even the vivifying breath of the wind 'goes forth from the Nun,' . . . and every night darkness returns, the state which for the Egyptians too was 'in the beginning everything.'"[23] Thus, when the soul is taken before Osiris, god of the dead, the deceased stands before one "to whom comes that which is and that which is not."

These concepts are very difficult to grasp because the modern mind believes it thinks in mostly conscious, rational ways. Grasping Egyptian cosmology requires the Western mind to lay aside its logical attempts to explain the world. To gain some idea of this ancient world we need more than accuracy and knowledge about the afterlife; again, we must change the way we think and in this case, look at reality.

Here I am reminded of an old Chinese story that illustrates the different cognitive styles between the Eastern and Western minds. A fierce battle is being waged in China, and eleven of the top generals convene a meeting to decide how to proceed. Should they fight or should they retreat? They decide to put the question to a vote. Three vote to fight and eight to retreat. It was unanimously decided that retreat was out of the question and they would fight on. Of course, in the end they were victorious. To a Westerner this would make little sense, since both rationality and democratic rule point to favoring the majority. But to these Chinese generals, the number three, being a symbol of wholeness, is a much better number than eight. And so it is that sometimes even we moderns might learn to act against reason and find success. There is no better science for understanding such paradox than alchemy, and for that reason we briefly turn our attention to the Royal Art in order to make some sense of Osiris and his mysterious ways.

2

ALCHEMY, MAGIC, AND OSIRIS

Wherefore we must be bold to say, that an Earthly Man is a Mortal God,
and that the Heavenly God is an Immortal Man.

—Hermes Trismegistus

lchemy is as complex and as old as Osiris. Both share a common source—the Nile and its rich symbolism. To understand this connection we must unravel the cryptic language of alchemy, just as we have to interpret the rich symbolism of the Osiris myth. Fortunately, C. G. Jung, the twentieth-century psychiatrist who coined the terms *individuation* and *collective unconscious*, took up the daunting task of deciphering what the alchemical riddles and recipes meant to the development of consciousness. In my view, his achievement is comparable to Jean-François Champollion's decoding the Rosetta stone; without either man's work the wisdom of the unconscious, both historic and psychic, and its relevance to modern thought would have remained inaccessible to us.

Jung was a contemporary of Sigmund Freud and for a time contributed to the development of Freudian psychoanalysis. When Freud began collaborating with Jung, the young Swiss psychiatrist had already established a world reputation with his word-association experiments. He demonstrated the existence of deep-seated complexes lodged in the human psyche, patterns that transcended a person's individual history. Freud, too, had shown evidence of repetitive patterns that could be traced back in time to explain how psychic energy moves, develops, and is expressed in thought, feelings, and behavior.

Jung credited Freud with having discovered the first archetype in the myth of Oedipus, in which Oedipus tragically kills his father and unwittingly marries his mother. From his analysis of the myth, Freud discerned critical dynamics of early childhood development that explain unconscious motivation, wish fulfillment, incest taboos, death wishes, etc. Discovering the Oedipus complex was a tremendous achievement in establishing that the past lives on in us, not just as archaic memory but more importantly as unconscious determinants in personality development. The Greek Oedipus myth became the cornerstone of psychoanalytic theory, and its description of the early psychosexual development formed the blueprint for many other psychological systems that followed in subsequent years.

What the Oedipus myth did for psychoanalysis and its profound influence on contemporary culture, the Osiris myth did for alchemy over the course of five thousand years. As I will show, Osiris provided a mythic foundation on which researchers continue to build, elaborate, and refine models that explain how the mind works.

Jung expanded the Freudian paradigm and showed that the Oedipus myth was only one among many myths describing how consciousness develops throughout the lifespan. In his elder years, Jung devoted all his attention to alchemy in an effort to support his theory of the collective unconscious and the individuation process. In his search for concrete evidence that showed how these concepts were not merely theoretical but actually existed in the historical record, he found many examples in the world's ancient mythologies.

Jung studied alchemy and its psychology for the last thirty years of his life. He mostly concentrated on medieval alchemy but was also well aware of the importance of Osiris to the symbolism of death and re-birth. Jung was convinced that alchemy's real worth had less to do with recipes for transmuting metals than with demonstrating psychophysical methods of transforming consciousness. The true intent of the alchemist, he believed, was to extend life and deepen the capacities of the human mind. Alchemy was not meant to replace nature but instead to facilitate its processes so that the time needed to transform gross matter into something exquisitely refined was markedly shortened. We might conjecture that instead of having to live many lifetimes, a person could accomplish the goal of individuation in a single lifetime by applying alchemical methods.

And what precisely is this goal? In my view, the goal is the creation of a Divine Self, one that enjoys the conscious union of ego and Self, instincts and archetypes, femininity and masculinity, psyche and soma—having an active relationship with the unconscious; mastering the technique of active imagination; integrating shadow; recognizing projections; and, finally, achieving "object love" with individuals, the collective, nature, and God.

Books on Egyptian history do not fail to mention *heka* (magic) and its importance to the ancient Egyptians' mythology, cosmology, and theology. Glaringly obvious, however, is that no mention of alchemy is made in the old hieroglyphic texts, and it is conspicuously absent in modern books on Egypt. On the one hand, this absence comes as no surprise since the first alchemical writing did not appear until 200 BC with Bolos of Mendes.[1] But it also seems especially strange, since the basis of alchemical theory appears to have been largely influenced by the myths and practices of the first Egyptians. We know that Cleopatra, the last Ptolemy to rule Egypt, practiced the Royal Art, but before her there is no record of alchemy being practiced (in any formal way) by any pharaoh. At the same time, I should add there are no records to show that the Egyptians made astrological observations despite the fact they developed a calendar and certainly used astrological data in constructing mortuary complexes.[2]

What I surmise from careful study of ancient Egypt is that alchemy in fact did not exist as a formal science, but there is no doubt that its principles were already in practice as early as the Old Kingdom— perhaps even earlier when we consider that the people living in Predynastic Egypt, some six thousand years ago, already knew the chemical process for tanning animal skins. Egyptologist Alison Roberts convincingly demonstrates a direct parallel between alchemical treatises and Egyptian sources. The correlation between Egypt and all manner of alchemical theory, symbology, and practice is much too close to entertain the possibility that the basic tenets of alchemy could have come from any other ancient place. As Roberts says, "In the light of everything that the alchemists have said about the origins of their tradition, it is implausible simply to explain away this European sequence [*Splendor Solis*] as merely a similar response to universal life-cycle challenges or some spontaneous eruption of the collective unconscious, entirely unconnected with ancient Egypt. The similarities are so striking that such explanations seem scarcely credible."[3]

No doubt, magic was the science of the day in ancient Egypt. Along with alchemy, no philosophical system or even evidence of a formal school of astrology exists, and yet we see the seminal operations of transmutation taking place in the mummification process and the supreme importance of the polestar in Egyptian cosmology. Certainly, neither alchemy nor astrology had yet eclipsed the hold heka had on the popular culture in which pregnant women made offerings to Hathor and the embalmer called upon Anubis for guidance; that would come with the Greeks and the great transference of knowledge via Alexandria to the rest of the world.

Yet, throughout history we find archetypal patterns and even gods that form a common thread connecting shamanism, magic, alchemy, and modern science. For alchemy in particular, we can identify a lineage that begins in Egypt with Thoth, followed by the Greek Hermes and Hermes Trismegistus, and finally, in the Middle Ages, we have Mercurius, who becomes the patron of the alchemical opus. In *The Egyptian Hermes*, Garth Fowden states that "Hermes Trismegistus . . . was the cosmopolitan, Hellenistic Hermes, Egyptianized through his assimilation to Thoth, and in fact known throughout the Roman world as 'the Egyptian' *par excellence.* To some extent this intermingling of Egyptian and Greek theology and Hellenistic philosophy produced a sum that was greater than its parts, a divinity who could deservedly be placed among the *dei magni* of the pagan pantheon that presided over the Roman world."[4]

Although exploring this mythological lineage further is beyond the scope of these introductory remarks, it is interesting to note that still other connections between Egypt and the modern world can be identified. To cite just a few examples, consider *heka*, meaning magic as well as referring to the Egyptian god of magic, Heka; the Greek goddess Hecate; and our modern colloquialism "heck." The early Christians described the most poignant result of these associations. They understood Osiris to be the prefiguration of Christ and similarly identified Isis with Christ's mother, Mary. Budge and, more recently, Mojsov show direct parallels between the major themes of Christianity, including the Trinity, the Resurrection, and the sacraments, with their antecedents in Egyptian rites. Other researchers go a step further and show patterns that relate religious rituals to their Egyptian antecedents. For example, there is a clear affinity between Nun-Nile-renewal-rebirth-baptism and the alchemical operation *solutio.* This chain of associations contains a fundamental paradox: we must die or surrender to the unconscious in order to attain spiritual life. Accordingly, we find traces of this ancient connection in the Bible: "Unless a man be born again of water and the Holy Ghost, he cannot enter into the kingdom of God" (John 3:5).

These archetypal patterns show that embodying the spirit of Osiris isn't as extraordinary as it may first appear. The past lives with us both in these concrete parallels and also in Jung's concept of the collective unconscious. Marie-Louise von Franz, a close associate of Jung, describes Osiris as "the personification of the collective unconscious, all that existed in the collective unconscious psyche, but which was not included in the conscious religious forms of that time."[5] If Osiris not only represents a dynamism that helped structure the human psyche but also is an archetype (of the Self), then with the use of Jungian techniques we should be able to empathetically engage this ancient god to access his wisdom. I hasten to add that I am not proposing any sort of channeling in which an individual acts as a passive catalyst to receive communication from a god, spirit, or deceased person, but rather a Jungian approach that employs active imagination and empathic engagement not unlike methods used by the Egyptians themselves.

I believe the roots of alchemy are buried deep in the Egyptian psyche. We have signs of its germination well before Cleopatra or Bolos of Mendes recorded their alchemical ideas. As mentioned earlier, the process of tanning was already in use as early as the sixth millennia BC. This process involved urine, alkaline lime, and salt, all ingredients commonly used in the alchemist's laboratory. Mortar was discovered a thousand years before the first dynasty, and gold mining in Upper Egypt used fire setting to soften rocks. All too often evidence of alchemy's existence in early Egypt is solely tied to its funerary rituals. I think alchemy as a protoscience was much more pervasive throughout the country than is generally recognized. Still, to whatever extent alchemy had advanced into the culture, its innovations were not enough to support Egypt's continued existence, in large part because its technology was mostly put to the service of religion. Certainly other factors contributed to the fall of a three-thousand-year-old dynasty. Overreliance on magic, the rise of Christianity, and a progressively weakened view of the pharaoh made Egypt increasingly vulnerable to foreign invaders. As sacred rites moved out of the temple, a shift away from the centrality of the pharaoh began. Priests were replaced by Hermeticists, and finally alchemists sought to materialize in laboratories the mysteries of their ancient Egyptian predecessors. The end of dynastic rule and a succession of conquests and occupations by Nubians, Libyans, Greeks, and Romans ultimately destroyed the last remnants of the old Egypt.

What had not been destroyed was assimilated by other cultures. One of the worst consequences of the Roman occupation was the destruction of the great library complex at Alexandria. Tragically, Julius Caesar's soldiers burned it down in 48 BC. With it thousands of magical and sacred papyri were lost. Yet, out of its ashes alchemy sprang to life in the period from the third century BC to the fourth century AD. What had been early simple transformations involving merely superficial changes in the surface appearance of a metal (gilding) now aimed at actually transmuting molecular structure. Recipes became less focused on magical spells and more like methodological formulae found in today's laboratories. Zosimos of Panopolis (third century AD) in particular advanced alchemy, providing its first definition, inventing various alchemical equipment, and describing in allegorical terms the transmutation of lead and silver into gold.[6]

The Osiris myth survived old Egypt because it possessed elements of both magic and alchemy, bridging an old magical tradition to a proto-science that eventually coalesced into formal laboratories and experimentation. In reading about Osiris, we must therefore look beyond magic and especially focus on psychological nuances that take us deeper into the nature of psyche and soma, the psychoid realm.[7] Since alchemy attempts to transform physical substances using both laboratory methods and psychic processes, we should not be surprised to discover the Osiris myth contains an alchemical recipe stating a fundamental principle underlying psychophysical change. In fact, I believe the Osiris myth may contain *the first alchemical recipe*.

This discovery most likely came initially to the pharaoh and his court of shaman-priests. Such a find was kept from commoners and embedded in the language of heka and the imagery of pharaonic ascension. If de Lubicz is right in his assertion that the gods are better understood as functions than states of transcendent being, then these gods—Osiris and his retinue—represent elements in a divine equation. This representation is the most mysterious part of the myth: we will be looking for secret recipes embedded in the myth's characters and their strange behavior. Again, we should recall the extreme lengths to which pharaohs and alchemists went to safeguard sacred knowledge. The alchemists were notorious in their efforts to protect hard-won insights gained in self-experimentation. Silence was virtually an oath taken by all sincere adepts. Just as pharaohs and court priests took pains to hide secret rituals, alchemists ingeniously concealed their knowledge in strange ciphers, misleading images, wordless books, seals, and even architectural structures.

Since the Osiris myth emerges from a time when magic was prevalent throughout Egyptian society, it is important to appreciate what heka meant to the people and how it differs from alchemy. To begin with, there was no word in the early Egyptian language for religion; the closest term is *heka*, but the two are far apart in meaning. Heka was a god, the "father of all gods," who alone could command other gods. While religion is an organized set of beliefs, Heka is a god with whom one enters into relationship by very prescribed rituals. Through rigorous training a magician becomes Heka and thereby attains the power to transform reality. "Magic," writes Naydler, "is a mysterious divine force through which the spiritual and physical universe becomes manifest, and hence a force permeating and linking all levels of reality from the highest to the most material." It is "the means by which the human being, and ultimately all creation, returns to the supreme Godhead, the unmanifest source of all that exists."**8** Without understanding heka, the Osiris myth is little more than a fairy tale. Appreciating the role that magic played in Egyptian life sheds light on the context in which the Osiris myth originated.

Osiris taught the people how to farm the land, while Isis, his sister-wife, showed them how to make bread. These tasks seem simple, but to those whose diets depended on raw fish, ox flesh, figs, sweet oil, and the most basic staples, the sprouting of grain and the making of bread from flour must have seemed like pure magic, a gift from the gods. In fact, Ra was believed to have given heka to his people as a protection against evil spirits, especially those who might poison the food supply. In word and image, the theme of food offerings is found throughout ancient Egyptian texts and commonly displayed on temple walls. From farm fields to kitchen to temples and gravesites, magic was the chief means empowering common people with a modicum of control over an otherwise hostile environment.

The threats facing these people came from every corner of life. Pestilence, famine, and disease were common, and defenses against such evil were as important as learning to till the fields. "In the opinion of the common people," writes Serge Sauneron, "it was less important to battle the physical cause of an illness than to exorcise the evil demon and constrain it to release its prey. To ensure such a result, there was nothing better than a good magic spell, and no one was better qualified to write it than a learned 'lector-priest' well versed in the lore of the old books of magic . . . thus, outside the temples, our learned celebrants fulfilled the role of village sorcerers."**9**

Included in the official duties of the lector-priest was a regular recharging of the divine energy, which might diminish over time or be stolen by ominous powers. The magician-priests were well schooled in texts like *Book of overpowering Apopis, the enemy of Re and the enemy of Wennefer* (Osiris) that contained explicit instruction for maintaining divine power. They were equally adept at "functioning as exorcists, copying down little spells against fever, scorpion stings, and maladies of every sort,"[10] not to mention concocting love potions and preparing elixirs to enhance beauty.

David Rankine, author of *Heka*, describes the nature of magical power: "One of the titles of the god Heka was The One who Consecrates Imagery, referring to the ability of the god to empower creative thoughts and actions and translate them into their physical equivalents in the physical world. So Heka was also perceived as the animating and manifesting force of every ritual act. In this context, heka is thus both intent and action: the cause, the act and the effect."[11]

This animating power relates to Jung's description of the anima, the soul that functions on the microcosmic level in a man's personality and, at the macrocosmic level, is seen as the Anima Mundi. In the first instance, the anima is an intermediary between the conscious and the unconscious personality; in a woman, the animus, or spirit, functions in a similar way. Ritual is a means of activating the energies of one's soul and guiding this force toward a specific purpose. One difference between magic and alchemy is that the former is a power employed *to* change nature at the direction of the magician's will, or *akh*, in concert with the god Heka. By contrast, alchemy works *with* nature because the source of power is not in the operator but in nature; accessing this power requires the alchemist's mind to be in sympathetic accord with the rhythms of nature.

Magic works in strange ways, often involving interplay between soma (matter) and psyche (mind). The god Anubis serves as a good example to show how this image evolved from a concrete, physical source and became a complex deity rich in symbolic power. We can trace a distinct line between his beginning in natural phenomena and his rise to power through human manipulation. Early on, people buried their dead in shallow graves, but as Seth's winds roared up, the bodies of corpses were exposed and desert dogs feasted on the remains. The magician-priests used ritual to honor the god that dwelled in these beasts. As a result, what had been an unmanageable predator animal was transformed through magic into the god Anubis. By the time his god image reaches maturity, we see that his powers stem from his canine nature and his close association with the dead. Just as the waters of Nun contain rejuvenating powers, so too do those who live in the soil. Anubis's animal nature and his association with the dead infuse him with powerful supplies of heka. Perhaps for this reason, his image commonly adorns the lid of the magician's box containing the tools of his practice. Priests, wearing full Anubis headdresses, used these tools in the embalming process to embody the god and apply his skills.

It is not by chance that Anubis, depicted with the head of a jackal or desert dog, became the god of embalmers. We see in many texts the evolution of Anubis from the desert dog to the jackal-headed god who prepared his father's body for the afterlife. Frankfort attributes the source of heka found in animals to their *otherness*. He explains, "The Egyptian interpreted the nonhuman as superhuman, in particular when he saw it in animals—in their inarticulate wisdom, their certainty, their unhesitating achievement, and above all in their static reality."[12]

At the same time, the observant Egyptians realized that the salt in the sand and the hot sun overhead dehydrated the exposed corpses. Thus, the first steps in embalming were revealed by a natural process of predation and preservation; both these processes are found in the alchemist's laboratory. The combination of heat and salt (natron) was nature's way of drawing out moisture from the corpse and led to the elaborate methods used in mummification and later, for other purposes, in alchemical practice. *Calcinatio*, for instance, became a standard alchemical operation used to reduce or eliminate the humidity of the *prima materia* (First Matter; undifferentiated substance) and return it to its original form by applying heat, both psychic and physical.[13]

In addition to natural elements, the Egyptians attributed the power of heka to a number of gods—Ra, Heka, Isis, Sekhmet—but ultimately it came under the dominion of Thoth, a god represented with the head of either a baboon or an ibis. The baboon suggests a human's lower nature and the ibis its highest spiritual aspect. Thoth used magic to conjoin these opposites in his nature, and oftentimes we see him assist other gods when their magic isn't sufficient to accomplish a difficult task. As we will see in greater detail in the Osiris myth, Thoth helps Isis find a critical member of Osiris's body and manages to curtail the interminable warfare between Horus and Seth. This power to bring warring opposites to peaceful resolution is later symbolized by the caduceus of Hermes, a magical wand that has its origins in ancient Egypt. The pharaoh was imbued with this same talent whereby he united "in himself the Above and the Below, and brings into manifestation a new divine-human axis, a channel for the energies of the spirit world to flow into the terrestrial world."[14]

Thoth was to magic what Mercurius became for alchemy, a god without whom the entire opus could not succeed. By contrast, Osiris is best understood initially as the prima materia, that is, the basic substance from which the gold or philosopher's stone might eventually emerge. He is sacred matter, passive, pliant, and pure, pregnant with life and possibility. He also represents the operations of decay and death—*putrefactio* and *mortificatio*—those same operations we saw when corpses were exposed to the natural furnace of burning sand and hot wind. Osiris is the movement of the Nile, whose waters bring life to the dry riverbeds and potency to the human body. "Osiris," says Egyptologist Rundle Clark, "is the spirit of becoming . . . no longer the Dead King, Fertility Daimon or Inundation Spirit but the personification of the coming into being of all things."[15] In other words, Osiris not only triumphs over death, but also represents the principle of continuous creation.

In *The Coming Forth by Day* we find Osiris navigating the duat, carrying the sun (consciousness) through the land of darkness (unconsciousness) and triumphing in the creation of each new day. He is both sun and shadow, symbolizing the "two paths" that each of us must travel and integrate as we strive to become whole. Michael Maier, the sixteenth-century alchemist, described this struggle in the form of a recipe: "The Sun and its Shadow bring the Work to perfection." In other words, we must integrate life-giving and death elements of the psyche in order to individuate. To strive for either enlightenment or goodness without accounting for the dark aspects of life isn't sufficient if our goal is to gain our own special form of divinity.

In summary, I know of no better example than the myth of Osiris to illustrate the original principles involved in this transformational process. Myths provide maps to help guide us through the labyrinth of life until we find the center of our being. The Osiris myth is part of a collective dream, and, like any dream, we can understand what and who Osiris *is* not only by interpreting the symbols of his life, death, and resurrection, but, ultimately, by embodying his spirit.

Before delving into the myth we might ask: What does Osiris have to tell us? Who are Osiris, his brother and sisters, and their children? What is the magical and alchemical significance of these ancient gods?

Just as an alchemist spends an inordinate amount of time selecting and meditating on the ingredients that will go into his vessel, it is important for us to examine the main characters of this myth. Their traits and nuances enrich our understanding of their function for one another and for the overall meaning of the myth. These details are important. For example, legend holds that the tears Isis shed after the death of her husband were so profuse that they caused the Nile to overflow its banks.

These tears can only have come from a goddess. They express the relentless love that propels her throughout the myth to accomplish extraordinary things; despite all odds, her love proves indomitable. Von Franz describes the source of Isis's hidden numinous image: "She always does what has to be done. She does the negative thing in order to dissolve consciousness, then the positive thing in order to bring forth the process of individuation. As the destructive and at the same time redeeming Great Mother she is everywhere. She is the feminine principle which furthers the inner transformation."[16]

Her love for Nephthys; her strength in resisting Seth; her perseverance in retrieving her husband's body; her protection of her son, Horus; and her ability to reanimate her husband all reach beyond the ordinary boundaries of human love and take us into an irrational territory that can best be called magic. Indeed, her magic is great.

While Isis is all about love, Seth inspires hate. His red hair is the color of the desert, and his black brow bespeaks evil. To do "red things" meant that harm would follow. Seth is odious and vengeful, qualities that make it hard to understand why he was worshiped. Sympathetic magic gives us some insight into how such an awful god might command veneration. Seth was symbolized as a black pig, a fitting image for such a swine. He was blamed when the Nile's waters rose too high or sank too low. Pestilence and disease followed the resulting flood or drought. To appease Seth and prevent such catastrophe, festivals were held each year in which a black pig was ritualistically slaughtered in an effort to pacify this dangerous god. More than pacification, worship of Seth paid honor to the necessity of limits he constantly demanded. He drives us to the brink of madness, and there we discover the limits of what we are capable of achieving.

Clouds, dust, darkness, chaos, and confusion symbolize Seth's sulfuric nature. For all the mischief and even death that he doles out, Seth is not morally evil. The Egyptians believed evil was inherent in the nonexistent world; gods and humans struggled to keep evil at bay, heka being their chief weapon. Seth is not a devil, but rather a divine trickster, black magician, and alchemist who creates "all necessary features of the existent world and of the limited disorder that is essential to a living order."[17] He forms a boundary that brings us to the extreme limit of sanity, passion, and even murder. In a strange twist of fate, it was the unlikely god Seth who in the end killed the demon serpent Apopis and, at the world's end, together with Ra and Osiris "evaded his day of death."[18]

Horus, too, has a very important symbolic role, one that is not immediately obvious in reading the myth. He was not just Osiris's son and avenger, but more importantly he was the reincarnation of Osiris—his future. "Osiris is past, Horus tomorrow," as written in the Pyramid Texts, suggests that we in the present exist between these gods in the ever-changing flux of reality. Actually, there are at least two images of Horus, one who is depicted as a bird perched on the horizon at the dawn of creation and the other who champions his father's spirit. In the first instance, the elder Horus is seen as a solar deity more commonly named Horakhty. The Pyramid Texts refer to him as the "god of the East," the place where the sun rises and the pharaoh is reborn. "The elder Horus," writes von Franz, "was a kind of pantheistic godhead who included the whole cosmos, matter, spirit, the world, the totality of nature and life."[19] He is typically shown as a falcon whose eyes represent the sun and the moon; his speckled breast represents the stars and his wings, the sky. His name derived from the Egyptian word *her*, "the one on high" or "the distant one" (referring to this solar image). This is the Horus that was born (again) on the fifth day following Thoth's gambit with Khonshu.

The younger Horus, whom we will meet in the myth, represents the divine child, commonly known as Harpokrates. Horus brings a human dimension to the myth. We see him as a child lovingly attended to by his mother and later as a man taking on the responsibility of avenging his father's murder. His power derives from his association with Ra, which came about through a trick played by Isis on Ra when she cunningly secured from him the most powerful of his names, which signified the secret essence of his being. This "Golden Horus" name was passed from Ra's ka soul directly to Isis's soul on the condition that this magical name be made known only to Horus.

Names possessed great power in the ancient world, and people had many names serving different purposes. Only one's mother (and Isis) knew her child's true name. In this way, a hex against a person failed unless the magician knew the individual's special name. Isis was the only god that had knowledge of everyone's name. This power was especially important since a person's secret name possessed the essence of their individuality. By absorbing the ka of Ra, Horus becomes the hero of identity, the one who vanquishes the shadow enemy of individuality, Seth, and represents Osiris's counterpart on earth. He is the perennial spirit of each living pharaoh.

Other than Osiris, the two remaining gods in the myth are Nephthys and her son, Anubis. In modern terms it would be easy to defame Nephthys because of her liaison with Osiris and the illegitimate birth of their son. Indeed, she is the only god of the Ennead, or "group of nine," who was not worshiped. But there is much more to this goddess than infidelity suggests. Her name derives from *nebet-hut*, "Mistress of the Mansion," or "Lady of the House." In early times, and even today in some cultures, it was common for a man to have many wives for a variety of reasons. It was not uncommon for the chief wife, Isis in this case, to be on friendly, cooperative terms with the mistress. Recalling the concrete style of thinking I have already described, we might conclude that a mistress serves only to provide sexual pleasure, but she also represents the distant feminine, the dark side of Seth; being an outsider to the family, she doesn't carry the obligations put on the first

ALCHEMY, MAGIC, AND OSIRIS

wife. While Isis is the feminine aspect of the Self, Nephthys is a more earthly goddess. In this way, she has a more nonpersonal relationship to her patron. In alchemy she is the *soror mystica*, the feminine counterpart who provides a connection between the laboratory and nature. Nephthys embodies qualities that give her more freedom and allow her greater movement throughout the myth. She represents beauty, home, and the distant feminine. In this way, Nephthys has archetypal significance, and we find shades of her in Demeter and Aphrodite.

Anubis, son of Osiris and Nephthys, is typically portrayed as a jackal-headed god. As with Horus, Anubis had his own divine life before being absorbed into the Osiris myth. In fact, Anubis was the chief Egyptian funerary god prior to Osiris's popularity. He is mentioned dozens of times in the Pyramid Texts in relation to the king's burial. Not unlike all these gods, Anubis is a complex figure. As his many epithets show, his range of power is great. Some of these include Lord of the Sacred Land, He Who Is upon His Sacred Mountain, Ruler of the Bows, He Who Is in the Place of Embalming, and Foremost of the Divine Booth (burial chamber). In the Osiris myth, his keen senses and instincts make him especially helpful to Isis, so much so that she is said to have adopted him as her own son. He, rather than Isis, is sometimes credited with reconstituting his father's body.

Without having to look too deeply, we can find important human qualities in each of these figures. Isis epitomizes love and loyalty; Seth, antagonism, opposition, and limits; Horus, identity and authority; Nephthys, dark femininity; and Anubis, earthy instincts. But when it comes to Osiris we encounter a psychological complex far more difficult to comprehend than that of most Egyptian deities. His relationship to life and death cannot be easily assigned certain fixed values. Rather than a state of being, his nature has more to do with the process of becoming. In the myth we will see him transform from the virginal prima materia to the golden Self. Such complexity and dynamism boggles our mind.

We cannot see him directly, but we can feel his presence in all living things. He cannot be known by the intellect because reason alone cannot explain the movements of God or his reflection in nature.

Unlike most Egyptian deities, Osiris is always shown in human form, either as a corpse tightly bound in white mummy bandages with only his face and hands exposed or as king of Upper and Lower Egypt. The bandages suggest a cocoon that will serve as the container for his metamorphosis. His skin is typically an earthy green or solemn black, symbolizing his life and death aspects. This greenness relates to Osiris's association with the vegetative kingdom, what alchemists referred to as the "blessed green." The deeper significance of this fertility lies in the fact that just as plants regenerate with each new season, so too does Osiris resurrect from death. In his kingly visage, Osiris bears the royal crook and flail, symbols that represent his mastery over animals and crops, the realm of our lower, unconscious impulses and instincts. At times, we see his erect phallus protruding from his bandages, an ithyphallic image reminding us that fertility and virility issue from the same source—nature.[20]

His head is adorned with the *atef* crown, symbol of supreme authority of a unified Egypt. Regal, yes, but the Egyptians always add some humor or pun so that we might avoid pomposity and not think too highly of the gods. Thus, it is said that Osiris often complained of the heat radiating from his crown. The heat is explained by the fact that Ra, the sun god, originally wore the crown. While we might be amused by this humorous connection, we again see the literalism of the Egyptian mind.

Osiris is often represented by the *djed* column (see frontispiece), a powerful symbol that will receive more attention when we encounter it in the myth. For now it is enough to point out that the djed column was associated with Osiris's backbone, and the image was often pictured on amulets tucked into a mummy's bandages. The djed column represents the stability I spoke of earlier. Osiris was known by many names, but his oldest is Khenti Amentiu, "Foremost of the Westerners." The west is of course the place of the setting sun and with it the twelve dangerous night hours that have to be traversed before consciousness is restored to earth. Another common name of the god is Wennofry, meaning "beautiful being" or "joy of existence."

While some 158 hieroglyphs are used for Osiris, the simplest is a chair situated below an eye. The name associated with this hieroglyph is Seat and Throne of the Eye. The chair refers to the seat of power and, more specifically, the motive power of consciousness. Just as we might say, "I'll *see* that it gets done," Osiris is the awareness that precedes and gives way to action. He is not, then, the god of the Nile, but rather the life energy that *causes* it to ebb and flow. For this same reason, the alchemist Fulcanelli points out that chemistry is about facts, but alchemy has to do with causes. More broadly speaking, Osiris enlivens the soul: he literally brings dead, inanimate things to life, over and over again—"a million times true." And life, in this sense, is not just physical being. "He channels the vitalizing energies of the spirit world," says Naydler, "into the realm of the living." And conversely, Osiris shows that "spiritual life . . . can be sustained even in the midst of the sphere of death."[21] This is the significance of the Eye, that divine organ of consciousness that enables us to see in the dark.

Osiris takes us into the night, where it is pitch black. It is a place we resist but cannot avoid. We go kicking and screaming. There is good reason to run the other way. All the things that go into the construction of reality—like the five adjustments mentioned in the introduction—are switched off in the dark. This is not ordinary darkness, but one the alchemists say is "blacker than black." Death is one word for it, but for the Egyptians it was the darkness that went into the fabric of creation. As part of the created world the duat is "utterly deep, utterly dark, utterly endless."[22] The fright of this darkness comes in thinking it will last forever, that there is no going back, and, for some, the possibility that an unfavorable judgment awaits them, one that will have them cast into flames, the Lake of Fire, the equivalent of nonexistence. What this god has to tell us is that *he is the light in the dark*—a light that appears at times to be extinguished but in reality never wholly disappears. His life is as tortured as any of us could imagine, and still he is transformed. He doesn't die in the usual sense, but rather dies to another realm of eternal reality. Osiris is a lunar deity, the "Man-in-the-Moon" who slowly dies for fourteen days and then resurrects.[23]

On his throne, Osiris is the lord of the underworld, presiding over all souls brought before him. He possesses intimate knowledge of the cycle of life, death, and transcendence. Osiris is not an object of beauty but rather the process of beauty. As we peer at the sunset of our life, we can rest assured that Osiris will guide us through the night, taking us from the material world into a timeless eternity of spirit.

Some might argue that I carry this myth too far, that it is, after all, nothing more than a figment of our imagination. Perhaps. But even today's physics is revealing a secret that has been the mainstay of Eastern wisdom for many centuries: *consciousness is an ever-unfolding creative force in nature, a force that gave rise to the physical universe.* The intuition of the ancestors—that matter arises from spirit, not the other way round—is proving to be true. This being the case, we must recognize countless generations of believers who have venerated, worshipped, and even "embodied" the concept of change, with Osiris being chief among those gods who personify this process.

By personifying gods, we recognize their autonomy and at the same time our relationship with them. We begin to see how they function in our life as well as how they act as intermediaries between this world and others. Osiris, in particular, exemplifies that part of our nature having to do with death and transformation. His personified form provides hope and comfort to an otherwise irrational and terrifying event in human existence.

Comfort is the least of what Osiris offers. More than pharaohs who sought to ascend into the starry night, Osiris is the resurrection beyond this short life. He holds our good name in posterity in this world and ensures that we will be remembered in the next life. History will account for us and remembrance connects us with our ancestors and with the gods. In Osiris's story, we find a familiar path. It is one that a person who knows something about the road to individuation will recognize. In his own words he proclaims,

> Whether I live or die, I am Osiris
> I enter in and reappear through you,
> I decay in you. I grow in you.
> I fall down in you. I fall upon my side.
> The gods are living in me for I live and grow in the corn
> That sustains the Honored Ones.
> I cover the earth,
> Whether I live or die I am Barley,
> I am not destroyed.[24]

We will follow the path he paved long ago and, like him, carry the torch of consciousness into a new day. Now, let us turn our attention to his myth.

3

DISTURBANCE
IN THE MATRIX

In the beginning there was the Ogdoad, eight gods associated with four principles of creation: Water, Hiddenness, Darkness, and Infinity. Nun, the god of Water, formed the primeval ocean. Atum, the "self-engendered one," emerged out of Nun in the form of a mound. He then inseminated himself and created a pair of male and female gods—Shu and Tefnut, the gods of air and moisture respectively. Nut, the sky goddess, and Geb, the earth, were created from their union. Conflict erupts when Nut angers Geb by swallowing the stars, their children. Shu separates Nut and Geb. Legend has it that these two gods then became lost while wandering the cosmos, and Atum sent his Eye to find them. On their return, Nut wishes to have children but Ra forbids it. Thoth intervenes and, using his magic, Nut bears five children; Osiris is her first-born.

We owe a debt of gratitude to Egyptologists for stringing together plausible narratives that help describe the history from which the Osiris myth was born. Unfortunately, most Egyptologists don't seem to appreciate the elusive mystery that is Egypt; acknowledging the mystical ambitions and experiences of pharaohs and priests is contrary to the goals of modern empirical science.

Scholars still debate whether this mystery is simply a romantic notion or whether Egypt was actually a mystical culture replete with cult practices, magical rituals, and other methods of achieving transcendental experience. Egyptologist Hornung flatly states, "The Egyptians never succumbed to the temptations to find in the transcendence of the existent release from all imperfection, dissolution of the self, or immersion in and union with the universe." Yet, even he "begs indulgence over inconsistencies."[1] Then there is writer and philosopher Jeremy Naydler who, in a chapter entitled "The Recovery of Ancient Egyptian Mysticism," says, "It would be entirely appropriate that mystical texts concerned with traveling into the realm of the dead while still alive should be employed for funerary purposes. But the texts themselves are clearly describing experiences of the living, not of the dead. That is why they are mystical."[2] I will leave this debate to the scholars and instead tell the story of Osiris that I believe reveals an intriguing, mystical conception. We begin the Osiris story with its mythological prehistory—how Egypt and its conception of the world came into existence.

At the very beginning were the *Neteru,* a word that has been translated to mean, according to Budge, "survey, holy, divine, sacred or set apart, renovation, power, force, strong, protect, mighty," and, perhaps most commonly, "gods." As noted earlier, Egyptologists of the Symbolist school view the Neteru as functions and "causal powers" whose attributes are personified by the gods. But even with symbolic interpretations of esoteric writings, we need to root these abstract principles in reality. The general belief is that the indigenous people who dwelt in Predynastic Egypt were uncivilized and that some wise race of people—perhaps the Dravidians or the Berbers—entered the land and established the great Egypt that for centuries ruled the world. John Anthony West, like others before him, describes a period when "Egypt was ruled by the Neters and then another, almost equally long period which . . . was ruled by the Shemsu Hor (the Companions of Horus)," making Egypt some thirty-five thousand years old.[3] As with many of the Egyptian gods, we are left to wonder whether certain gods actually existed. Some believe that such luminaries as Osiris, Seth, and Hermes Trismegistus once walked the earth.

Another definition of the Neteru, one I prefer, comes from the German Egyptologist Heinrich Brugsch, which he says incorporates both the Greek and Latin meaning of *natura*, a possible cognate for our word *nature*. According to Brugsch, the Neteru represent "the active power which produces and creates things in regular recurrence; which bestows new life upon them, and gives back to them their youthful vigor."[4] This definition isn't very different from the Greek root *physis*, which signifies "something that becomes, grows or develops," or the Latin root *natura*, "she who will give birth."

This definition not only resonates with nature but also strikes a familiar chord with Jung's term for the psychological gods, *archetypes*. Certainly, archetypes are found with "regular recurrence" and are reinvigorated by the attention we give them. This phenomenon being the case, the Ennead—Osiris's immediate family—represents archetypes of the collective unconscious. Therefore, any means of bringing increased awareness to them, like reading this book, clearly has a revitalizing effect on them as well as on the reader. Here, I suggest, is an important step toward embodying Osiris, namely—*attention paid to a god is answered kindly*. The road to the unconscious is not a one-way street; rather, it is a living part of the psyche that responds in its own mysterious way to all that happens in our conscious lives. Building an image of a lost god revives ancient memories, and in this way Osiris is psychically recalled and brought back to life.

Westerners certainly do not ordinarily think of gods in this way. Perhaps somewhere in the evolution of the Christian God we forgot that praying to him not only serves our needful purposes but also adds some measure of life to his divinity. Recalling Abt's words from chapter 1, the archetypes "have a tendency to fade in their vigour and die

71

away." Our efforts allow us to reconnect with archetypal reality, and in return we, too, are renewed in the process.

The first archetypal gods, known as the Ogdoad, were first mentioned in the Coffin Texts circa 2000 BC. These gods, grouped in four pairs, each with a male and a female, were personifications of the four fundamental qualities—Water, Hiddenness, Darkness, and Infinity— that make up the world of existence.

> Nun and Naunet—Water
> Amun and Amaunet—Hiddenness
> Kuk and Kauket—Darkness
> Huh and Hauhet—Infinity

They represent psychoid functions that are the original structuring principles giving form to all psychic and physical existence. What we will find in examining the Osiris myth from an alchemical, psychological perspective is the formation of the modern-day psyche. We will see successive battles resulting in critical separations that helped form a psyche composed of consciousness and unconsciousness. Further, we will witness the creation of familiar archetypal powers like the ego, the shadow, and the feminine. As with so many myths, the creation story that provides the context from which Osiris and his family emerge begins with water.

All things, gods, demons, and humans, issue from Nun, the boundless, primordial sea of existence. We might imagine this ocean as a matrix of dark, hidden, infinite water that serves as the font of consciousness. Freud was quite right in describing the unconscious and the moods that stir within it as being "oceanic." We cannot know how long Nun existed since there was no time to measure its duration—it simply existed. The waters of Nun are sacred and powerful. This precious liquid is the source of many mythologies, symbols, sacred rites, and religious ceremonies. It is holy water, the *aqua permanens* of the alchemists and the water that is transmuted into the blood of Christ in the Catholic Mass. Osiris was often symbolized as a cup or golden jar containing water from the Nile; the vessel, say the alchemists, is as important to the symbolism of wholeness as its contents.

Figure 3.1. Nun supporting the Solar Boat.

The created world begins when Atum coalesces with the sun god Ra to create a primeval mound from his own spittle or semen, both of which represent internal "waters." Atum and Ra are solar deities, and together as Atum-Ra they represent the setting sun, an allusion to the descent of consciousness into the duat. Tum and Atum are believed to be one and the same god; both names mean "to complete" or "to finish," suggesting that they bring closure to Nun's limitlessness. This self-contained power complements Nun, and from his own secretions Atum-Ra creates Shu and Tefnut, thereby furthering the ongoing process of creation.

Atum-Ra brings about their birth by masturbating into his own mouth, a strange image that reminds us of the ouroborus. While this act sounds abhorrent, it holds profound symbolic meaning. Like the circle that forms its basic design, one arch represents the rising or evolution of consciousness, while the descending arch represents the falling or involution of consciousness. This process demonstrates the self-perpetuating power of a god as well as the continual cycle of transformation. Alchemists believed that lower, base metals were devoured by the noble metals of silver and gold; thus, the ouroborus represents the ongoing transmutation of the cosmos.

In ancient Egypt, this symbol is associated with a more primitive, sinister image. A number of Late Period texts have various references to "the Serpent in the Primeval Darkness." From the Coffin Texts, we find a haughty description of creation by autofellatio. The Serpent exclaims:

> He [the Indwelling Soul] it was who made the universe in that he copulated
>   with his fist and took the pleasure of emission.
> I bent right around myself, I was encircled in my coils,
> One who made a place for himself in the midst of his coils.
> His utterance was what came forth from his own mouth.[5]

In addition to the curious creation of the world by a serpent—a creature we in the West have come to perceive as lowly and evil—the last line is remarkable in that it conflates creative utterance with seminal emission. In many world religions, sound, vibration, and words are the vehicle that create *ex nihilo*, a concept that has made its way into modern physics. The serpent as a creatrix is typically shown in the form of an ouroborus, the "tail eater," and at the same time represents the Neter of infinity. These circular images and recycling secretions are symbolic representations of the life-giving waters of Nun and play a significant role in the Osirian cycle of death and rebirth. This Serpent of Darkness is a primeval image of God, and since the Egyptians believed that, in the end, Atum reverts back into the form of a serpent, we have God existing at the beginning of the world and at its end. "After the 'millions of years' of differentiated creation," explains Hornung, "the mayhem before creation will return; only the primeval god (Atum) and Osiris will remain 'in one place'—no longer separated in space and time." In the end, all that remains are these two gods, now transformed into "another snake which men do not know and the gods do not see."[6]

Atum-Ra creates the gods of air and moisture, Shu and Tefnut, respectively. From their union Nut (sky) and Geb (earth) are born. According to the Pyramid Texts, Geb is enraged when Nut swallows the stars, their children, and Shu has to separate them. After Atum's initial separation from Nun, there is no greater cosmogonic act than Shu's division of the earth from the heavens (Geb from Nut), for now there is room enough for the birth of human beings and a consciousness alchemically composed of the critical elements of life: warmth, moisture, and air.

An alternate, more psychological interpretation of these events tells of Shu becoming enamored with Nut, and for this reason Nut and Geb are separated. And yet another version of the story has it that Nut and Geb were so in love that Shu, the great divider, had to separate them, and as a result earth and sky became distinct parts of the world's ecology. In each version, the common theme is love and with it the wish for reunion. For the love that persists between Nut and Geb causes them to long eternally for each other. Thus, coffins were often painted with Nut on the lid and Geb on the bottom; closing the coffin signified the reunion of sky and earth. Following their separation, Nut forms a physical canopy over the earth with her fingers and toes gently pressed upon the earth's surface; through her body, the sun makes its daily sojourn from the eastern to the western horizon. She is the sky in which all other deities—the stars—are contained.

Figure 3.2. Nut, Geb, and Shu.

While Nut arches her body to form the firmament overhead, Geb puts earth under our feet. Geb is often shown in the act of performing a somersault, suggesting the earth in rotation, a concept that clashes with an outdated belief that the Egyptians viewed the earth as a flat surface.[7] In any case, Nut and Geb create a world capable of supporting human life. Again, we see a reversal in gender identifications. Ordinarily, we think of Mother Earth and Father Sky, but for the Egyptians, the opposite was true.

Humans (*remetj*) were created when Nut and Geb, wandering in this new world, lost their way. We understand this to mean that even gods sometimes slip back into unconsciousness. But, a greater god, Atum-Ra, comes to their rescue. An important logic is shown in this cosmology. Nut and Geb are closer to the plane of earthly reality, whose trappings can ensnare ego consciousness and cause one to lose his or her way. Atum-Ra represents the higher powers of the Self archetype. While the ego engages earthly reality, the Self is the all-encompassing archetype of consciousness and unconsciousness. One of the most difficult tasks of individuation is to align these two great powers of psyche: ego and Self.[8] Atum-Ra sends his Eye to find Nut and Geb. The Eye of Ra represents his omniscience, psychologically understood as the organ that enables us to see the Divine. With the return of Nut and Geb, Atum-Ra cries out, "I wept tears . . . the form of my Eye; and that is how mankind came into existence."[9]

By separating Nut and Geb, Shu creates an atmosphere that divides the sky from the earth, a graphic display of differentiation. Separation (*separatio*) is followed by differentiation in making the world, both physical and psychic. Differentiated consciousness indicates a significant development in the personality; alchemically, it represents a new and more refined generation of consciousness. All critical moments in the process of individuation are precipitated by separation, so to become one, integrated human being, we must first become two.[10] This step is followed by differentiation, which works internally to create even more refined aspects of consciousness. The soul is a good example of differentiation, especially in the case of the ancient Egyptians, who believed that every individual had nine souls. Each of these souls had a particular function (see chapter 9). For now I want to mention only one of these souls, the heart, since at this point in the myth when humans enter the world, mention of emotional expression is made for the first time.

The heart was considered the seat of intelligence, and from it issued a stream of affects, moods, and emotions. These contents were not just sentimental but had wisdom that served one just as well in the underworld as in this life. For this reason, the heart was left intact during the mummification process. As with any type of intelligence, the feeling function needs to be developed; the more refined or differentiated the feeling function, the more one is able to draw from a wide palette of emotions.

Just as we distinguish mind from brain, the Egyptians had two words for the heart, one denoting the human organ that circulates blood and therefore animates the human body into a whole, living organism, and another (*haty*) conveying a sense of "individuality, consciousness, and personal identity."[11] For them the haty heart was divine intelligence. As the center of intelligence, the heart contained its own truth, and this included all memory of past behavior, good and bad. As a result, people feared that the haty heart might disclose their transgressions to Osiris in the Great Judgment Hall. To prevent the dire consequences of being judged unworthy of resurrection, the living sought to keep the heart from betraying them by reciting protective spells. In the "Invocation to the Heart" a person declares:

> Get away from me, messenger of whatever god thou may be! If thou have come to take away the viscera of my human heart, it will not be given to thee. . . . My heart is in my possession, it will certainly never be taken from me! I am Horus who dwells in the hearts. . . . May terror be removed from me and oppress me not while I am in the breast of my father Geb and my mother Nut. I have not committed any abominable offense against the gods, I did not lose my honor as I have had my righteousness proclaimed.[12]

This intelligence is displayed throughout the Osiris myth, especially in the love Osiris had for his people; the loyalty of his son, Horus; and the devotion shown by Isis and Nephthys. Legend has it that Osiris and Isis were already in love and mated while still in their mother's womb. They are biological soulmates whose love enables them to overcome difficult challenges and perhaps even death.

Returning to the myth, we find that a cosmic bubble forms in the great sea of Nun as a result of separating Nut and Geb. All sentient life emerges within this sphere. The existent world is bounded by Nut above with Geb forming the earth below. Wonderful pictures in the Valley of the Kings depict Nut's body forming the sky with Shu representing the atmosphere standing between her and Geb (figure 3.2). The stage is set for further differentiation of the gods and even humans, but first resistance must be overcome in order for future progeny to come into being.

The jealous Shu (sometimes it is Ra) declares that his daughter, Nut, will not give birth any day or night. Distressed, Nut turns to Thoth, the magician-trickster god, and pleads with him to act on her behalf. Knowing Khonshu, the moon god, to be a gambler, Thoth invites him to a game of draughts. Khonshu loses miserably. With each loss, the moon god gives up some of his luminosity, until as a last resort he wages all his light and again is defeated. The new moon is evidence of this final loss. Having gained enough light to form five days, Thoth gives them to Nut, thereby sidestepping Shu's command. Nut proceeds to give birth to five gods on the extra days, and Osiris, Isis, Seth, Nephthys, and the younger Horus are delivered into this world. We have then the pantheon of creation known as the Ennead (although Horus is not considered part of the Ennead, he plays a curious role toward the end of the myth):

CHAPTER THREE

Atum-Ra
Shu and Tefnut
Nut and Geb
Osiris, Isis, Seth, Nephthys

In the first chapter, I pointed out that the 365-day calendar came about when the pharaoh decreed that five days be added to the 360-day calendar based on the seasons so that the Nile's flooding could be tracked with reliable regularity. Here, however, we have a story, not a pharaoh's declaration, that gives us insight into the genesis of calendrical measurement. Time isn't viewed mystically or even astrologically but as a myth introducing the gods who help humankind establish a civilized society.

The presence of gods lovingly presiding over different locales and seasons was welcomed far more than any edict. Not only did this correction allow people to anticipate and plan for the Nile's flooding, but now Osiris and his siblings enter the world, each bringing further refinements to creation. Specifically, their introduction into the existent world heralded a shift of power from dependency on the gods to individual control over one's life and death. The ability to cultivate the land meant that people could now feed themselves and, as noted, abandon their taste for human flesh. This newfound independence marks the beginning of individual autonomy and the development of a personal psyche. With it begins the slow, gradual process of the transformation of the gods from external deities to internal archetypes; along with the existent world so, too, are the internal members of the psyche being put into place.

4

DARK DEEDS

Osiris rules Egypt and teaches the people the skills of civilized society. Egypt prospers as farmers learn to till the fields using the Nile's waters. Isis teaches women how to make bread from wheat and barley. While Osiris visits other nomes (settlements), Isis assumes the throne. Seth is maddeningly envious and begins to hatch a scheme to kill Osiris. Meanwhile, despite his love for Isis, Osiris sleeps with Nephthys, Seth's wife, and as a result Anubis is born.

The Black Land is gone. All that is left are the remnants of a grand civilization lying mostly buried beneath the parched sands of the Sahara. So much attention is focused on imagining the living reality of this mythic place that we forget a nameless land once existed long before pharaohs took to the throne. Narmer is regarded as the first pharaoh, who unified Egypt into a country about 3100 BC. Before him, very little is known. Archeological evidence shows that a number of different cultures existed in this region between 10,000 BC and the beginning of the First Dynasty. Of these various cultures, the Naqada, in the Qena district of Upper Egypt around 4400–3000 BC, is the most relevant to us. This cultural period derives its name from Nubt, a town whose name means "gold."

Although little indigenous gold was found in Egypt, deposits were known to exist in the Eastern Desert near Nubt. This area is important to the Osiris myth for two reasons. First, during this time a number of developments there contributed to the earliest beginnings of a civilized culture. These include copper tools, mud-brick buildings, the tanning of animal skins, and the veneration of deities. Secondly, these developments involved alchemical operations, including the use of copper implements and the invention of mortar around 4000 BC. Gold, of course, is both the physical and spiritual metal symbolizing the ultimate achievement of the alchemical opus.

The period from 4000 to 3000 BC evidenced an increased concentration of hunters and gatherers in the Nile region because of extremely arid conditions. With the Nile supplying an abundance of resources, people adopted a more sedentary lifestyle as they settled by the river as far north as the Delta and south to Nubia. "The beginning of the First Dynasty," writes Professor Kathryn Bard, "was only about 1,000 years after the earliest farming villages appeared on the Nile, so the Predynastic period, during the 4th millennium B.C. was one of fairly rapid social and political evolutions. . . . With the influx of people into this region some form of central governance became necessary and by ca. 3,050 B.C. the Early Dynastic state had emerged . . . controlling much of the Nile Valley from the Delta to the First Cataract at Aswan."[1]

Myths and gods are timeless, so we do not know when Osiris first introduced farming and agriculture to the early Egyptians. As noted, the concept of an Osirian god probably derived from Nubia, and with the evidence cited above we can entertain the possibility that the myth's origin coincides with the late Naqada period. It must have been an exciting time, with people migrating from the desert to the Nile and bringing with them remnants of their own cultures. It was a time of radical change that brought Egypt from a chaotic assortment of various cultural groups to an ordered society. We find this theme echoed mystically in the alchemical opus as a transformation from chaos to cosmos.

The myth doesn't speak of a central government but rather of a pair of parental gods who teach people how to work the land. While Osiris gives instruction in farming, Isis teaches simple methods of making bread from wheat and barley. These seem like simple tasks and yet, in the context of history, they represent a major transition from a hunter-gatherer society to an agrarian civilization. The significance of this change is no small matter in the development of consciousness since it signifies a real beginning for people taking control over their destiny. It marked the emergence of an entirely new concept of what it means to be human, one that does not depend on a pharaoh and, to some degree, a god. It will take many thousands of years to elaborate the idea that God is contained *within* a person and that through deep mystical practice one can virtually become a god.

Despite the achievements of modern humanity, in the hubbub of contemporary life surprisingly few of us know how to make bread or have any idea of what it means to till the land. The poet Wendell Berry gives us a sense of the farmer's life and his rootedness to the land; with a few words, we discover Osiris rising from the winter fields in "The Man Born to Farming":

> The grower of trees, the gardener, the man born to farming,
> Whose hands reach into the ground and sprout,
> To him the soil is a divine drug. He enters into death
> Yearly, and comes back rejoicing. He has seen the light lie down
> In the dung heap, and rise again in the corn.[2]

In the Coffin Texts, Osiris is referred to as both wheat and barley. In one text we learn of the identity between wheat and the gods: "It was Atum who made me wheat, when he sent me down to the earth, to the fire island, when the name Osiris was given to me, the son of Geb. I am life."[3] This "life" finds its parallel in the alchemical belief that gold germinates within the ores of the earth as a result of the sun's rays. In addition to mummifying the dead, the Egyptians also mummified animals and corn, believing that new life sprouts from the dead body of Osiris. The dead come to life just as vegetation undergoes endless life cycles. Commonly believed was that grain sprouted from Osiris, the seed, and that Isis was the earth and Seth the heat necessary for germination. The farmer possesses this knowledge in his hands and in his heart because he is part of the cycles of nature.

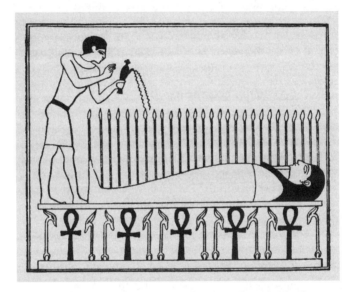

Figure 4.1. Osiris with wheat growing from his body.

Isis also provided women the skills needed in the kitchen, where the crops are taken in from the fields and transformed into foods that nourish our bodies and sustain life. With a hearth at its center, smoke rising from crude pots, and pungent odors wafting upward, a kitchen is difficult to distinguish from an alchemical laboratory. Any good cook knows the secrets of the alchemical kitchen. The fifteenth-century alchemist Paracelsus, describing Vulcan, the god of fire, says, "What is accomplished by fire is alchemy—whether in the furnace or in the kitchen stove. And he who governs fire is Vulcan, even if he be a cook or a man who tends the stove."4

Osiris and Isis were greeted with great love and devotion. But such adoration became the inspiration for Seth's malicious plotting. Since he is lord of the desert, the very place where these people came from, it is not surprising that the popularity of Osiris and Isis aroused envy, anger, and ultimately vengeance. To make matters worse, Osiris leaves Isis to assume his duties while he goes off to other towns and settlements to teach agriculture. Having a woman, even a goddess, serve as pharaoh was as rare then as it is to see a woman serving as head of state in today's world.

To think of Osiris as a teacher isn't sufficient. The gods of Egypt represent functions and principles, not specific roles. Since all realities begin with psychic images, so, too, did the gods first appear in the dreams and visions of the Egyptians. The mixed form of gods that typically combine the head of an animal and the body of a human did not appear until the Third Dynasty (2650–2575 BC) when Horus was depicted with a hawk's head. Before that time he was shown, as were all gods, in animal form.5 "Egyptian gods," observed Hornung, "do not mingle freely with people on earth; they may be encountered only in liminal areas where the world of mankind and the world of the gods come into contact—on a distant island . . . or in a dream."6 In attempting to embody the spirit of Osiris, we should not be thinking of the image of one bound in mummy bandages. Rather we will want to find that liminal space where the boundaries between the existent and nonexistent worlds are blurred, what Jung called the psychoid dimension.

Rundle Clark describes this realm: "Osiris is nature itself or, to speak more accurately, nature as experienced by the farmers and stock breeders of the Ancient Near East [where agricultural methods were first invented]."7 He goes on to describe the listlessness of the dry land during times of drought as if "the spirit of life had departed" and the joy that came with the Nile's flooding—a true metaphor for the death and resurrection of Osiris. Throughout much of the myth Osiris is listless and asleep until his son—new life—awakens him. This sentiment also described the "weariness" of Atum while still immersed in the waters of Nun. Weariness and awakening are common themes that run throughout many Egyptian texts. Again and again we read words that describe a wide range of human emotions, something all too often overlooked by Egyptologists. Fortunately this point is not lost on Clark, who suggests, "It is not yet generally recognized that the Egyptians sometimes explained their myths in psychological terms."[8] In this sense, weariness or sorrow is at once the lethargy one experiences prior to establishing an independent identity and the impetus that gives rise to awakening following the separation from nonexistence and the Great Mother.

All these considerations help explain Osiris's affair with Nephthys. Here we must invoke our nonmorality clause, for it is easy enough to form a judgment of Osiris and miss the larger point. Some interpretations attribute the affair to Nephthys, and others suggest that Osiris, being asleep, was not at fault! That Osiris succumbs to Nephthys, "the Lady of the House," is very significant. We've already described her as the detached feminine; she has no temples or cults. Her Egyptian name, Nobt-Hut, indicates that she is of noble status; in a positive way, she is above the law or outside it. This position allows her to perform unsavory tasks without the interference of untoward sentimentality—doing things we detest but that must be done. Her love is bound by divine loyalty that exists between souls rather than one legitimized by human law. In fact, legal marriage did not exist in ancient Egypt, and loving relations between a man's wife and a mistress were common. Nephthys is also referred to as Mistress of the Mansion and, as we shall see, she becomes a trusted ally of Isis, a true Lady of the House of Osiris.

Morality, in this case, gets us nowhere. We are still dealing with the embryonic development of psyche when individuation is in its nascent state, and moral issues will not arise until critical separations have been accomplished. Apparently, for Osiris to break free of the mother by marrying Isis is not enough. The bond between Osiris and Isis began in Nut's womb, and separation will be difficult. An outside force is apparently required to separate them. This force turns out to be Nephthys, who is Osiris's sister and Seth's wife. The affair puts Osiris at odds with his dark brother. Nature, which appears boundless, finds its limit in the person of Seth. He, like nature, violently imposes limits with no regard for human sensitivities. Nature is, after all, blind, unconscious, and independent of the Egyptians' wishes, and it ushers in change with a relentless force. Seth and Nephthys are dark figures residing closer to the earth than to the heavens. We can better understand them by appreciating their affinity to nature.

Nature is the realm of mystery. It is mother and father to us all. It feeds us and provides materials for shelter. Nature is home to animals and our instincts. Our physical being is also nature, or, as the philosopher-poet John O'Donohue describes it so beautifully in his book *Anam Cara*,

> It is mysterious that the human body is clay. The individual is the meeting place of the four elements. The human person is a clay shape, living in the medium of air. Yet the fire of blood, thought, and soul moves through the body. Its whole life and energy flow in the subtle circle of the water elements. We have come up out of the depths of the earth. Consider the millions of continents of clay that will never have the opportunity to leave this underworld. This clay will never find a form to ascend and express itself in the world of light but will live forever in that unknown shadow world.[9]

He further describes an ancient Celtic belief about a tribe that was banished to the underworld, where it ultimately "controlled the fecundity of the land above."[10] For this poet, liminality is "luminosity" and the landscape is "numinous," both qualities that easily describe Osiris as a fructifying spirit.

The Egyptians believed that dreams occur in a place where it is possible to encounter a god. The realms of dreams and the dead are liminal places—intermediary spaces between life and death. Marie-Louise von Franz reports the dream a dying man she was treating had shortly before his death. It captures this same power of Osiris, a force so strong that it engenders all forms of new life. "He saw a green, half-high, not-yet-ripe wheat field. A herd of cattle had broken into the field and trampled down and destroyed everything in it. Then a voice from above called out: 'Everything seems to be destroyed, but from the roots under the earth the wheat will grow again.'"[11]

Both earth and body are of the same substance, so the body can know things well before we become consciously aware of them. Heka, god of magic, has this physicality about him. He was seen as a god, but also as a substance that could be consumed. The Pyramid Texts contain many "cannibal spells" that involve ingesting magical substances. Magical power comes only from the god Heka. The king or magus "becomes" Heka, and only then can he command the elements. "An image expressing the thorough integration of magic into the person," writes Naydler, "is that of swallowing it and digesting it, so that it resides in a person's belly." This is physical embodiment. Naydler cites the Cannibal Hymn, where the magus "eats the *heka* of the gods and 'enjoys himself when their magic is in his belly.'"[12] While there is little magic and cannibalism in the world today, we still see this "body wisdom" in symbolic form.

I saw an example of this wisdom in a middle-aged man I treated for a few years. More than his words, I observed how his body spoke through his dreams, anticipating events he was not consciously aware of. Shortly after he fell wildly in love with a young woman, she became pregnant with their child. They mutually decided to have an abortion, but he felt terribly guilty. When I inquired about his dreams *prior* to knowing that his girlfriend was pregnant, he told me, "There are two rivers and I am in one of them holding a lion cub close to my chest. I have to protect it, otherwise it will run off. At times we are underwater. We surface where the two rivers meet. I climb up onto the land barely holding onto the cub."

The timing of this dream is just as important as its interpretation. Mythic time is not linear, and certainly this dream has a prophetic quality. If we posit that the cub represents the fetus, the two rivers the fallopian tubes, and the place where the two rivers join, the vagina, then the dream graphically depicts the birth process. The fact that the patient had the dream before knowing of the pregnancy indicates that *his* body was *already* well aware of what had happened a week before he had knowledge of his girlfriend's condition. Such knowledge transfer is not unusual with married couples, but sometimes we find it occurring when libidinal energy is excited (heated up) in a new relationship.

In another dream told by a woman, mythic time takes on a synchronistic quality. In this dream, the patient is in my waiting room. She is preparing to write a check for me when another woman walks in through the front door. Before I enter the waiting room from my office, my patient is uncomfortable and pretends not to be a client of mine. Immediately after she tells me this dream, the session ends and I open the door to allow her to leave. At that very moment a woman, also a patient, arrives carrying a check to give me. The two women pass each other silently in the narrow hallway between my office and the waiting room.

How the dreamer could have anticipated this seemingly random occurrence is impossible to know. Again, interpretation is less important than the overlap between two sets of very different realities. In the same way, this overlap is the liminal sphere where gods and humans make contact, sometimes for a known reason and sometimes not.

Thus, we can only speculate about the reasons why even gods come into contact with one another. While it would have been more likely for Osiris to have his first child with Isis, instead we find him fathering an illegitimate son, Anubis, with his brother's wife. As a result, Osiris is tainted with some of his brother's darkness, and in turn Set is bitterly angry. We might imagine these dynamics in physical terms, as when one chemical contaminates another by contact. Jung said, "The meeting of two personalities is like the contact of two chemical substances: if there is any reaction, both are transformed."[13]

The differences between Horus, son of Osiris and Isis, and Anubis are striking. Whereas Horus becomes patron to the pharaohs, Anubis remains in the realm in which he is most at home, cemeteries. There he is a scavenger who feeds on the flesh of the dead; his name derives from the word meaning "putrefy" or "king's son." His black skin reminds us of his father. Black, in alchemy, has numerous associations to the prima materia and the nigredo, both of which are variously described as "blacker than black." In his canine image Anubis possesses keen senses that will later help Isis in her search for the scattered pieces of her dead husband. Whereas Horus stands by each pharaoh, Anubis stays at a distance, like his mother, attending to the deceased as they make their way into the afterlife.

As we will see later, a serious problem arises with Horus's birth: who will inherit the throne once Osiris is gone, his legitimate son or his hateful brother? This question will become a central theme at the end of the myth. At this point in the story, Osiris is very much alive and enjoying his place in the world.

5

PARTY TO A MURDER

Seth puts his murderous plot into action by announcing that he will be hosting a party. He has secretly taken Osiris's physical measurements and built a beautifully constructed coffin. Many people attend the party including seventy-two coconspirators. Seth announces that the coffin will be given to the person who best fits in it. Once Osiris settles into the coffin, Seth has his assassins quickly seal the lid with lead bands. He then casts the coffin into the Nile.

Still railing from all the adulation given to Osiris and Isis, Seth puts his malicious plot into action. No mention is made about how Seth "sized up" Osiris for the coffin tailor-made to his measurements. In our time, a tomb is an odd prize to offer at a party, but in Egypt a tomb was a prized possession, especially one made of stone. Others of lesser value were built of elm or cedar. A stone casket signified royalty, since it lasted longer and offered better protection against grave robbers. We are not told what the coffin at Seth's party is made of, only that it is either bound with leaden straps or had lead poured over it. Both the coffin and the lead are especially significant in the alchemical laboratory.

The alchemists believed there were seven metals—lead, quicksilver, tin, iron, copper, silver, and gold—that had psychic and physical qualities ranging from inferior and gross to remarkably refined. Lead, the least refined, is not simply a metal. It symbolizes a state of mind best

described as lethargy, melancholia, and depression, so we can understand Osiris's weariness as representing a dark, unrefined condition.
Lead's more positive attributes include restriction, discipline, and te-
nacity. Long before Saturn was associated with lead because of his affinity with death, Seth was the agent of limitation, constriction, and
the operation of *coagulatio*. That Seth should choose lead to bind the
vessel containing Osiris reveals a perfect metaphor for the beginning
of the alchemical work. In this first stage, the nigredo, the prima materia, is constricted, strangled, and dried out in every imaginable way,
for only by applying these operations (calcinatio and separatio) can all
the metal's poisons be leached out and new life begin. Unlike other
metals, lead does not respond to light, yet it contains its own light. If
the metal is pulverized, it instantaneously bursts into flames. As such,
lead was believed to contain its own redemption. Jung, quoting from
Elias Ashmole's seventeenth-century opus *Theatrum Chemicum Britan-
nicum*, says: "For as lead burns up and removes all the imperfections of
metals . . . so likewise tribulation in this life cleanses us from the many
blemishes which we have incurred."[1]

Seth and Saturn make up a pair we can easily hate and call evil. And
yet, like lead, they possess important qualities that redeem them. Both
are limiting agents. We may not appreciate limits imposed on us, but
sometimes we need an external agent to end things we lack the wisdom
to stop. Often these gods do our dirty work. Individuation typically
involves some dirty work in its formative stage; darkness is the tincture
that helps make a person whole. Light alone doesn't get the job done!
"One does not become enlightened," said Jung, "by imagining figures of
light, but making the darkness conscious."[2] This work is precisely what
the alchemists were willing to do and what today is the dirty job handed
over to therapists. At times, it is hard to separate the analyst who daily
confronts the demons hiding behind symptoms and complexes from
the alchemist. "In many ways," writes Jungian astrologer Liz Greene,

"the ancient art of alchemy was dedicated to this end: for the base material of alchemy, in which lay the possibility of gold, was called Saturn, and this base material, as well as having a concrete existence, was also considered to be the alchemist himself. Modern psychology, which is paralleling more and more the path of the alchemists, also seeks to make a friend of Saturn although here he is called by other names."[3] Seth was one such name, and lead was his primary metal.

Seth was also associated with Mercury. Each of the children of Nut and Geb was thought to endow the stars with particular functions. Thus, Horus was associated with Mars, Jupiter, and Saturn; Ra or Osiris with Venus, etc. "As for Seth," writes Dimitri Meeks, "although he was identified with planet Mercury, he was above all associated with the constellation of the Great Bear, in which he was visible at all times."[4] This constellation was tied like a stake to the North Star, and it therefore never sank below the horizon, the place of Osiris's eventual home. In this way Osiris is protected against being further harmed by Seth. Still, it is somewhat surprising to learn that Seth's presence—his astral light—is constant in the night sky. He seems to earn this special place by virtue of the danger he poses to Osiris or, in psychological terms, the threat posed by the shadow, a threat that cannot be avoided. Through conscious suffering, one confronts and transforms the shadow into something productive to the individuation process.

The alchemists viewed lead as an ideal metaphor for human beings, for in the midst of our very darkness we contain the light and fire of consciousness. Even without developing our conscious mind we have an innate awareness of the latent Self within. Not surprisingly, lead yearns to be silver, that bright, glittering metal. If lead is cut into pieces, a silvery film becomes visible for a brief moment. Unlike lead, silver is very responsive to light, another trait seized upon by the alchemist to show how metals behave like human beings. Similarly, much can be learned from the mineral and vegetative kingdoms. For instance,

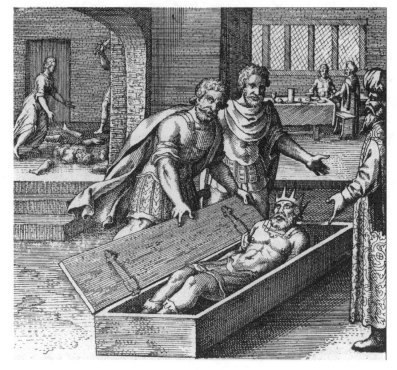

Figure 5.1. Entombed King.

we share the same natural tendency—phototropism—as plants to move toward light.

Sealed within the coffin, Osiris is thrown into pitch darkness and is presumably dying. This tragedy must have been too much for Egyptians to bear, for it is only with the Greek historian Plutarch (AD 46–120) that fragments of the Osiris myth are collated and made into a complete, reified version.[5] Nevertheless, this woeful tale is of supreme symbolic importance. Osiris's suffering is akin to entombing some part of nature, cutting it off from its life-giving source of light. Closing the coffin lid is tantamount to rejoining Nut and Geb, ending life in this world. In this case, it is Osiris, not Shu, who lies between sky and earth, here having a very different meaning. With Shu, it was opening a space for life to begin, but with Osiris, "putting a lid on things" means the end for an old king and the start of a different order of existence. Notice in the alchemical image in figure 5.1 the upper left-hand corner showing a dismembered body, which is the same fate that awaits Osiris in his death and resurrection.

Creation is not the same as transformation. Osiris didn't die a natural death but was murdered. In medieval times, when the natural order went awry a deadly shout rang out demanding the king's head. Killing a king is an extraordinary event, something akin in modern times to killing the Pope or a Supreme Mullah; in this instance, it is a ritual murder of a god, which has profound mystical implications. To understand the significance of Osiris's murder, we must look beyond its human dimensions. We are seeing a profound shift in Egyptian cosmology in which the god of fertility actually "becomes earth." It is a central mystery that must be understood for us to get beyond the horror of the murder and discover its deeper meaning.

For centuries, alchemists pondered this mystery and realized insights that may have been unavailable to the Egyptians. The ancients lived the myth and did not have the advantage of conscious reflection that comes with an individual ego and the passage of time. This sad turn of events must have been very distressing to the Egyptian people. As we will see momentarily, the people reacted with perplexity on finding their hero god dead. Centuries later, the alchemists realized the necessity of this murder and its symbolic use in the psychological laboratory. In their manuscripts is an old recipe instructing the adept on how to begin the work: "The King must die for the Son to be born," a formula that echoes the cry of medieval people. Egyptian texts have allusions to this same idea. For example, in the Book of the Dead we read, "Yesterday is Osiris and Tomorrow is Re on that day when the enemies of the Lord of All are destroyed, and when his son Horus is established as ruler."[6]

These statements point to the fact that Osiris had to die in order for Horus—the *filius regulus*—to be born. "No new life can arise," says Jung of the alchemists, "without the death of the old. They liken the art to the work of the sower, who buries the grain in the earth: it dies only to waken to new life."[7]

"Osiris," writes Rundle Clark, "was nothing without Horus, just as the latter was no true king unless he was able to guarantee the continuous fertility of his land."[8] It was not enough that Osiris gave life to the land and to its people; he also needed to possess the power to regenerate the soil, bring it back to life long after it appeared dead. This regenerative power is what the Egyptian meant by describing Osiris as "becoming earth." The fields had to be replenished with each successive season, and, symbolically, the soul of every deceased person had to survive the death of the body in order to be rejuvenated in the afterlife. This regenerative power must pass from one season to the next, from the old king to the new one, from Osiris to Horus.

This transition of power begins with Atum-Ra's emergence from Nun. With him, Atum-Ra brings Ma'at (order) to the world. From this viewpoint, Osiris's murder recapitulates Atum-Ra's "weariness" while still immersed in the chaos of Nun. Atum-Ra rose up from these Stygian depths, and Osiris did likewise, first by bringing civilization to humankind and then by continuous regeneration, the necessary nourishment for going forward. These transformations begin with Atum-Ra, continue with Osiris and Horus, and eventually are transmitted by the pharaoh to each and every human being. Despite the great gift this murder-sacrifice gives to the development of human consciousness, the news of Osiris's death must have been received with equally great horror and despair.

Imagine reading in the newspaper, pictured on temple walls, that the god who brings life to the soil and food for the soul has died! Given the close affinity between Osiris and the reigning pharaoh, the death of either left the people immediately cut off from the divine realm. As a result, their concept of the afterlife radically changed. Henceforth, people would be left to their own devices to find a way into a life beyond death. This turn of events probably took place with the decline of the Old Kingdom. At that time, the Pyramid Texts were intended for the sole use of the king in his ascent into the afterlife. But in successive periods, other texts followed that opened the gate for everyone, or at least anyone having sufficient funds to purchase a painted coffin! With Osiris dead, the instruction manual that helped one gain access to the eternal realm was no longer a royal privilege. For now, Osiris lay unconscious as his entombed body was cast into the Nile.

The etymological tree from which the word *alchemy* emerged has two basic branches: *khem* meaning "black" and *chymia* meaning "to cast." *Khem*, of course, refers to the Black Land, but *chymia*, from the Greek, is a bit more complex. At first, we might think it has to do with casting a metal and finishing it off, which of course relates directly to the metallurgic aspects of alchemy. But *chymia* has another meaning relating specifically to this scene in which Osiris is "cast down" and thrown into the river. A more esoteric interpretation points to the relationship between magic and alchemy. Since heka is considered a substance, one needs a net to gather it. In the ninth division of the Book of Gates, Apopis is subdued by being captured in a net. For a net to be of any use it must be cast out. In our time, we have the Internet, which is cast into the world to capture information. In alchemy, the image of the net takes the form of a spiderweb, and together both symbolize the matrix that is the fundamental substratum forming in the *vas hermeticum*, the vessel of transformation. With Osiris being cast down, the work is thrown into the waters of the unconscious. In alchemy, this operation is the *solutio,* whose action is to break down "differentiated matter into its original undifferentiated state—that is, to *prima materia.*"9 The waters of the Nile are, in other words, dissolving Osiris's body

Figure 5.2. Dissolving King.

in order to sacralize the earth. In essence, Osiris is transformed into spiritualized earth.

In the picture above we see the drowning king, a medieval image that recalls Osiris being thrown into the Nile. As I mentioned earlier, the Egyptians believed that rejuvenation was brought about by immersion in the waters of Nun. Thus, another alchemical recipe directs the adept to "dissolve the Matter in its own Water." In this case, Osiris's body is submerged in the Nile, not Nun. The primeval Nun was the source of Atum's origin, whereas the Nile becomes the matrix for the transformation of Osiris's body. The Nile was traditionally associated with sacrifice. Until recent years, corn dolls (*el arusa*, "the bride") were thrown into the river, a sacrifice intended to cause the water to rise— the very thing needed to resurrect Osiris's dead body. Sacrificing Osiris's body to the Nile is an expression of dissolution that both rejuvenates his spirit and causes the living waters of the Nile to move him forward on his journey toward rebirth. At the same time, "The king swimming in the sea cries with a loud voice, 'Whoso shall deliver me shall obtain the great reward. . . . Whoever saves me shall live and reign with me forever in my brightness on my royal throne.'"[10] And, what is this reward? For the Egyptians, it was embodying Osiris and gaining his great insights into the darkness we call depression, despair, and death. For this reason, the name of every Egyptian changed with death, such that Osiris became his or her first name.

We must pause here and ponder the image of Osiris trapped in the darkness of his tomb. Personally, I cannot imagine anything more gruesome than being buried alive and experiencing the air slowly being snuffed out of my lungs. This fear might explain my personal decision to be cremated when I die—I'd rather be offered to the sky gods than be buried in the darkness of the grave. Tibetan Buddhists go a step further in their funerary plans. They believe that the death of each person requires a specific type of funeral. The type is determined by selecting from the four elements the one that aligns with the astrological significance of the exact time of death. I suppose that I, having a Leo sun sign, would be given a fire funeral, or at least this would accord with the homeopathic principle that "like cures like." In any event, the Egyptians were of a totally different mind on this subject. For them, cremation was a cruel punishment reserved for their worst enemies. Without a body or tomb—the vessel of transformation—the deceased had no chance of an afterlife. "The tomb," comments Frankfort, "was the instrument by which was overcome the disintegration of a man's personality as a result of the crisis of death."[11]

Taken symbolically, the dying Osiris has an altogether different meaning. In fact, this image is a central one of alchemy and Hermetic philosophy, to say nothing of the profound influence it had on the world's great religions. The image of the light trapped in darkness is a metaphor beautifully described in Hermetic mythology. There, the main motif is based on light trapped in nature and the adept's attempts to rescue it. The fifteenth-century alchemist and healer Paracelsus called this light the *lumen naturae*. Jung distinguished between this light and *lumen Dei*. The former is the light that remains hidden in nature until we, through alchemical means, are able to set it free. The latter refers to divine consciousness that comes directly from the spiritual realm through revelation.

The image of Osiris trapped in the tomb, where he undergoes magical transformation, recalls the passage taken by the pharaoh as he moves through Nut's celestial body. At each point in her sacred body, the pharaoh undergoes a particular transformation. Nut's body is the vessel similar to the tomb in which Osiris's flesh is being transmuted. Egyptologists like Dimitri Meeks correlate particular anatomical parts of Nut's body with specific transmutations. For instance, he attributes Nut's liver as the organ having to do with matters of the heart and representing the defeat of Osiris's enemies; the gall bladder, a digestive organ in the bilious region, insures against further attack. Since these operations are all taking place in a postmortem state, Nut is referred to as the "coffin goddess."

In the Book of the Dead, the idea of a god embodying specific powers is extended to the deceased. In Spell 42, the notion that every part of the deceased embodies a divine substance is made clear:

> My hair is Nun; my face is Re; my eyes are Hathor; my ears are Wepwawet; my nose is She who presides over her lotus-leaf; my lips are Anubis; my molars are Selket; my incisors are Isis the goddess; my arms are the Ram, the Lord of Mendes; my breast is Neith, Lady of Sais; my back is Seth; my phallus is Osiris; my muscles are the Lords of Kheraha; my chest is He who is greatly majestic; my belly and my spine are Sekhmet; my buttocks are

the Eye of Horus; my thighs and my calves are Nut; my feet are Ptah; my fingers are Orion; my toes are living uraei; *there is no member of mine devoid of a god*, and Thoth is the protection of all my flesh.[12] [Italics mine]

The Egyptians shied away from describing any details of Osiris's death. Instead of saying that he died in that coffin, they simply said he was "asleep in the water." In psychological terms, he is deeply unconscious. We are left to our own devices to imagine what this journey might have been like as his coffin drifted along the Nile's currents. The image is a powerful one in that it describes Osiris entombed in a vessel making its way toward another land or level of consciousness. The light of his physical being may be extinguished, but his soul is drifting toward liberation.

Each of us contains an inner light that has many names. The world soul, *Anima Mundi*, and the transcendent Self envision this light that is trapped within our decaying body, a self-serving ego, and, more generally, the unconscious. From time immemorial there have been taboos to keep one from discovering this divine inner light, for unless we are ready to receive it we will either misuse this sacred light or destroy ourselves.

We cannot simply consider the importance of light without speaking of it in terms of darkness. In the modern era this dichotomy is more sharply divided than it was for the Egyptians. While they had Ma'at, an angelic goddess who stood for order, they had no corresponding god to singularly represent disorder. Rather, disorder was a concept reflected in different ways in different gods. *Isfet* is the hieroglyph that represents disorder. It literally translates as disorder or falsehood. As we have seen, Nun represents the part of isfet that is chaos and Seth the part that is ethical disorder. Again, we need to set aside our modern ideas of morality, for it is more accurate to regard Seth as a limiting agent necessary for the transformation Osiris is to suffer (undergo).

Seth brings us to excess, to the brink of desire and madness—so much so that we are unavoidably confronted with the ultimate limit of desire: death. Examples abound to illustrate the ravages of excess. For the alcoholic who has exhausted the capacities of his liver, death is one last drink away. The concupiscence of the pedophile priest is doomed to a spiritual death in hell. Ironically, excess of desire brings either death or redemption. We will either submit to temptation and die or, as we shall see in the case of Osiris, transcend it and live eternally. Seth isn't alone in conducting his demonic deeds. While he brings death, his confederates are the agents of decay and dissolution.

Osiris's suffering is a model for all of us, since without suffering the hidden light cannot be achieved. Seth is something of an alchemist who unconsciously goes about blindly transmuting sleeping nature into a fully awakened state. This view of evil is radically different from the one most of us are used to, but when we consider that Seth had many followers (and even Seti I, the architect of Osiris's tomb at Abydos, was the "son of Seth"), we are forced to reevaluate his function in the transformation of consciousness. We might then consider this murderous scene a necessary sacrifice, a *felix culpa*, which is executed by a higher wisdom. Just as a plant dies only to become compost for the next generation, Osiris dies in order for a new and more conscious life-form to evolve. Alchemists said, "The corruption of one is the generation of the other."[13] This generation takes him out of the conscious realm and deep into the collective unconscious.

Osiris's coffin is the vas hermeticum, the vessel in which the god's transformation takes place. In various interpretations the coffin is referred to as a chest, tomb, and sarcophagus. Alchemists believe that this sacred box is just as important as what occurs inside it. We may recall that one of Anubis's epithets is Foremost of the Divine Booth (tomb) and that his image is imprinted on the magician's box, sure signs that corruption always precedes generation. The box is sometimes depicted as a skull or the *vas mentalis*, where the chief elements and stages of the Work are insulated from outside contamination.

The skull of course associates with the mind, and it is within this sphere that transformations become possible. "The hermetic vessel," says Jungian analyst Esther Harding, "is oneself. In it the many pieces of psychic stuff scattered throughout one's world must be collected and fuse into one, so making a new creation."[14] Many alchemists referred to themselves as "Children of the Golden Head," a name we will discuss further in chapter 8. The skull also relates to death, and by contemplating death we are able to see beyond the ego. In *Anatomy of the Psyche*, Jungian analyst Edward Edinger explains this critical connection: "The outstanding example of death as the genesis of religion and consciousness is the elaborate mortuary symbolism of ancient Egypt. This is also clearly the origin of alchemy. The embalming of the dead king transformed him into Osiris, an eternal, incorruptible body. This is the prototype of the alchemical opus, which attempts to create the incorruptible Philosopher's Stone. The alchemical vessel has been equated with the sealed tomb of Osiris, containing all the limbs of the god." Edinger further suggests, "The psyche cannot come into existence as a separate entity until the death of the literal, the concrete, and the physical."[15] Thus, we can appreciate the importance that death served in the views of the ancient Egyptians, for without restriction and limitation put upon the material world, no insights into the nonmaterial world can be had. Seth, then, is a vital part of the individuation process. He is a catalyst that upsets the status quo and forces us to exercise a dark part of ourselves that makes us extremely uncomfortable.

The fact that the coffin is precisely fitted to Osiris's physical measurements tells us that a process is to begin that is aimed solely at his transformation. Like Cinderella's glass slipper, the coffin is the vehicle designed specifically for him to individuate. At this point, we might imagine an alchemist enclosing the prima materia in the alembic as he prepares to reduce it to its most elemental form. In this way, the materials used in alchemy were thought to suffer and die as they dissolve in the purifying waters of acid. In much the same way, a therapist goes about dissolving his or her patient's problem through analysis—*lysis* meaning "to loosen." This work is not pleasant and often requires confronting resistances, challenging rationalizations, and regressing the patient to the original source of the problem. In order for this nasty work to be done safely, the therapist relies on the healing relationship that has been constructed for this purpose. Even the therapist's office serves as a container in which these operations can be safely performed. Few go willingly into the unconscious. Just as Osiris was trapped, so too must patients be gently guided or even tricked into reckoning with the destructive aspects of their personality.

Osiris may be dead, but he is not nonexistent. While the Coffin Texts describe him as "sleeping in the water," we do not know what Osiris is experiencing locked up in the coffin. We would guess that he is gasping for air until every cell in his body is starved of oxygen, and he may even be dead by the time the coffin is thrown into the Nile. But Osiris is a god, and we can't know what a god might do in this circumstance. On a personal level, this death motif is the "dark night of the soul" a person must experience in order to be born anew. At the same time, this point is precisely the one at which Osiris leaves the above world and takes permanent residence in the underworld, where he is god of the dead. Osiris, then, continues to be with us in this unconscious realm despite his death sleep, and as a result we will need to understand the new role he plays in our conscious awakening.

6

RISE UP!

Isis is grief-stricken when she learns what has happened to her husband. She immediately goes in search of his coffin. Children tell her that it drifted to the far north. At Byblos the coffin is thrown up onto the shore by a wave and lands against an acacia tree in a forest. Nearby is the kingdom of Alcindor and his queen, Astarte. By the time Isis arrives, the tree has completely grown over it. The sweet scent of Osiris's corpse attracts the attention of the king, who has the tree cut down and made into a column for his palace. Isis sits by the shore, transformed into an old woman with braided hair. The royal children, playing by the seashore, notice her. Isis befriends them and braids their hair. Soon after, the girls run home to the queen mother and tell her of the old woman. She notices their strange hairstyle and invites the woman into the palace. The queen has Isis stay the night and puts her infant child into her care.

Even today duty requires that a wounded or dead soldier's body be brought home. Heroism of this kind often requires courage that blinds one to the danger of such a mission. We see this valor in Isis when she learns of her husband's death. She is inconsolable about Osiris's murder, but rather than retire into mourning, she seems driven wild by the death of her husband. Oddly, Seth is the one who stirs up this reaction in her, for it is his energy that moves people to put aside their personal feelings and selflessly act in the service of a higher principle. In this case, Isis is driven by duty to her lost love—to find him and bring him home.

The thought of leaving a dead comrade, much less a brother or spouse, in a foreign land was unthinkable to the ancient Egyptian. If the body were not returned home, there would be no possibility for a proper funeral or any chance of resurrection. Unless sacred rites were performed on his native soil, the soldier would suffer the worst fate imaginable— his soul would simply disappear into the realm of the nonexistent.

Isis is initially at a loss about where to go in search of her husband's body. Children point the way. They tell her that the coffin drifted to the far north, well beyond the Nile's delta and into the Green Sea. It traversed the coast of Lebanon and arrived at the ancient city of Byblos. Children often represent fresh consciousness and new insights. Their innocence is untainted by any agenda. They are "true of voice" in that they speak their mind. Here children guide Isis to her husband, enabling the two to be reunited. As will become clearer in the following chapter, this reunion will have a profound effect on the further development of the psyche.

Nothing in the myth occurs by chance; every detail is filled with meaning. If we simply follow the narrative without questioning its symbolism, we miss a major transformation taking place in the emergence of Osiris into a new state of being and the implications for further development of the human psyche. We must ask, why was Byblos the place where the tomb washes up on the shore? What is the meaning of the wave that sends the coffin crashing into a tree? Why an acacia tree? What is the meaning of Isis's braided hair? Why is the tree, containing the body of Osiris, cut down and made into a support for the king's palace?

Shedding light on these details opens up exploration of even more challenging mysteries. What, for example, does it mean that the horizontal position of Osiris, lying outstretched in his tomb, changes, and he is turned upright to the vertical position? Is he still dead? What is the meaning of a tree that envelops the tomb? What is happening to the trapped light we've discussed, the lumen naturae, which now shines darkly within the hollow of a tree in an unknown land?

Before taking up these questions, we might imagine the emotional state Isis would be experiencing on learning of her husband's murder. I think the news would be overwhelming, leaving her shocked, dismayed, and filled with grief. But Isis is a goddess, and she exemplifies extraordinary strength. Instead of submitting to mournful despair, she gathers herself up and sets out to retrieve her husband's body. Most texts indicate that Osiris was killed at Nedit, near Abydos. If so, Isis traveled many thousands of miles to a faraway city. For someone living in Los Angeles, that would be something like going to the Amazon, a strange and bewildering experience, even for a goddess.

Osiris's tomb could have come to rest at any number of cities along the way from Nedit. But, Byblos, said to be the oldest city in the world, was the most likely choice for several reasons. Its antiquity dates back to the Neolithic period. We have the sense that Osiris is returning to very ancient times, perhaps the First Time before the origin of the world. The myth is telling us that something happened here eons ago. Before revealing what this might be, let me add that Byblos was originally called Gebal, a city that still has remnants of early Phoenician civilization. The Greeks later gave the city its name because of the large trade in papyrus (βύβλος) that came through its port. Papyrus plays many important roles in the Osiris myth. In addition to providing the parchment used to inscribe sacred mythologies, the papyrus marsh also serves an important function for Horus; even Isis's boat is made of papyrus.[1]

We find in these many clues an intersection of history and mythology that distinguishes Byblos from other possible places where Osiris's coffin might have landed. As the myth unfolds we will recognize the importance of these clues.

Given the close, friendly relationship that existed between Egypt and the inhabitants of Byblos, it is not surprising that Osiris's body would mythologically find its way to this ancient place. Moreover, we might expect that the king would have been an ally and welcomed Isis with open arms. Yet, we are not told why Isis adopts such an unusual, stealthy approach to gain entry into the palace. For whatever the reason, a direct approach was not warranted, and instead a more feminine, darker, and magical strategy is used. Isis transforms herself into an old woman with braided hair as she sits beside the acacia tree. By now the tree has grown old, and even Osiris's ba, which alights on a nearby limb, is weary.

A cursory examination of the mythological roots of the acacia tree shows it was no accident that Osiris's tomb would be embraced by this sacred tree.[2] The acacia is well known for purity and endurance of the soul, and, given its role in the Osiris myth, Freemasons still regard it as a symbol of resurrection and immortality. The acacia is strong and gives off a sweet aroma. In Egypt incense was used to cleanse the pharaoh and venerate the gods. But, intoxicating odors also emanated from the gods. Egyptologist Richard Wilkinson informs us that incense was "magically significant for the transformation of the deceased into a divine state, and this is reflected in the relation of the Egyptian name for this substance, *senetcher*, with the word *senetcheri* 'to make divine.'"[3] We might conclude then that the reason for the tree's embrace was to infuse Osiris's body with its sacred fragrance, making both tree and its contents divine. Odors travel virtually unseen, calling up memories, carrying us off to distant places. We can only imagine what effect the odors of this tree might have had on Osiris's body. Certainly, incense was common among the funerary equipment used to purify the dead. In alchemical imagery, smoke and incense are commonly depicted as a medium by which spirits ascend to the heavens.

The divinity of this tree lies in the durable quality of its wood. It was used for making furniture, and, in the Bible, God himself instructed Moses to "make an ark of acacia wood" and a "table," as well, of this sturdy wood (Ex 25:10, 23). Not only do we relate the making of the Ark of the Covenant to the acacia, but some believe that the burning bush was also the very same tree. Incense from the acacia was known to put demons as well as gods in a pleasant mood, perhaps because an alcoholic beverage derived from the fruit of this tree has a strong intoxicating effect.

These are some physical reasons that explain how this tree, and not the famous cedars of Lebanon, emerged as the cradle of Osiris's tomb. The acacia's intoxicating effects also call to mind Dionysus, a god well known to be associated with wine and agriculture, and one who dispels worries through reverie and debauchery. This connection wasn't lost on Plutarch, who saw a striking similarity between Osiris and Dionysus, going so far as to declare them as two faces of the same god.[4] Although we usually read about Dionysus in Greek mythology, his origins have long been suspected to have come from another country.

Herodotus, the famous Greek historian, mentions other significant details that draw a connection between Osiris and his Greek counterpart, Dionysus: "As soon as Dionysus was born, Zeus sewed him up in his thigh and carried him to Nysa, above Egypt in Ethiopia; but they cannot say where Pan went after his birth. So it is quite clear to me, at least that the Hellenes [Greeks] learned the names of these gods later than those of the rest, and that they attribute to each of them a birth-date corresponding to the time when they first learned of him."[5]

This strange image of Dionysus being born from Zeus's thigh echoes the words spoken by Isis in Spell 74 of the Coffin Texts, where she pleads, "Osiris, live! May the Listless One rise upon his side." According to Rundle Clark, "The request to rise on one side is one of the most important themes in the Osirian cycle. The waters of the annual inundation came from the thigh of the god."[6] Clearly, we can surmise that the thigh of a god refers to his phallus.[7]

In figure 6.1, taken from a fourteenth-century manuscript, we see a tree that looks very much like the acacia growing from the thigh of an injured man. The caption attached to this picture reveals its meaning: "From death comes new life. While the body remains below, the volatile part rises, just as the human soul and spirit leave the body when death releases them."[8]

Figure 6.1. Phallic Tree.

This tree grows from the man's genitals, indicating once more the fertility of the god who will "Rise up!" These words call to Osiris, pleading and nearly commanding him to rid himself of the weariness of birth and the grave. It follows, then, that the king has the tree cut down (castrated) and made into a column supporting his palace, an image of the erect phallus. The alchemist Frabricius adds further interpretative information that reveals other features in this picture: "It [the *arbor philosophica*] appears in an alchemical vision of the sleeping Adam in the Garden of Eden. Bathed in the light of the moon mother, Adam is united with the tree of knowledge and with an Eve still existing as 'bone of his bone, And flesh of his flesh' (Genesis 2:23). The trunk grows out of Adam's lap as his erect penis extending into the crown of apples. The hand of *Mercurius philosophorum* has broken through the sky and pierced the heart of Adam with an arrow (signifying death in love)."[9]

The sexual imagery in all these themes is so obviously phallic and captivating that it is easy to overlook more subtle clues to the mystery embedded in these scenes. I will therefore point out two symbols that take us out of the mythic realm and bring us squarely into the mystical dimension. The first is found in Isis's braided hair. According to Denise Dersin in *What Life Was Like on the Banks of the Nile*, Egyptian women of this time did not weave or braid their hair.[10] In fact, due to the ever-present problem of head lice, women as well as men often donned wigs, and, as is seen in virtually every painted image of Egyptian women and goddesses, their hair was never curled or braided. In some instances Isis's hair is "disheveled over [her] face and the hair on [her] head was ruffled,"[11] indicating that she is being presented in the form of a flame or is saddened by the fate of her husband. The braided hair signifies much more when considered from a mystical perspective.

The interlacing pattern of braided hair indicates that two things of the same substance are separated and brought together in a graceful, complementary way. This form recalls the twin, opposing snakes that entwine the staff of Hermes, the caduceus. We see a much earlier form in the scepter held by Thoth on the engraved walls at Abydos. There the snakes represent the uniting of Upper and Lower Egypt. They combine to form the uraeus serpent that adorns the pharaoh's crown. It is a warning against would-be enemies as well as a symbol that expresses a synergistic flow of energies necessary in the process of integrating disparate and often conflicting parts of the psyche.

Isis's braids, taken on a cosmic level, point to an elemental form—the spiral—that is found above, in the great spiral galaxies, and below, in the helical structure of DNA. The vortical energy bound within the spiral is an archetypal force ubiquitous throughout nature and ancient cultures. Dozens of beautiful examples can be seen in Jill Purce's book *The Mystic Spiral*. From the simple design of a conch shell to mandalas, labyrinths, and the swirling dancing dervishes, the spiraling action of opposites is brought into harmony. "Weaving, two threads, by themselves," says Malkowski, "cannot be situated. Yet, when woven together, they become an intersection, which gives rise to form."[12]

Some of these ideas were well known to the Egyptians. They, for example, believed that meditating on the basic symmetrical geometric solids produced healing effects.[13] We also see the spiral protruding from the pschent, the double crown that depicts the energy shining forth from the pharaoh's forehead.[14] The double crown signifies not only the union of two formerly divided lands, but also the synergistic power emanating from the third eye in the form of a cosmic spiral protuberance. In this regard, I would also like to recall the djed pillar or column, which we presently find in the myth where Osiris's body is stood upright, enveloped by the acacia tree, and taken into the king's palace. The wave that precipitated these actions is another fine example of the vortical action of the spiral.

Figure 6.2. Spiral Pschent Crown, detail.

The spiral action in the braids and the wave are very dynamic. This archetypal form expresses energy moving and evolving. Often I explain to therapy patients that healing can be envisioned as a spiral moving one from old fixation points in their lives to higher levels of consciousness. Instead of a flat circular movement in which the patient is stuck repeating old, dysfunctional patterns, healing offers the opportunity to apply greater consciousness to the conflict and, as a result, brings fresh insights, attitudes, and new behaviors. The movement of energy is not confined to fixations, but more generally, raises the entire spectrum of consciousness. It is more accurate to call this action a shift rather than a developmental movement since there is a sudden death or shedding of an old self and the emergence of a new one. "No creature can attain a higher grade of nature," writes Ananda Coomaraswamy, "without ceasing to exist."[15]

Some speculate that the Egyptians developed techniques for transmuting energy and that yoga may well have originated in Egypt. Yoga is one of the very best systems for the transformation of psychic energy. Kundalini yoga in particular demonstrates this same spiral transmutation of gross energy into its subtle form. In this system, the Kundalini serpent awakens in the root chakra and through meditation moves up the spinal column as it awakens each of the seven chakras. Each chakra represents a center of psychophysical power. As we've seen in figure 3.2, Nut assumes the yoga position now popularly known as "downward-facing dog."

In what we might call Egyptian yoga, such practice would be based on correspondences between chakra points and Nut's body. We will recall that Nut was a celestial goddess. In theory, the sun's energy is regenerated as it moves through the twelve hours of night as represented by particular parts of Nut's anatomy: "Her lips correspond to the second hour, her teeth to the third . . . her throat and bust are crossed during the fourth and fifth hours. . . . In the tenth hour, the sun finally reaches her vagina and is reborn."[16] Before the deceased's soul embarks on this journey, it must first find its way through the labyrinthine underworld where Osiris reigns. The djed column expresses the strength and stability gained by the ba soul once it becomes one with Osiris.

In its simplest form, the djed pillar represents Osiris's spinal column. In human anatomy the spinal column, together with the brain, comprise the central nervous system (CNS). All operations requiring higher cortical functions are mediated through this system. As important as the CNS is to maintaining critical thinking and purposeful action, the organism still requires a more fundamental system that carries out basic housekeeping tasks such as respiration, blood circulation, and fight and flight defenses that are unconsciously mediated and react reflexively. This is the province of the autonomic nervous system (ANS). Despite its preeminence in the modern human, the CNS existed only

Figure 6.3. Raising the Djed Pillar.

in nascent form in the earliest days of civilization. "In the beginning," writes ethologist Lyall Watson, "there were only automatic responses; everything was unconscious. Then, when a critical level of complexity in the community of cells was reached, there were the first glimmerings of true conscious awareness, bringing both vigor and vulnerability."[17]

The vulnerability Dr. Watson speaks of stems from the power of reflection that comes with excessive conscious awareness. Like looking in a mirror, this attribute fascinates humans. But there are dangers associated with such preoccupation. In regards to hunting, for example, self-absorption can distract the hunter's aim and cause the arrow to miss its target. Vanity, arrogance, and righteousness are other dangers whose roots stem from the same cause. This kind of obsessive attention also caused problems in the alchemists' laboratories, something they called *fascinosum*. Years spent gazing into the fiery vessel and watching for any sign of success caused the adept's mind to wander. For this reason, "dissociation is vital" in order to protect the organism, says Watson.[18] In other words, scientists came to believe that consciousness had to be partitioned from the unconscious in order to ensure survival. As an unintended consequence, many people still either are unaware of the unconscious or wholly deny its existence.

While both nervous systems are essential for life, it is the CNS that somehow lifted itself up from its lowly place on the evolutionary ladder. And what was the impetus for this great evolutionary event? We don't know. What we do know is that abstract thought and the birth of modern consciousness resulted from this profound change. Still, such confessions don't come easily, especially for materialistic scientists. Theories abound. Ironically, great discoveries come precisely out of the mystery of the unknown. In his old age, a great biologist, Loren Eiseley, confessed, "In the world there is nothing to explain the world. Nothing to explain the necessity of life, nothing to explain the hunger of the elements to become life, nothing to explain why the stolid realm of rock and soil and mineral should diversify itself into beauty, terror and uncertainty."[19] Here we find ourselves at the brink of the imaginal world staring into the darkness with "holy curiosity."

Without the benefit of the sophisticated individualized ego consciousness of modern humans, the Egyptians did not struggle with questioning reality. The world was an open canvas, unrestricted by the need to make rational sense of existence or even be bothered with unconscious complexes. "Ancient thought—mythopoetic, 'myth-making' thought," explains Frankfort, "admitted side-by-side certain *limited* insights that were held to be *simultaneously* valid, each in its own proper context, each corresponding to a definite avenue of approach."[20]

This multiplicity of approaches allowed for rational thought to coexist with nonrational beliefs. Demons lived among the Egyptians while they were building some of the world's most complex structures. Theirs was a simpler world, neurologically speaking, where contradiction and lack of logical continuity did not interfere with a more organic, magical reality. Thus, for example, they experienced no discontinuity in discovering that the final resting place of the dead was actually located in more than one place. Some positioned it in the Field of Offerings beyond Sirius, the polar star in the north sky, while others thought it was in the west, beyond the horizon where the sun sets each night. Of course, the rational mind presumes that this "field" should be in a fixed place, leaving out the possibility that it actually exists wherever the mind locates it. Notwithstanding the impossiblity of integrating this morbid geography into a coherent map, the Egyptians had a keen sense of direction and amazing technological methods to locate adequate geological surfaces to support massive stone structures.

Any careful study of Egyptian temples shows the meticulous care they took to place each statue, engrave every hieroglyph, and even cut openings in the ceiling so that shafts of sunlight would shine on particularly sacred spots throughout the day. Therefore, it would be a serious oversight to ignore the attitude of Osiris's body—south to north while floating toward Byblos and vertically as his tomb is stood upright against the acacia tree.[21] Accordingly, we see that his spinal column also shifts from the watery realm and rises up to take an upward, sky-directed orientation. Physically, the spinal cord becomes the pillar or foundation that supports the brain, freeing humans to use their hands to make things and defend themselves with the added resource of more highly developed cortical functions. The transition of human beings from sea creature to land-based animal represents a major advance in the history of consciousness.

Is it possible that the Osiris myth is at this point depicting this radical change in human evolution? Might this be the reason why ancient Byblos was chosen as the spot where consciousness initially moved to the land and stood upright for the first time? Is the myth retelling Atum's ascension from chaos and the elevation of the human mind? Early humans were certainly quite intelligent, and yet they did not possess a well-defined individual ego. I seriously doubt, therefore, that this myth was a recipe for spelling out the transformation that must have occurred as humans took to the land. But we should not be too quick to dismiss the secret meaning of the myth, for it derives not from ego consciousness but from nature herself. Nature is, for the alchemists, their guide and teacher. "He who would understand the Book of Nature must walk its pages with his feet," instructed the fifteenth-century alchemist Paracelsus.[22] What we are observing in this part of the Osiris myth is nature's way of showing the progression of human evolution, both physically and psychically. The sequence of Osiris's tomb moving from sea to tree to palace represents an evolution of the human species from the wiles of nature into a new, civil dimension of reality.

The "rising up" of Osiris represents a new alignment of the spinal cord, a new spatial orientation, and the seminal emergence of individual identity. As we have seen, we cannot separate myth from history. Thus, we see a kind of early resurrection taking place as the tree concealing Osiris's body is brought into the royal court. To this point, individuation was a collective phenomenon, with the exception of the pharaoh, whose destiny it was to attain the status of the Divine Self.[23] He was the access point by which people observed the full expression of personality development as best symbolized by the archetype of the Self. As such, he alone was the conduit through which people made contact with the transcendent world. This, however, all changes in the rising up of Osiris's body. Just as we saw in Akhenaten's reign, the center of power shifts from pharaoh to god, and with it a new, more personal relationship with divinity is born. Although the king in the myth is unaware that it is Osiris who provides stability to his kingdom, *we know* that a god—and not the king—is supporting the central pillar of the world.

This central pillar has evolved into an image, the Axis Mundi, that is ubiquitous in world mythology. Furthermore, it takes on innumerable forms in religion, ecology, architecture, spirituality, and different mystical systems. Whether seen as the Tree of Life, Jacob's Ladder, the Temple Mount, Mount Kailash, or the Great Pyramid of Giza, the Axis Mundi is considered the central pillar around which psychic energy swirls, transforms, and ultimately holds the world together. The Pyramid Texts describe this axis as a stairway that takes the pure of heart to heaven: "A stairway to heaven shall be laid down for him, that he may ascend to heaven thereon."[24] In alchemy, the Axis Mundi is the golden chain of Hermes that unites opposing forces and connects the human being with all dimensions of reality—earthly, astral, and spiritual. At the core of these images is the djed column, the spinal cord of a god who supports all life.

We should not let these amplifications disguise the fact that Osiris is dead and far away from home. And meanwhile Isis, in the guise of an old woman, is greeted by the queen and put in charge of her infant son.

7

ISIS, HEKA, AND ALCHEMY

Isis, appearing as an old woman, is welcomed by the queen and shown to a room where the column containing Osiris's body is located. During the night, strange sounds are heard coming from the room, and the queen decides to investigate. In horror, she sees her child burning in the fireplace as a kite flies around the column. When she pulls her son from the burning embers, the kite transforms into Isis. The goddess announces her true identity to the queen and admonishes her for having interfered with the magical operation that would have bestowed immortality upon her son. She then requests that her husband's tomb be given to her. Before returning home with it, she gives instructions to have a temple built in his honor.

Plutarch tells us that the queen's name is Astarte, which raises the question of whether the queen is a goddess. Historically, Astarte was an Egyptian goddess whose popularity reached its height during the Amarna period (ca. 1353 BC) of the Eighteenth Dynasty, when Akhenaten, Tutankhamun, and Hatshepsut ruled Egypt. Astarte, the goddess of fertility, sexuality, and war, was worshipped in Egypt at this time. The Greeks adopted her into their mythology as Aphrodite. Astarte was often associated with Anad, another goddess of war; the two goddesses were wed to Seth.

CHAPTER SEVEN

Is this the Astarte of our myth? If so, we would expect her to have recognized Isis as a goddess and to have used supernatural powers to determine the source of the cries coming from the bedroom. Instead, the queen steals into the room and hides behind some furniture. She seems to have no magic and does not understand what Isis is doing to her son; much less was she able to cure him of his affliction. This behavior isn't what we would expect of a goddess. Perhaps she is a goddess in name only. For hundreds, even thousands of years, it was not unusual for men and women to adopt cover names in hopes that substituting a god's or goddess's identity would endow them and their work with supernatural powers.

We should not confuse this type of appropriation of a god's identity with embodying a god; the former is an example of sympathetic magic, and the latter is sympathetic engagement that involves "entering into" and empathizing with the religious object of study for the purpose of bringing it alive. "Only then," writes the Dutch philosopher W. Brede Kristensen, "can insight be achieved into the religions of the past *from the standpoint of their adherents.*"[1]

With sympathetic magic, the belief is that a god's power is transferred to the seeker through a process of contagion. A hero-warrior's sword, for example, transferred his powerful spirit to the person who touched it. In a similar way, the name of something is very nearly the equivalent of the thing itself. Ra's chief means of creation is accomplished by naming things. Thus, a pharaoh's ability to maintain the rule of Ma'at stemmed from two sources: *Sia* (perception) and *Hu* (utterance). The first enabled him to "perceive the plenitude of meaning and to keep it in his mind (in Egyptian, 'in his heart'), whereas Hu gave his word the power to become a reality immediately."[2]

One's name transcends the label we give our human body—it carries a person's history, testimony, soul (*ren*), essence, etc., into the annals of time and posterity. Temple walls often showed a list of pharaohs, with many kings sharing the same name. For instance, there were six Ptolemys and four Cleopatras. While the repeated use of a name was intended to keep the spirit of the royal blood in the family, it was also meant to bestow a cumulative power on descendents of earlier, powerful ancestral kings. The art of naming, as we saw with Ra, is an act of creation, but it also can re-create the original energy and transfer it into another person.

This magic is accomplished by recreating the First Time. "This was achieved," writes Naydler, "through an act of invocation in which the supramundane or archetypal reality was brought down into the mundane, suffusing the latter with spiritual power."[3] The principle involved here, as mythologist Sir James Frazer tells us, is based on the belief that "things act on each other at a distance through a secret sympathy, the impulse being transmitted from one to the other by means of what we may conceive as a kind of invisible ether, not unlike that which is postulated by modern science for a precisely similar purpose, namely, to explain how things can physically affect each other through a space which appears to be empty."[4]

Sympathetic or imitative magic stems from the concrete idea that all life is One Thing that has infinite expressions. Life in this view is infused with consciousness, which shows itself externally as matter and internally as spirit. By controlling the latter, the magician is able to direct energy from or into an object. This ability was especially useful in the afterlife, where one expected to encounter demons; donning the face of a god was essentially the same as enacting a spell.[5] Thus,

> The one who knows the spell
> Will be like the sun god in the east
> The one who executes this pattern
> Is like the Great God himself.[6]

Magic of this kind was just as useful in everyday life. According to Naydler, in the "toilet ceremony" the pharaoh underwent an elaborate daily ritual in which he was "washed, censed and given balls of natron [salt] to chew." Each of these acts "corresponded to the cosmic and mythical events of the sun god's rebirth from the waters of Nun." Naydler explains what happens next: "The king then ascended the stairs of the Temple of the Morning at exactly the same moment as his heavenly father Ra rose above the horizon. Just as the sun was purified and reborn each morning in the Temple Beneath the Horizon, then ascended into the sky, so the king underwent the same daily ritual. In this way, the toilet ceremony projected him into the First Time in a repeated fusion of temporal and eternal realities, through which his identity as image of Ra on earth was daily reestablished."[7]

I'm sure few of us attach this kind of meaning to our toilette, but if we adopt a divine vision of the world, everything holds within it a bit of grace and transcendence. Sympathetic magic is quite symmetrical in that there is a correspondence between higher and lower realities that not only reflect one another but also penetrate one another. We might add that above and below can also be understood as within and without; in this case, we are at the intersection of these four dimensions. Applying our name is a way of fixing our spiritual location at this central point. But unless we are mindful every moment of this conjunction, we are misaligned and reap no lasting benefit.

Constructing this vessel of consciousness is akin to the creation of the vas hermeticum in which alchemical transformation can occur. As a psychotherapist, one of my tasks is to establish such a vessel in which the processes of healing are performed. A psychotherapist "holds space" for his or her patient by relying on formal and informal means. Strict rules of confidentiality are part of the therapeutic contract that safeguards a high level of privacy. Building and maintaining an alliance in the relationship helps build trust. In practice, however, such forms of secrecy are an art that require the therapist to weigh a patient's right to privacy against potentially imminent danger posed by withholding critical information.

An alchemist has to handle truth in much the same way as a therapist. Putting secret knowledge to good use is a subtle, tricky art requiring a high degree of integrity. The lengths to which fake magicians will go to deceive their sponsors are extraordinary. Discerning Astarte as a real goddess or the kite as Isis is a task that only a true magus might achieve. To distinguish the true adept from a charlatan can be very difficult at times; often, mistakes lead to tragedy.

It is likely that the queen took Astarte's name to embolden her image in the court. Her suspicion of Isis and failure to recognize her in her kite form shows that Astarte was neither a goddess nor skilled in the ways of magic. We will therefore regard her as purely human, with all the flaws that come with humanity. It is no surprise, then, that the first thing we learn about the queen is that her infant son is ill and that he is put in the care of one whose powers are greater than hers. Still, questions remain. We do not know what the boy suffers from or why the queen would entrust him to a perfect stranger.

Moments like these make myths appear like dreams. Indeed, this scene is one of the most magical in the myth—an eerie blend of Egyptian magic, heka, and alchemy. I think it is most profitable to approach this section of the myth as if it were a dream. Since the scene is enacted principally by two female figures, Isis and Astarte, it is worth our time to delve a bit more deeply into feminine psychology to explain what is really happening.

The appearance of a male figure in a woman's dream typically signifies the animus, an archetype that expresses the essence of masculinity in a woman's personality. In her book *Animus and Anima*, Emma Jung points out that the animus typically shows itself in dreams and fantasies "as father, lover, brother, teacher, judge, sage; sorcerer, artist, philosopher, scholar, builder, monk."[8] Any of these would provide some insight into the woman and her relationship to the animus. This archetypal man is most obvious in dreams. In my work with a happily married woman who had been sexually abused by various men in her childhood, I gleaned a great deal of knowledge about her current life by a dream she reported. She dreamed a young, handsome, and muscular man lured her away from her husband. He took her to his expensive condominium by the ocean many miles away from her home. He was a surfer, and later he broke his back in an accident. While his drunken father was taking him to the hospital, they were in a terrible car crash and the young man died. Following this tragedy she discovered that she was pregnant with his child. We can readily see in this dream the power of the negative animus to hold this woman in his grasp.

The animus, like any other archetype, is neither good nor bad. Archetypes are like gods and goddesses in that they serve the individuation process by amplifying powers innate within our nature. These powers can serve us or, as in a complex, mesmerize us into unconsciously repeating dysfunctional behavior patterns.

Were a woman to dream often of men who wield authority, we would suspect she possesses a large reservoir of masculine strength to draw from. Depending on how conscious her relationship with the animus is, she may exhibit positive masculine traits. In a business meeting for example, she may offer her opinions freely and be able to hold her position in disagreements with colleagues. A woman having a mature relationship with the animus is able to call forth the masculine energies of the unconscious as needed. She can be appropriately assertive when necessary; temper her emotions with reason; and be focused, deliberate, and structured in her thinking. By contrast, a woman lacking this kind of integration is subject to the autonomous impulses of the animus. She may be impetuous and aggressive or, just the opposite, find herself unable to contain her emotions. Recalling how Queen Hatshepsut donned a beard, demanded that she be addressed as king, braved long travels to foreign lands, and undertook enormous building projects, we might speculate that she was dominated by her animus, much to the expense of her femininity. Such a woman is oftentimes domineering, lacking in compassion, and out of touch with her body.

In our present circumstance, we find Queen Astarte with an ailing son—a sign, perhaps, that points to a weak condition of her own animus. "Sometimes," Emma Jung adds, the animus "is represented by a boy, a son or a young friend, especially when the woman's own masculine component is thus indicated as being in a state of becoming."[9] In other words, a woman in this state is only just becoming aware of the animus—it is young, poorly developed, or, in this case, infirmed. The queen is vulnerable and in danger unless something is done to correct her relationship with her sick son and undeveloped animus. Seeing the queen's son and knowing what ails him, Isis applies healing magic. And here we find a strange juxtaposition in the myth. As the queen watches, she sees her own infantile animus being healed and transformed, while unrecognized nearby stands the body of Osiris, the archetypal symbol of becoming.

Isis is attempting to facilitate the boy's individuation by the alchemical use of fire and at the same time help his mother develop a more mature relationship with the animus. Often the childish ways of a woman must be burned off in order to transform her insecurities. History often repeats itself. An insecure mother may coddle her child and in the process overlook the divine powers that can only become conscious when she adequately detaches herself from the child. Isis is well aware of what is required. By putting this child through a trial by fire she intends not only to burn away the mother's dependency needs, attachment desires, and projections, but at the same time transform him into a god. Had the queen not interfered with Isis, her undeveloped animus would have attained its rightful place as a god within her psyche. As an added benefit, the queen's son would have become his own man, free from his mother's needs or who she thinks he should be. And finally, burning away the boy's human attributes might further transform him into a god in the likeness of a true pharaoh. We will see this dynamic played out when Horus must separate from Isis to become the archetypal model of the pharaoh.

By understanding the personality of Queen Astarte, we begin to see the alchemical implications of this scene: Isis uses the hearth as an alchemist utilizes the furnace for performing the "Operations of the Sun." Here Isis employs calcinatio, the operation of fire that reduces gross, physical matter to purified ash. While there are precious few things in everyday life that give us a tangible image of transformation, fire is certainly one of them. Whether it is the sun above or the fire in the hearth that causes things to change, we are reminded that the world is constantly undergoing transformation.

For the Egyptians, the sun was everything—life itself. In his beautiful poem *The Great Hymn to the Aten* Akhenaten says,

> When thou settest in the Western horizon, the Earth is in darkness after the manner of death. . . . Darkness lurks, and the earth is silent when their Creator rests in his habitation. . . . The earth brightens when thou arisest in the Eastern horizon and shinest forth as Aten in the daytime. Thou drivest away the night when thou givest forth thy beams. . . . All ways open at thy dawning. The fish in the river leap in thy presence. Thy rays are in the midst of the sea.[10]

In this lovely passage, fire is associated with light as a generative force that brightens the day and illuminates the soul. Fire, as Paracelsus points out, is the operation that bestows immortality by separating "that which is constant or fixed from that which is fugitive or volatile."[11] In our myth, this is precisely what Isis is attempting to do with the queen's son—dissolve those things that will die from others that will live forever. The fire-bath establishes a connection "between the ego and the archetypal psyche, making the former aware of its transpersonal, eternal, or immortal aspect."[12] This task is not easy. To illustrate, Edinger recalls the Greek myth of Persephone in which her mother, Demeter, wanders off after losing her daughter to Hades. The king and queen of Eleusis take the distraught Demeter into their care. Like Isis, Demeter attempts to make their son, Demophoon, immortal "by holding him in the fire." But just as Queen Astarte interrupts the transformation, so too does Queen Metaneira scream when she sees what is happening. Her ego is no more able than Astarte's to recognize and sustain the intensity of the archetypal psyche.

We are of two minds when it comes to fire—we are drawn to it like moths to flame but cannot bear the heat and the danger it poses. In alchemy this ambivalence is especially true since the psychological process can be grueling. "One is roasted, roasted in what one is. . . . For you roast in what you are yourself and not in anything else; one could say that one is cooked in one's own juice."[13] So many of my patients want to become more individuated, but when it comes to the inevitable trial by fire, most shrink from the task. We would sooner hold on to our troubling complexes because they seem familiar and, curiously, closer to the great potential hidden in our darkness. Von Franz explains this strange paradox:

> When someone is stuck in a neurotic complex, the same problem goes round and round in his head. . . . There is also something numinous hidden in the complex, and in the very worst center of the neurosis or psychosis there is generally a symbol of the Self and that causes the fascination and makes people hang onto it. If one contents oneself with repression of the illness, the symbol of the Self is thereby also repressed, and that is the

reason why people often fight against being cured. They have a hunch that the best of themselves lives in their worst suffering, and that is the awful difficulty.[14]

Individuation means adopting an entirely new orientation to life, and that can be frightening. The old ego simply does not know how to adapt—nor should it, since individuation is *not* about adaptation but about transformation. The ego is simply not equipped to experience immortality, for it exists within the confines of space and time. Thus, just like the queen, the ego is horrified when her son—representing a new level of reality—threatens to upset the status quo. She simply is not ready to sustain the transcendent reality of the Self. For the Egyptians, this achievement was left to the pharaoh, and it was enough that he acted as a conduit connecting others with the transpersonal realm. With the eventual fall of the pharaoh and, more generally, reliance on representation by others—be they priests, popes, or prophets—modern humans are faced with a daunting choice: either resist becoming more conscious or change!

Every therapist is saddened when a patient resists undergoing transformations necessary for his or her individuation process. I once said to a patient I'd treated for five years, "I shook the boat, but the wrong person fell out!" I was trying to shake him loose of his entitlement and dependency on his family so that he could "learn to swim" on his own, but instead I found myself out of the boat. This is the feeling that Isis must have experienced when the queen interfered with her work: a mix of annoyance and regret. Still, as a goddess she raises herself above the human pale and with the compassion of a bodhisattva allows the boy to live on in the mortal world—at least for a while. In exchange for her husband's coffin, Isis blesses the kingdom and instructs the people to construct a temple in her husband's honor. Ironically, the queen's son accompanies Isis back to Egypt, but when he is unable to curb his curiosity and opens the crypt, Isis gives him such a stare that he dies instantly. We see these two aspects of the goddess existing side by side—she is full of compassion, but also inspires terror.

8

SOLVE ET COAGULA

Upon returning to Egypt, Isis hides her husband's coffin in the papyrus marsh. But Seth, while out hunting, discovers it, and in his rage he cuts Osiris's body into fourteen pieces. He scatters the body parts throughout Upper and Lower Egypt. Again Isis transforms into a kite and along with her sister, Nephthys, goes in search of her husband's severed limbs. Wherever she finds one, she performs sacred funerary rites. She collects all but one of Osiris's body parts, his penis. Thoth comes to her aid and discovers that the member had been cast into the Nile, where it was eaten by a fish. Thoth recovers the penis, and Isis reassembles her husband's body. She then spreads her wings and magically reanimates Osiris just long enough to be inseminated by him. In this way, their son, Horus, is born. Isis and Nephthys then sit in vigil, protecting and mourning Osiris, while Anubis embalms his father's body and Horus lives on into maturity.

If any doubts remain that Seth is evil incarnate, then this scene surely raises an important question—is he purely evil or is he, as I've suggested, the necessary catalyst that ultimately causes Osiris to assume his position as lord of the underworld? Despite Seth's despicable acts, I still submit that Seth is not evil, but that another character, who does not appear in this myth, is a much better candidate for the role of devil— Apopis. In fact, we learn in the Pyramid Texts that Seth, the dark god of limits, kills this destroyer of consciousness. Additionally, we should not forget that Seth is part of the Ennead. Nor should we ignore the fact that it was Osiris who seemingly instigated Seth's wrath by sleeping with his wife. For now, we will delay judgment and await the trial of the gods to decide the fate of both Seth and Osiris.

The Osiris myth stands out against a mythic background that shows Ra sailing through the night sky battling monsters and demons to restore the light of consciousness to the world. Ra's archenemy is Apopis, whose only ambition is to snuff out this light and render the world lifeless—an empty shell cast back into the sea of Nun. If true evil is unconsciousness, then Apopis is this devil that is the agent of annihilation. Seth's motives are far closer to being human. He is filled with hate, envy, and murderous impulses, to be sure, but these are emotions that temper and define their opposites. By contrast, Apopis is a serpent of the lowest order—blind to the motives of men and women, acting out of destructive impulses that lack human emotion and reason.

Whereas Seth takes humans to the outermost limit of humanity, Apopis seeks to end humanity altogether. And yet, these dark gods each belong to a powerful complex that defines the limits of human consciousness, delineating a limen that separates order from chaos. While they draw us back into darkness, countervailing forces remain to prevent total collapse. Certainly Isis, using love and magic, is a vital force who is there at every turn to confront Seth and have him undo the havoc he has wrought. As the story continues, we discover that she is not alone in this mission. It is tempting to get caught in the drama of the story at this point and miss the hidden meaning concealed in the myth, but before we are finished with this part of the myth we will discover an archetypal recipe that offers a basic law of the universe.

Seth is enraged when he again sees the dead body of his brother, Osiris. He tears the body into fourteen sections and, according to Plutarch, scatters them throughout Egypt. Once again Isis goes in search of her husband's body. She is accompanied by Nephthys, another indication that this wily goddess is her own woman. The Pyramid Texts say that "Isis comes and Nephthys comes, one of them from the west, one of them from the east, one of them as a 'screecher', one of them as a kite, they have found Osiris, his brother Seth having laid him low in Nedit."[1]

As noted earlier, Osiris was killed and dismembered in Nedit, a name that derives from *nedyet*, meaning "to fall to the ground." Phrases like "laid low" and "fall to the ground" are ancient expressions indicating death, killing, and murder. But in the case of Osiris the murder is especially savage and, at the same time, symbolic. On the human level, dismemberment evokes hideous images of cruel punishment: decapitation, drawing and quartering, the rack, and the guillotine. If we consider the human form as a star-shaped body—an observation not lost on our ancestors—then the tearing apart of an astral form proffers symbolic meaning. "Beheading," writes Jung, "is significant symbolically as the separation of the 'understanding' from the 'great suffering and grief' which nature inflicts on the soul. It is an emancipation of the '*cogitatio*' which is situated in the head, a freeing of the soul from the 'trammels of nature.'"[2] Anyone suffering from a severe migraine will appreciate the relief to which Jung refers. People whose racing thoughts keep them from a good night's sleep or the manic person who simply can't stop thinking (or talking) might welcome a symbolic decapitation.

Admittedly, to suggest that anything positive might result from such a hideous act is difficult. But from an objective standpoint we need only consider how the world evolves to realize that dismemberment is an implicit operation occurring at every level of reality—including the inner world of psyche. We exist in a process of continual dismemberment in which supernovas are exploding and subatomic particles disintegrate, each followed by a reciprocal process of reintegration that creates new and more refined forms.

I indicated earlier that an Egyptian god's or goddess's power is to some extent determined by the number of his or her manifestations. In other words, this breaking down process is not simply a means to an end, for death in that case is the ultimate decapitation of life. Rather, the myth presents us with the very real possibility that dismemberment serves to increase power and bring new life. As evidence to support this view, we find new settlements springing up where each of Osiris's body parts comes to rest. In one version of the myth, Isis uses her magic to create an effigy of Osiris's corpse from each body part, leaving each town to believe that they alone possess the whole of his sacred remains. These settlements, or nomes, grow from the generative power contained in the "juices" of Osiris's decaying limbs. Eventually, the fourteen colonies born from Osiris coalesce to form a nation. In our own time, the motto *E Pluribus Unum* echoes the same principle, namely, "Out of the Many, One." Mythically, this principle is illustrated by the two missions undertaken by Isis, first to retrieve Osiris's dead body, then to retrieve the severed limbs that have been dispersed throughout Egypt—first one, then many that are magically reunited.

As we've seen throughout this myth, every detail, when examined carefully, has meaning. That Osiris is cut into fourteen sections and not twelve or nine must therefore be significant. Thinking in concrete terms, it is easy to see how the number may have come about: dissection at the ankles, knees, wrists, elbows, and shoulders, with the final cuts to the neck, waist, and the penis. Butchering Osiris in this savage way resulted in fourteen body parts, a number having symbolic significance.[3]

The numerologist Annemarie Schimmel, in *The Mystery of Numbers*, describes in some detail why the number fourteen is considered to have protective and healing powers. She reminds us that the human spine has fourteen vertebrae, a reference that recalls the significance of the djed column. Given Osiris's connection to the moon, it comes as little surprise that these powers relate to the fourteen days needed for the moon to achieve full luminosity and an additional fourteen days for its decay. Each piece of Osiris's precious body is then infused with lunar energy that has the power to regenerate his spirit. In a similar vein, we find this theme of dismemberment and regeneration at critical stages in the alchemical opus. Many examples of these reciprocal actions are found throughout alchemical art and literature.

Figure 8.1. The Golden Head.

Figure 8.1 is a plate taken from the fifteenth-century alchemical treatise *Splendor Solis*. It depicts a gruesome image of dismemberment, explained by the accompanying text: "In [the murderer's] left hand was a paper on which the following was written, 'I have killed thee, that thou mayest receive a superabundant life, but thy head I will carefully hide, that the worldly wantons may not find thee, and destroy the earth, and the body I will bury, that it may putrefy, and grow and bear innumerable fruit.'"[4]

To fully understand this passage we need to consider the preceding plate in *Splendor Solis* (not shown), which depicts a winged hermaphrodite holding a sun disk. Jungian analyst Joseph Henderson provides a good explanation for what is happening here. In *Transformation of the Psyche* he points out that the union of opposites represented by the hermaphrodite is a prefiguring image of the Self. "The hermaphrodite," he writes, "as a resolution of the problem of the opposites is contrived, facile, or too intellectual." The opposites are, in other words, simply pieced together. In this case, "There is always the danger of getting fixated upon the insight without the embodiment of the transformation."[5] We cannot rush transformation. Alchemy is a slow, deliberate process that steers its way through the narrow strait of fixation and exuberance. The "worldly wantons" destroy the earth by settling for superficial "insights" that lack thoughtfulness and responsibility. Only by uniting the opposites with care and patience are we able to enjoy the lasting benefits of alchemical transformation.

Haste, warned the alchemist, can ruin the most well-conceived experiment. With this in mind, I recall an old saying that cautions, "Don't push the river, it flows by itself." We must, in other words, attune ourselves to the rhythms of nature, as well as our own, or suffer untold consequences. Impulsive action, poor judgments, and unbridled passion usually lead to disaster. When we neglect to stay true to our inner rhythms and properly care for and incubate a decision before taking action, not only do we risk losing our bearings, but, worse, we suffer a loss of integrity. "Psychologically," says Henderson, "the rendering of false integrity is often experienced inwardly as a bodily dissociation or dismemberment."6 This was certainly the case of a middle-aged man I treated for grief and depression stemming from a long history of early maternal abuse and the death of his daughter in childbirth. Despite being highly intelligent, articulate, and well educated, he generally lived on the brink of financial ruin, was unable to complete his doctoral dissertation, and frequently exhibited bouts of explosive anger. The grief he shared with his wife, whom I was treating separately, brought both of them to the brink of suicide.

My first impression of him was, how can such a smart man be so unsuccessful? He looked like a broken man who, despite his intelligence, simply couldn't pull his life together. Clearly, the loss of his daughter was a shattering experience, but it seemed that her death not only reopened injuries he sustained as a child, but in a more positive light offered a mortificatio that was long overdue. Painful memories had to be confronted and symbolically killed if he was ever to have a healing, transformative experience. He lacked the golden head (see figure 8.1) that appears when one undergoes a successful dismembering experience. The gold head, Henderson writes, "signifies the coming into consciousness of the Self, beyond the opposites. [It] represents the lasting and unique value of . . . [preventing] the danger of slipping back into a conventional or an infantile form of adaptation [i.e., the solution sought by the 'worldly wantons' in the above quote from *Splendor Solis*]."7 This explanation is supported by the Egyptians' use of a mummy mask, called "mysterious head" or "the head of mystery," that preserved an ideal image of the deceased.

Ironically, the theme of this man's dissertation had to do with the process of initiation, which in many cultural traditions involves some form of symbolic dismemberment. As we worked in therapy, this theme showed itself in a dream. He recalled being in a cemetery, standing before a grave that had two headless bodies buried one atop the other. Under his arm he held a head that he knew had to be attached to one of these corpses but he didn't know which one. Nearby was a bridge, which he couldn't cross until he attached the head to the right body.

In discussing his associations to the dream, the patient identified the two bodies as being young and old; the older body buried the deepest. He could not identify the head he carried beneath his arm. After much deliberation, he felt the head needed to be connected to the older corpse. This was his old self, which he had long lost touch with, the one buried deepest in his psyche. Connecting the head would revitalize his old self, allowing him to act without doubting himself, or as he said, "I won't be of two minds." This decision came after a visit to his family, who had gathered to celebrate his mother's eightieth birthday. He described his family as "metal cutouts," incapable of feeling or receiving love.

Years of criticism from an unfeeling, demanding mother had left his soul drained. As Henderson describes, this patient became "fixated . . . without the embodiment of the transformation."[8] More simply put, he took refuge in his head, with the result that he was overly intellectualized; his feelings were concepts, not felt experiences. As a result, his confidence suffered and he generally felt incomplete. It was as if his mother's harsh voice resided in his soul, and unless he could evacuate it there would be no chance of dissolving the complex or successfully mourning the loss of his child. His mother had decapitated him many times by "biting his head off" with cruel, cutting criticisms.

This man had to heal the split between his Real Self and the False Self[9] that protected him from his mother's blows; thoughts and feelings had to be integrated. He had to find a way to connect his soul with the "golden head," for this would give his old body new life. Given his deep religious history, we associated the golden head with the idea of Divine Mind, a concept that reflects the integration of all psychological opposites.

Following the dream he had an experience that offered hope. While hiking in a wilderness area, he came upon a large dead snake. Being knowledgeable in mythology as well as ophiology (the study of snakes), he took this as a sign that things were changing for the better. Snakes and double dream images (in this case, dead bodies) are symbols of imminent change. Specifically, he felt that his grief over the loss of his child was lifting and he could find new channels for love. In fact, love is the countervailing force that not only could heal his soul but also, as the text indicates, allow him to "bear innumerable fruit." Accordingly, he resigned from a dead-end job, joined a new business group, and retained a dissertation coach. He was ready to cross the bridge.

Isis and Nephthys find every piece of Osiris's body save his penis. The penis is of course a symbol of masculine fertility. Why Isis especially cannot locate the penis, despite her vast magical powers, is disconcerting and very mysterious. From a Jungian perspective, it appears that Isis's search for her husband and gathering up of his body represents her need to *incorporate* her own masculine self, the animus, in order to achieve union and wholeness. That she is unable to find his penis tells us this is something so central to masculinity and so contrary to her nature that she cannot grasp it, that only by way of an intermediary will she be able to obtain it and integrate it. This idea is very alchemical since mercury, friend to all metals, acts as a catalyst in joining "unsociable" substances. While the story continues to focus on the transformation of Osiris, we are left to imagine the profound change Isis undergoes once she achieves union with her husband and inwardly with her animus. This urge to individuate explains Isis's motivation and the incredible lengths she goes to in order to retrieve her husband's body.

The penis plays no small part in this transformation and therefore deserves further discussion. Perhaps it is unsurprising to learn that the etymology of the word *penis* contains the root stem for our word *pen*. Stanford literature professor Tom Hare demonstrates in his semiotic analysis of the Osiris myth that many meanings can be drawn from various associations with the glyph for *phallus*: semen, urine, and "the humors of the body."[10] Just so, a pen "projects" words that can have any number of effects on the world. In Egyptian symbols, the pen or stylus used to write the hieroglyphs was thought to be the quill-shaped beak of Thoth in his ibis form. Without the penis, the rest of Osiris's body would not be able to regenerate. Even Isis's magic could not help her locate and retrieve her husband's penis. Once again Thoth comes to her assistance. Like a trickster spirit, he is able to cross an important threshold and deliver the sacred member into Isis's hands.[11]

The penis was thrown into the Nile, where it was swallowed by a fish, or in some versions three fish.[12] Because these fish had consumed the sacred flesh, eating any of them would have been strictly forbidden. It is possible that the image of a fish emerged in the myth due to its physical similarity to the phallus—the body of the fish resembling the shaft of the penis and the back fins, the testicles. Much later the fish image gained a more abstract association when it became related to Christ, the *ichthys*, and was given symbolism in the sacrament of the Catholic Mass, the Eucharist. These images recall Atum's autoeroticism and the culture of cannibalism in ancient Egypt. The fish may have become a Christ symbol because, lacking eyelids, it signified omniscience, the all-seeing power of the gods that recalls the Eye of Horus.

Isis now proceeds to reconnect the lifeless pieces of her dead husband. She first transforms herself back into a kite and, by fluttering her wings, not only reassembles his lifeless limbs but also reanimates his body just long enough to copulate with him and conceive a child. This is described in a hymn from the New Kingdom:

She shaded him with her feathers and gave him air with her wings,
She cried out for joy and brought her brother to land.

She revived the weariness of the Listless One and took his seed into her
body, [thus] giving him an heir.[13]

The phrase "gave him air" reverberates throughout alchemical literature and other sacred texts. Hermes Trismegistus, in the Emerald Tablet, writes, "The Wind hath carried it in its belly." The phrase refers to the One Thing that joins the multiplicity of all things. In John 20:21–22, Jesus appears to his disciples following his death and says, "As the Father has sent me I am sending you. And with that *he breathed on them* and said, 'Receive the Holy Spirit'" (my italics). We gain further insights into the meaning of these references to air from the Upanishads, where this element, known as *prana*, is a vital life-sustaining force that comes from the sun. We have already seen many references in Egyptian texts to the sun and its power to enliven physical bodies and illuminate consciousness. In the final chapter we will again revisit the importance of the sun god Aten as he represents the Self.

It is precisely these miraculous acts of Isis that inflame Seth and cause him to protest. He does not believe that Isis and her dead husband mated and produced a son. Instead, he accuses her of being a harlot and Horus, her illegitimate offspring. As we will see later, his interpretation of events will become the foundation of his claim against Osiris in a court of law. He contends that he, not this bastard child Horus, is the rightful heir to the throne.

To my mind, Isis is exhibiting her most powerful magic in four critical actions—reassembling Osiris, reanimating him, sexually joining with him, and bearing an heir. These events have a special place in alchemy. Osiris's dismemberment is a personification in mythic image of the first of the two operations that form the alchemical recipe solve et coagula. In the laboratory, this recipe involves cutting, dicing, masticating, reducing, and dissolving, followed by joining, combining, fusing, melding, and "marrying." The laboratory is a sacred place where the primary forces of separating and uniting are used experimentally to replicate and transform mundane matter into spiritualized substance. "In many places," observes Edinger, "the whole *opus* is summarized by the phrase, 'Dissolve and coagulate.'"[14]

Modern astronomy and particle physics inform us that these very same forces are at work at every level of reality, from star-making quasars to the cellular mechanics of the human body. A prevailing theory maintains that the universe began expanding with the Big Bang and that it will someday reverse its course and begin contracting. Similarly, these same two actions, dissolving and coagulating, are occurring constantly in the life and death of every cell in the human body. There is virtually no end to the list of phenomena that follow these actions: the contraction and expansion of world economies, the rise and fall of ocean tides, economic expansion and contraction, physical growth and decay, social isolation and integration . . . life and death. Clearly, the early Egyptians possessed this incredible insight many thousands of years before it became a formal core recipe in the alchemical opus.

Many more dualities can be added to this list. Philosophers have used various terms to describe the dynamic flow of life in explaining how meaning is produced from psychic energy. Some examples: Heraclitus described the *logos* from which all things flow from one extreme to the other—"what is drawn together and what is drawn asunder. . . The one is made up of all things and all things issue from the one."[15] Hegel's model posits a synthesis resulting from the union of thesis and antithesis. Egyptologist Jan Assman captures the essence of this movement and what it meant for the Egyptians. "Death," he writes in a chapter aptly titled "Death as Dismemberment," "was the principle of dismembering, dissolving, isolating disintegration, while life was the principle of integrating animation, which conferred unity and wholeness."[16]

Death was for the Egyptians the secret means by which one escaped the restraints that tethered an individual to the material world, allowing him or her to pursue Ra's course to the stars. There we rejoin the gods in eternal bliss. But the interpretation of Osiris's dismemberment and reunion we are considering is a radical view contrary to this traditional understanding of Egyptian cosmology. Assmann's explanation holds true for life on earth but does not explain the larger view of what happens after death. Instead of following Ra on his journey to the stars, Osiris "becomes earth." Or, in modern terms, he transforms into an archetype of the unconscious whereby we today can embody his spirit and heal the split between psyche and matter. This path is the way of modern individuation: liberation is within, not without, or, as alchemy would have it, "As above, so below, for the making of the One Thing."

The dualities I described above are different variations of the rhythms of life and death of psychic life. Obviously, these rhythms of separation and reunion do not oscillate at the same rate in every situation. We cannot begin to imagine the endless fields of resonance created by ongoing oscillations created by these rhythms; yet, despite being in sympathetic resonance or not, taken as a whole they create what we know as reality. Furthermore, each person becomes real by the individuation process in which consciousness develops and the push of psychic energy advances the personality through life stages. Later research in developmental psychology elaborated this concept and described a process of physical detachment from a primary caregiver (typically the mother) that precipitates progressive integration of the personality, a process known as "separation-individuation."[17] The same process that governs many physical operations also describes the movement of psychic energy between an endless array of opposites. Once a child separates from the mother, new individuated behavior contributes to newfound independence; while separation-individuation is most active in the early years, it continues throughout the lifetime of an individual. Physical death is the final material separation from earth, and, as we have seen in Egyptian cosmology, it precipitates further individuation that ultimately leads to immortality and reunion with the Kosmos (conscious universe).

Not only is this recipe the foundation of all operations in alchemical work, but it also describes the essential formula for life. As I mentioned in the introduction, I was utterly amazed when I realized that this central recipe was concealed in the Osiris myth. Such a possibility sheds new light on alchemy and on the mysteries of ancient Egypt, to say nothing of the value this recipe plays in the individuation process. In fact, the separation-individuation process is a psychological derivative of this same recipe. As already mentioned, secrecy was mandated to protect and conceal sacred knowledge. Perhaps the originators of this myth used it as a device to transmit this secret, powerful recipe to those who were sufficiently enlightened to recognize it and use it responsibly. If so, they were incredibly successful, for it wasn't until the end of dynastic rule that we discover any literary evidence of alchemy and the eventual inclusion of this recipe into the alchemists' most sacred doctrines. What we see in the whole of Egyptian cosmology and history is, to varying degrees, "unconscious alchemy"—an art that hadn't been fully realized but whose effects in spiritual, architectural, and funerary practices produced miraculous results. It wasn't until the fourth century BC when alchemy rose to the surface of literary awareness and another millennia for it to reach its height in Arabia and Europe.

It took many centuries before this recipe became well known throughout the alchemical world. The concept was developed by brilliant minds that recognized the flow of psychic energy within human beings and the "urge" to integrate opposites into a cohesive whole. The early church father Origen (ca. AD 185–254), an Egyptian teaching in

Alexandria, said, "You can see how that man who is considered to be one person is not at all one, but there seems to be in him as many persons as mores [patterns of behavior] according to the scripture that the fool changes like the moon."[18] We find this same idea expressed much later in the alchemist Gerhard Dorn (ca. 1530–1584), who wrote, "Thou wilt never make from other things the one that thou seekest, except there first be made one thing of thyself."[19] At the heart of the recipe solve et coagula we find the initial impetus for a defined process describing the movement of mind and matter that eventually gives rise to an integrated universe in which the margin between above and below steadily moves toward sublime complementarity—what Jungian analyst Robert Johnson termed "Conscious Wholeness."

The priests and pharaohs of Egypt must have possessed similar knowledge and possibly incorporated it into spiritual disciplines. How else might we explain their deep mystical understandings or engineering feats that to this day cannot be adequately explained by conventional theory? We can only guess how many complex elaborations of this seed recipe were used in performing amazing transformations and transmutations. Sacred knowledge of this kind of experience could never adequately be submitted to writing, so it is quite possible that further insight into this ancient wisdom will forever remain a mystery. Perhaps this recipe may well be one of those divine thoughts Einstein meant when he said he wished to know the mind of God.

Earlier, I described a couple that struggled with profound grief following the death of their stillborn daughter. While the father lacked the emotional resources to process grief, the mother was overwhelmed by feelings. He suffered from a profound contraction that had a stultifying effect on his ability to think and process feelings, whereas his wife suffered from the reciprocal expansion—explosion—of feelings. Her pain was palpable and paralyzing. As she learned through therapy, her daughter's death brought to light many of the failures she'd suffered throughout her life. The promise of a daughter meant that she could begin life anew. But, unlike Osiris and Isis, this couple was denied an "heir," and for some time they seemed to have no hope of regeneration. Then, after nearly a year of intensive therapy, she had two significant dreams.

The first dream she recorded as follows: I am lured into a photographer's studio. He shackles me, strips me, rapes me, and then photographs me. Then, after releasing me he says, "You could have left at any time." As I leave, the photographer transforms into a woman who desires me and as a way of holding onto some part of me keeps the film. Then, I see an etching of an old man with a long beard in some kind of laboratory. He is stirring bones in a big cauldron while adding some kind of black, tarry substance. Then, I hear the word *coagulate*.

This woman had little knowledge of alchemy, and yet much of the dream suggests an alchemical process. A photographer's studio is often referred to as a laboratory, replete with acid baths, chemical pans, and glass vessels. The inner chamber of the laboratory, where the film and photographs are developed, must be kept in total darkness. The photographer is a master of light—directing its beam, lowering and raising its intensity, and adjusting lenses as he exposes the photographic paper, transforming the invisible image and making it visible.

The many cruel operations that the patient suffers are part of her dismemberment process. Rape is the worse of these, and it is a motif often seen in alchemy. Morality aside, it represents a violent, coercive act, removing resistance so that fresh material erupts from the unconscious. In psychophysical terms, the resistance results from a fixation on something that is by nature elusive. A fixation typically occurs as a result of a traumatic experience; it is meant both to protect the psyche by shutting it down until it can regain its senses and to deal with the injury when calm is restored. At the same time, however, the fixation can stunt developmental processes, and unless the traumatic content is dissolved it becomes part of the person's identity. We see here then that fixation has two faces, one that serves psyche and another that can also impair normal personality development.

Mercury is an excellent example of a material having this duplex quality, which shows itself in positive and negative ways. People with a mercurial personality can just as well be shamans or psychopaths, depending on their moral disposition. There are others we simply "can't pin down." In such cases, a forceful act is needed to get at the truth. Mercurius, being a trickster god, often causes awful accidents and crises to occur in order to open our eyes to higher truths. In the case of this woman, the dream seems to be saying that she can no longer avoid a painful stage requiring a breaking down of those elusive aspects of her personality that prevent her from seeing her true self.

One of these impediments appears to be a large degree of idealism. Her history certainly supports this hypothesis. She had, for instance, spent many years in a religious cult whose leader was a very well known, charismatic, controlling woman. During this time my patient lived in a sheltered environment cut off from the outside world while remaining chaste. All her efforts to assert individuality were stifled and met with staunch recrimination. This situation persisted for twelve years until she was finally told to leave. Pinned down in the dream, the unconscious uncovers this unhealthy idealism, smashes it, and exposes it. The photographer tells her the real chains holding her down are this inflated view of the world. In other words, she made herself small by making everything around her so big. In fact, her physical stature is short, made worse by a disease that affects her spinal cord; worse, perhaps, were her derogatory self-references. Jealousy and envy are links in this chain and they had to be broken for her to get her feet firmly planted on the ground.

The dream goes on in a rather dramatic way to recapitulate this message by using alchemical imagery. The adept is transforming her

149

bones—the prima materia that represents the physical foundation, what in alchemy is called the *matrix*. The antidote to idealism is having sturdy bones like those we saw when Osiris's spine supported the king's palace, a metaphor for the created world. In the end, this healing dream completes the recipe: having been torn apart, she is then "stirred" back together, coagulated.

Ten days later, the patient had another auspicious dream. Despite having little knowledge of ancient Egypt, this dream could easily have been dreamt by a high priestess. In the dream, she finds herself standing before a golden "sun throne" on which her dead daughter sits, holding a staff. As she stands there, a falcon pierces her right hand with its sharp talons. To her left is a lion-headed goddess. Although she couldn't recall what was said, she and her daughter communicate telepathically. The goddess grows weary of their talk and tears open the dreamer's chest and back. At that moment, the word *coagulate* appears to the patient.

Again we witness ritualistic acts performed on the woman. She stands at the center of a trinity of heavenly bodies: her deceased daughter above, Horus in his falcon form to her right, and the lion-headed goddess Sekhmet to her left. Recalling that both the spirits of the dead and the gods possess abundant heka, it is reasonable to conclude that the dreamer is an initiate being infused with powerful magical energy. In this case, the psyche provided the right god and goddess to help heal the patient, for one of Horus's roles is to guide the recently deceased through the early stages of their trial, the negative confession. If they succeeded, he took them by the hand and presented them to Osiris for final acceptance. Sekhmet is a goddess whose ferocity would complement to some degree the patient's timid nature.

Another legend sheds light on the relationship between Horus and Sekhmet. According to a myth in the Book of Gates, "The Egyptians were once the only race on earth. . . . Horus and Sekhmet joined together to create those people who dwelled in the desert beyond the so-called Black Land. . . . Horus created the black race and Sekhmet created the fair-skinned Libyans. The two gods consequently became responsible for protecting the souls of their creations in the afterlife."[20]

My patient took great comfort in knowing that two mighty gods were attending to her daughter. But at the same time she was being ripped open so that new life could emanate from her Self. And as it turned out, one month after this dream, the patient's husband lost his job. Although having been out of work for nearly eight years, this woman found the inner strength to quell her grief, soothe old wounds suffered from prior jobs, and restart her career. She described this remarkable change as "feeling more solid." Clearly, the time to coagulate was at hand.

The point of telling these dreams is to show that dismemberment and coagulation are essential dynamics involved in the process of healing and becoming whole. They are vital operations involved in rites of passage, which are not reserved solely for the initiation that helps boys and girls become full-fledged adults. These operations occur at critical points in adult development when radical shifts and changes are needed to break up obstacles impeding further individuation. To experience a complete transformation of the personality within one's lifetime is entirely possible. We might consider the elaborate funerary rites undertaken by Egyptians in preparing the dead for the afterlife as one such rite of passage, but it is equally likely that similar rites were practiced throughout their lifespan.

When Osiris's body is physically whole again, Anubis presides over the lifeless corpse and for the first time creates a mummy ready to take the long, arduous journey into the dark realm of the duat. Anubis must have applied the principles of solve et coagula, since mummification involved a process of removing (dismembering) certain "wet organs" in order to preserve the body. Additionally, we know from the Opening of the Mouth ritual that the deceased body is systematically reanimated (coagulated) so that its senses are prepared for the darkness of the duat; what had dissolved in death is repaired through the coagulatio operation. In this rite, the operation involves "aspersion and libations, always accompanied by prayers," all efforts aimed at reanimating the senses and readying Osiris to become an active force in the underworld.[21]

Solve et coagula is a recipe for growth and regeneration, here exhibited in patients' dreams and in our myth, with Osiris undergoing a process that delivers him into the underworld, where he becomes a font of energy regenerating all living things. Osiris is shedding his body and is making his rite of passage into another realm, where he represents the essence of becoming. Anubis's work done, Isis and Nephthys hold vigil for their brother while Horus grows into a mighty warrior whose only mission is to restore justice.

9

CHANGING OF THE GODS

After Osiris has been mummified, his soul takes residence in the under-world. Although Seth now rules Egypt, he is still not content. He goes in search of Osiris's young son, Horus. Isis hid the boy in the papyrus reeds, but, bent on vengeance, Seth finds him. Seth then transforms himself into a scorpion, and, as Isis is praying to Khonshu for protection, the scorpion strikes and kills the child. Unable to revive her son with magic, Isis turns to Thoth for help. Thoth prophesies that Horus will be reborn in the form of the Benu bird and that after a time in the duat he will return to earth healthy, whole, and ready to serve. While in the duat, Horus informs his father of Seth's malicious acts. For the first time Osiris grasps the deep-seated evil that dwells within his brother. After questioning his son, Osiris declares that Horus is ready to fulfill his destiny: avenge his father's death and reclaim the throne.

Osiris is dead and gone. While myths are potent messages from the past, they tell us nothing of how people reacted to these stories. One day a farmer is venerating Osiris in hope that the god will bless his fields and bring a rich harvest, and then suddenly Osiris is gone. The writing is literally on the wall: Osiris has been murdered, and his mummy rests in the underworld. We can only imagine how the whole community reacted. The god who causes the Nile to flood its banks and the soil to blacken with life, the one who rouses the spirit in all things,

153

is dead? He no longer exists among his people—he has died and now resides in the invisible world of the duat. As god of the underworld, Osiris lives beneath the earth; the sanctuary at Abydos is without its god. What will happen to this year's pilgrimage? We no longer see or feel his power directly; henceforth his spirit moves the currents of life in dark, mysterious ways.

What is known is that he resides outside this world and that his duties are threefold: he presides over the judgment of the dead; he accompanies Ra in the solar boat as it sails through the night; he is the god of becoming and rejuvenation, the "substance of being." Adoration of Osiris now turns to an abstract belief in a spirit rather than a living god. He has moved inside us and become an aspect of consciousness that is no longer visible.

We are left to see only reflections of his labors. When the sun rises in the morning, we know that Osiris has again successfully carried the light through the labyrinthine maze of the duat. We know Osiris is there when seeds break through the sodden earth and become fruit-bearing trees. Rundle Clark describes Osiris's new incarnation: "He is the sufferer with all mortality, but at the same time he is all the power of revival and fertility in the world. He is the power of growth in the plants and of reproduction in animals and in human beings. He is both dead and the source of all living. Hence to become Osiris is to become one with the cosmic cycles of life and death."[1]

In his death, Osiris resides in the dark places that make us real—places like the shadow, the unconscious, the duat, the dark nights of the soul, dreams, the land of mystery, etc. Joining him in life and physically in death causes us to become part of nature's rhythms. When we fall ill or depressed, we can rest assured that Osiris is there, not so much as a healer but as a god whose knowledge of darkness carries us gently through the night. When we die, he is there to attest to our worthiness as we reenter the cycle of creation. We take his name and his eternal spirit embodies us. Osiris has become a reflection of a divine force in nature that lives in the shadows of the collective unconscious. His resurrection created a vast underground world that supports nature and the conscious psyche.

For the Egyptians, a person consists of many souls, the shadow being only one part of this numinous dimension. The list below, adapted from Ramona Wheeler's book *Walk Like an Egyptian*, describes nine souls, or "parts or layers of being." Since Osiris is associated with the underworld, we will concentrate on the shadow and how this concept differs in some ways from our modern understanding of this archetype.

1. *akh*: the divine substance of the human soul
2. *sekhem*: the energy pattern of the divine spirit
3. *ib* and *haty*: the territory of the heart[2]
4. *khat*: the soul's container, that which decays
5. *shuit*: the living shadow, proof of reality
6. *ren*: the magic of your name, divine identity
7. *ba*: the you whom only you can know
8. *ka*: the you as others know you
9. *sahu*: the natural boundary of the psychic self

In ancient Egypt, shadow carried two meanings: *shuit*, one of nine souls possessed by every person, and s*utekh*, blind habits. Shuit is the literal proof of existence. In a land of abundant sunlight and relatively few trees, the shadow was living evidence that only solid matter is capable of blocking the sun's rays. While this method of proof is founded on concrete, archaic logic, it offers some real benefits. Wheeler calls attention to the fact that "the shadow faithfully duplicates every move and gesture. The shadow is a unique possession. Whatever a person might lose in life, your shadow is proof that you cannot lose *yourself*."[3]

CHAPTER NINE

A shuit shadow is living proof of our substantiality, evidence that in our darkest moments, when all seems lost, we still possess a body with all the scars and wounds attesting to our triumph over life's challenges. We should not take these things for granted. Sadly, however, there are many who only tentatively cling to life; even the physical body fails to anchor them in this world.

These people are not psychotic or split off from reality, but rather lack the ability to fully participate in life. For them, life is unreal, harsh, and distant. They live in a borderland between the solid, real world and one they can hardly imagine. In fact, their basic problem is a failure of imagination. Without an adequate capacity to imagine, the body is no more than an object they dress up and lug around. Despite oftentimes being quite intelligent, these people are typically fragile, despairing, and not fit for the harsh realities of life. They feel that they don't fit in; *if* they dream, the content reveals an alien, cold, and bizarre world. Many diagnostic terms are used to describe this type of person: schizoid, "as-if" personality, false self-identity, and borderline personality disorder. Whatever term we use, these people suffer in lonely silence. On some level they are aware of what the Egyptians meant by the nonexistent, that it is everywhere, most especially within them. Theirs is a gray-toned world where the light of day never shines. There is not sufficient light for them to clearly distinguish their shadow.

In one such case, a middle-aged engineer decided at my suggestion to attend a church in hopes of overcoming his isolation and social anxiety. I was surprised that he selected a Buddhist church, since he was raised Christian and long ago disavowed all forms of religion. Still, despite the fact that English was rarely spoken he enjoyed the service. He'd been attending for nearly a year when Christmas arrived, and he looked forward to a special holiday service. But when he arrived at the church on Christmas Day, not a soul was around. Stunned and disappointed, his despair and mistrust of the world deepened. But as he walked out of the church, a familiar voice called out to him. It was the Buddhist monk who led the services every week. He explained that services hadn't been planned for that day since it wasn't a special occasion in their faith. The explanation spoke to the engineer's mind but it did not touch his soul. The monk intuited this, and what occurred next illustrates a wonderful constellation of light and shadow. For the next ninety minutes the monk performed a complete service to a congregation consisting of one person! By embodying the spirit of Buddha, the monk responded to the need of the moment with true compassion and selfless service. This is a wonderful example of what it means to embody a god.

The second type of shadow, *sutekh*, is none other than Seth. Here we find him as Horus's shadow. Whereas Horus represents the heroic ego's struggle to secure an identity, Seth symbolizes unconscious habits that run counter to individuation. The struggle between these two gods is a contest between two forces: habits and will. Seth diminishes consciousness and defies individual choice, while Horus symbolizes a development that leads to the formation of a unique identity. In their mythology, the Egyptians depicted this struggle as a battle between Horus and Seth, each fighting for control of the solar boat, the carrier of consciousness through the jaws of darkness.

Wheeler compares this contest between Horus and Seth to Robert Louis Stevenson's novella *The Strange Case of Dr. Jekyll and Mr. Hyde*. In this story, we learn of the well-respected Dr. Jekyll, who experiments with a potion that transforms him into the hedonistic, murderous Mr. Hyde. Despite abhorring the uncontrollable impulses of his dark side, Dr. Jekyll secretly experiences a sordid pleasure in a life unbridled by the strictures of conscience. The story illustrates the two aspects of human nature, one that promotes life and the other that seeks to destroy it. This theme is played out in the brewing war yet to be faced in our myth by Horus and Seth, a contest of creation and destruction—alchemically expressed in the recipe "Dissolve and coagulate."

In modern psychology, the shadow archetype has two aspects. It is that part of the personality containing our repressed desires as well as our unlived life. If a person's life can be summed up by the decisions he or she has made, then always present is that lingering question about how life might have been different had a different path been taken "knowing what I know now." How much of our life do we actually choose? This question lies at the heart of Jung's concept of individuation. By increasing conscious awareness, we gain more control over habits, routine, group pressure—all the things that rob us of our individuality. On this point, Jung wrote, "I am not what happened to me, I am what I choose to become."[4] This isn't to say we can control everything that impinges on the development of personality, but at least by increasing awareness we also open our eyes to the dynamics of darkness. We can have our own Opening of the Mouth ritual in which we learn the ways of the unconscious, entering into partnership with it rather than being blindsided by it.

In the first half of life we are defined by others, by nature and circumstance, but in the second half we are faced with the challenge of defining ourselves. Much of the first half of life is experienced as a nigredo, a dark period when two extremely difficult tasks are undertaken: transforming the shadow and dissolving the false self. Though the shadow appears dark, it is not necessarily evil, nor is it the sole evidence of our being. Sometimes called the golden or white shadow, this archetype portends opportunity for new growth and development. Time and again, the alchemists maintained that their gold could only be made from crude black lead.

The two types of shadow described by the Egyptians form the basis of these psychological concepts. Again, we discover some of the original soil from which archetypes like the shadow came into existence.

Much has changed in the intervening years; archetypes and our relationship with them have become more complex. Religion portrays the struggle between light and dark as a moral battle. Suicide bombers kill in the name of God while killer flying drones answer with a terrifying response. What, I wonder, is the difference between either side's claim to moral superiority? The habits of tradition can cause good men and women to unwittingly sacrifice the gifts of darkness such as doubt, piety, and humility. A lack of self-reflection is no better in the extreme than its opposite.

Today, we would say that darkness is not just a place of death or even evil. It is far too simple to associate all that is good with light and denigrate darkness as an evil place. Recalling the image of the arid desert soil made black with the rich nutrients from the Nile, we see that, for the Egyptians, darkness had very positive associations. Peter Kingsley, in his book *In the Dark Places of Wisdom*, describes the place where these opposites find common ground: "The underworld isn't just a place of darkness and death. It only seems like that from a distance. In reality it's the supreme place of paradox where all the opposites meet. Right at the roots of western as well as eastern mythology there's the idea that the sun comes out of the underworld and goes back to the underworld every night. It belongs in the underworld. That's where it has its home, where its children come from. The source of light is at home in the darkness."[5]

Osiris is in the underworld, naive to the realities that put him there. As the story continues, Seth finds Horus on the island of Chemmis. While Isis prays to the moon god Khonshu for protection, Seth transforms into a deadly scorpion and kills the child as he lies sleeping in a small hut. On discovering her dead son, Isis immediately sets about to revive him using her magic. But all the heka she possesses fails, and in desperation she turns to Thoth. The great god again helps her, this time assuring her that Horus is not dead, but that his spirit has gone to the duat only temporarily to visit his father. Horus informs Osiris of the circumstances surrounding his two deaths—one by suffocation and the other by dismemberment. With this act, the underworld, or in psychological language the unconscious, is activated and becomes a vital resource for the living.

The unconscious is not separate from reality but, like the duat, is coexistent with it. Thoth may well have been responsible for sending Horus to the underworld; clearly he assures Isis that her son is not dead but is in the duat. Thoth is known for his healing skills and as a psychopomp who escorts the dead into the underworld. This trickster god, like the alchemical god Mercurius, easily crosses boundaries with impunity, transferring knowledge from one realm to another. In similar fashion, Horus becomes a messenger whose words enlighten Osiris. Horus returns to this world and becomes the patron of all future kings (the Self). Having awakened his father, the conscious and unconscious domains of the psyche are activated and are henceforth a powerful resource for humans. Anyone who works with dreams or other contents of the underworld appreciates the wisdom that can be gotten from the unconscious.

The Egyptians understood the importance of having this father-son relationship continue well after Osiris's death. While every pharaoh became the embodiment of Horus, the Egyptians wondered, what would become of Horus once the king died? Would Horus then also die? Some kind of mythological reconciliation was needed. Thus, it came to pass that when a pharaoh died, Horus served as spiritual guardian for the next pharaoh, while the deceased king went on to become Osiris. Eventually, this transition became the standard for all humans who proved themselves worthy; in death, they too became Osiris.

Horus's apparent death raises interesting questions. While we might imagine that his descent into the duat occurred psychically, what was done to his body? Where Seth is involved we must consider possibilities that may be worse than physical death. Horus awakens his father, but he himself is dead, or at least that is how it first appears. The symbolism is fairly transparent: the sting of death is a sexual rape, not murder.

H. te Velde makes this rape abundantly clear. In *Seth, God of Confusion,* he writes, "The 'poison of the scorpion' is the seed of Seth."[6] The seed, of course, refers to Seth's semen. That te Velde refers to the semen as poison suggests that the damage inflicted on Horus involves penetration and ejaculation. The "poison" spreads through mind, body, and soul. This is the tragic consequence in cases of rape—the harm isn't limited to the body but is spread to the victim's spirit and soul, to say nothing of its toxic effects on the personality. Something dies when children are raped or sexually molested. Certainly the innocence of childhood is stolen from them. They are dehumanized and made an inanimate object of forced pleasure. This type of pleasure has no meaning and certainly is not love. The victim experiences mostly mindless sensation at a primitive, animal level, creating a fixation that can extend far into adulthood. Perhaps more damaging than the abuse itself is the damage to the child's personality. While sexual assault is a terrible episode in the child's life, the injury done to his or her personality distorts, undermines, and misdirects future behavior. As we shall see, this instance will not be the last example of Seth's demonic sexual proclivities.

On a symbolic level the contamination has an altogether different meaning. Without being touched by darkness, the hero runs the risk of hubris, self-righteousness, and an insidious inflation. Again, we see that Seth, despite his malevolence, has a redeeming value. His "seed" is henceforth in Horus as he grows to maturity. Ironically, this same seed induces the very aggression that in the end defeats Seth.

Thoth consoles Isis by telling her that Horus will return in the form of the Benu bird. This detail serves to make a significant connection between Horus the Elder and Horus, son of Osiris and Isis. We may recall the former was envisioned as a bird that existed at the beginning of time. Here again, Thoth associates Horus the Younger with the Benu bird that flew over the waters of Nun, rested on a rock, and with its cry broke the primeval silence. That cry determined all that was to unfold in creation. Referring to a passage in the Coffin Texts, Rundle Clark notes that the two birds are "compounded," and as a result both images of Horus have cosmic implications. This is quite fitting since Horus the Younger is at this point in the duat. Clark says that the bird "flies up and across the night sky of the Underworld to land on the edge of the world, bringing with him the twilight that comes just before full day. . . . The appearance of Horus in the sky just before dawn is the mark of the New Year. Out of the fear and confusion of Seth's reign, the time of troubles, has come the herald of the new dispensation. The world's great age begins anew."[7] In other words, we find a parallel meaning for these two Horuses despite their appearance in very different parts of the myth. Their actions have similar significance: life is created and re-created, once at the beginning of the world and again with Osiris's awakening.

Centuries later the Benu bird becomes the Greek phoenix, an immortal bird that sets its own nest aflame, dissolves into ash, and is born anew.[8] The phoenix is the chief symbol of alchemical transformation and is associated with the coagulatio operation. This symbol also raises another issue yet to be settled: who will be heir to the throne, Osiris's brother or his son? The phoenix symbolizes the heir, and as the alchemist Dennis Hauck states, "The Heir is the final result of human genesis: a spiritual, indestructible form of life in which the soul is exalted." Thus, the question of who will follow Osiris is of paramount importance. "This Phoenix," Hauck adds, "will be his Heir."[9] The father has examined his boy and found him fit to inherit the throne. But Seth, having different ideas, is a formidable adversary.

Will the heir be Horus, the essence of ego consciousness—warlike and ever ready to protect the state, the person, and individual identity—or Seth, whose fiery, sulphuric nature returns the personality to a world of chance and chaos?

10

COURTING OPPOSITES

The Great War between the "Two Fellows," as Seth and Horus were known, went on for eighty years. Thoth intervenes and convinces the combatants to settle their differences in a council of the gods. Although the two agree, they are still eager to fight. With Thoth's help, the court appeals to Neith, goddess of wisdom, who decides in Horus's favor. Ra is not satisfied with the verdict but is calmed by the wiles of his daughter Hathor. He orders that the trial continue. This time Seth prevails. But Isis, using her wit, persuades the court to reverse its decision. Seth is furious and complains to Ra that Isis is unduly influencing the gods. Ra, fearing Seth's reaction should he lose the trial, moves the venue to an island and bars Isis from attending. Ignoring Ra's order, Isis uses magic to get to the island. Once there, she transforms herself into the likeness of Nephthys, who by this time has left her husband. Seth, beguiled by the disguised Isis and rendered weak by her magic, promises that their son will rule Egypt and that no harm will come to him. The council of gods is amused by Isis's trickery, and by his own oath Seth is ordered to relinquish the throne to Horus.

Like leaves blown from an ancient tree, the many fragments of a myth are caught in eddies of cultural, religious, and political currents until they come to rest and solidify into a narrative form. In the case of our myth, two endings present themselves, one called by

Professor Armour an epic[1] and the other, satiric. While each suggests something of the Egyptian mind, I believe the latter has more to offer an alchemical interpretation of the myth. The italicized prefaces in these last chapters of our myth are from the satiric version.

Seth, having killed Osiris, is prepared to murder his grown son Horus, whom he believes is the illegitimate offspring of Isis. Seth's real argument is with Osiris, but with him dead, Horus acts as his proxy. To this point we might have some sympathy for Seth's position and his hatred of Isis, but much of this will change as the story continues. Horus by now has become a warrior who prefers an hour of battle to a day of festivity. The bloody battle that ensues is necessary to determine who will be the rightful heir to the throne. It is a contest between barbarism and civility or, in psychological terms, between primitive instinctual forces and the more measured actions of the ego. Added to these dynamics is the fact that chaos often follows the death of a great leader. In this case, a god has died, and the question of whether a new order can be established will be determined by the outcome of the Great War. The physical and psychic landscape of Egypt lies in the balance.

Will the Egypt that has emerged from Osiris's teachings be salvaged or will it collapse into anarchy and barbarism? Will the pharaoh's court fall under the weight of Seth's bloody rule or proceed according to law and order (Ma'at) established by Horus? Another less obvious possibility is raised: will the traditional line of inheritance that up to this point (3000 BC) passed through the mother now shift to a patrilineal rule of succession?

Two battles will decide Egypt's fate—one fought by land, sea, and sky and another waged in the underworld. Horus will fight Seth on land while Osiris puts solid ground under his son's feet. Both Isis and Thoth ready Horus for battle.[2] Isis adorns her son's boat with golden garlands, and Thoth endows him with the ability to transform into a sun disk with flaming wings. Still, with all his weapons in place, Horus needs to be psychologically prepared. No fight is ever won solely by brains or brawn. Something entirely new has been added to the Egyptian psyche—the resources of the unconscious.

Just when the two are ready for battle, Thoth jumps into the act. He manages to persuade the two combatants to lay down their arms, at least temporarily, and take their case to court. In a world where conflict was commonly decided by brute force, submitting the matter to a legal process represents a radical shift in consciousness. The gods are assembled, with Ra serving as chief magistrate; Geb, father of Seth and grandfather of Horus, oversees the proceedings. With Shu arguing that "justice should prevail over sheer strength," the verdict comes quickly. Horus is declared the rightful heir, but Ra is unhappy with the decision, in part because he anticipates a violent retaliation from Seth. As we might expect, Seth ignores the court and challenges Horus to a trial by combat. Thoth again intervenes and asks if there might not be a better alternative. The court has Thoth draft a letter explaining the situation to Neith, long-honored as a wise goddess. She, too, rules in Horus's favor but suggests that Seth be given two beautiful goddesses to quell his temper.

Ra, whose might once served him well, is contemptuous of the court's decision. Some palliative is needed to calm his fury. As we may recall, Ra created Hathor to stop the bloody goddess Sekhmet from devouring the entire human race. This time Hathor is called into service to calm her raging father. She charms him with a wild dance in which she exposes herself. Ra's anger subsides as he is amused by his daughter's display, and he orders Horus and Seth back to court.

The "Two Fellows" present the same arguments, but this time the gods rule in Seth's favor. Isis doesn't accept defeat easily, and she assures the court that in the end Horus will be king. Seth is furious and refuses to have anything to do with any further legal proceeding until Isis is banished from the courtroom. Ra orders a change in venue.

167

Henceforth, the trial will take place on an island, and the ferryman, Anty, is ordered to stop Isis at the water's edge, making certain she isn't permitted to step foot onto the boat.

These melodramatic events thinly veil the real issues being played out in the myth. From today's perspective the haphazard legal proceedings of this council of the gods are almost comical. Not only are the gods easily swayed, but their judgments don't stand. Instead we see verdicts swinging back and forth. The humor is lost when we consider what lies in the balance. We can only imagine what Egypt might have been like if the verdict held in Seth's favor. It would have been a world dominated by might, brutality, and plunder. There would have been no room for deliberation, fair judgment, or human rights; whoever wielded the sharpest sword would have ruled. Certainly, many empires have risen through bloody conquest. Viewed from a psychological perspective, the real contest was between physical strength and mental judgment, a theme that reverberates throughout the ages in both the individual and collective society. In the preceding chapter, I mentioned Stevenson's novella, an excellent example of one man's struggle with this very same issue.

On the simplest level, the issue at hand is whether Seth's brute strength should trump Horus's call for order. Seth represents the instinctual powers of the unconscious while Horus symbolizes the dawning of a moral conscience. A second level of the problem involves rules of succession. The fact that Seth has murdered his brother seems to be forgotten in these deliberations. Instead, it is Seth's power—relentless instinctual force—that might best serve the future needs of Egypt. We should recall here that succession follows bloodlines, a theme that becomes especially apparent in the next chapter.

The dramatic swings in judgments not only reveal the inevitable errors that accompany a brand new way to settle disputes, but, perhaps for the first time, the gods are ambivalent, suggesting a weakening in their power. They face issues that are not simply black or white; both Seth and Horus have a viable argument in laying claim to the throne. Whatever the outcome, the new god-king will need Seth's impersonal, brute force as well as the psychological strengths of Horus in order to preserve Ma'at. Another important factor must also be weighed in the judgment. Will this be a decision made by and for men, or are we seeing a resurgence of the feminine? It is significant that three major female figures are introduced at this time to quell fiery passions and ensure that, in the end, civility wins out.

First there is Neith, goddess of war and wisdom, who, in later times, came to be known as Sophia. At the request of the gods, Thoth writes to Neith: "What are we to do about these two fellows who have now been before the court for eighty years without our being able to decide between them? Please write us what we should do."[3]

The judgment at hand will require wise counsel and a methodology that can fairly integrate opposing arguments. We can appreciate why Neith is a good choice by looking closer at the Greeks' concept of Sophia. The legacy of Sophia has a long history, but of special importance to alchemy is her significance to the Gnostics. She was considered the bride of God and responsible for the creation of matter. By virtue of having created the four elements, she brings soul and matter into existence. She is the Divine Spark and Cosmic Mind hidden in the flesh of every individual. This spark is the latent wisdom that, once realized, rejoins the individual with the Divine Light, God.

Neith's response is given without explanation. She simply says, "Award the office of Osiris to his son Horus. Don't commit such blatant acts of inequity which are illegal, or I shall become so furious that the sky will touch the ground. The Universal Lord, the Bull who resides in Heliopolis, ought to be told: Enrich Seth in his possessions. Give him Anath and Astarte, your two daughters, and install Horus in the position of his father Osiris."[4]

Despite the gods' immediate agreement with Neith's pronouncement, Ra recoils at the judgment. He fears that handing the kingdom over to Horus will come at a very high price. This is truly remarkable, that no less than Ra, the god of gods, should concern himself with Seth. But, we should recall that Seth, along with Ra and Osiris, are the only gods who are truly immortal. Each contains an essential power, without which everything in the created world would completely vanish. Might these three essences correspond to the alchemical Salt, Sulfur, and Mercury?[5]

Hathor, wife of Horus the Elder, is the second "cooling" agent who dampens Ra's fury. Using her body through dance and promiscuous exposure, she lightens Ra's spirits, rouses his humor, and calms him down. Such is the power of sex and humor to quell the fiercest among us, provided a deft master knows how to handle these agents.

The third goddess who influences the proceedings is Isis. Her powers of magic and healing are so effective that she manages to have the gods reverse their decision. She continues to be the adversary Seth most fears. To this point, she alone has cunningly dealt with Seth, has never backed down, and has outwitted him on several occasions. So, once more, we will see how she uses her ability to alter her appearance to gain entry to the court. She is never to be taken lightly. We saw how she extracted Ra's secret name, and in battles yet to be waged we will find her restoring Horus's wounded eye. This healing was celebrated throughout Egypt where the Eye of Horus, or the Wedjat, protected the king in the afterlife.

While there can be no doubt that men ruled ancient Egypt, we should recall that the origin of power lies in the Great Mother. Indeed, a woman is behind every throne! Tom Hare, in his postmodern, semiotic study *ReMembering Osiris*, points out that "upsetting and deconstructing the entire phallocentric hierarchy of the *kamutef*, is the reading of not 'bull of his mother,' but 'the bull is his (own) mother.'"[6]

We see glimmers of this feminine power in Isis's cunning. She subdues Seth's brute strength with her guile and clever words. We've seen her shape-shift into a kite and an old woman, and in the present situation she transforms into the image of Seth's estranged wife, Nephthys. In another version of the myth she is a "seductive temptress" who tells Seth her long sad story: "She had been the wife of a cattleherd and had borne him a son. Her husband had died and her son had begun to tend the cattle. A stranger appeared, though, and told the son he would take the cattle and threatened the son with violence. She appeals now to Setekh for protection, and Setekh, in his naiveté, blurts out, 'How could the stranger make a claim on the cattle when the son is there!'"[7]

In either version the result is the same: Seth has undermined his own legal argument, that he the uncle, or in this tale the violent stranger, should inherit the throne or be given the cattle. Horus triumphs, but only by virtue of his mother's intervention. In alchemy as well as in much of ancient Egyptian history, the role of women has been far underrated. "Women," says Hare, "had far greater rights and freedoms in the supposedly despotic Orient that was ancient Egypt, than in the supposedly democratic Occident that was classical Athens." But, to appreciate this status we must not ignore the "androcentrism" that was Egypt and the "abstract preference for male power in government, economy, and the various modes of written discourse." We recall that a masturbating god (Atum) gave rise to the created world, leaving us with "the inescapable relation between the phallic body and existence."[8]

"Ritual phallus," writes Jungian analyst Eugene Monick, "points to the essential importance of the masculine as co-originating factor of creation." He reminds us of Jung's earliest dream in which he saw a huge phallus in an underground vault. Only in old age did Jung realize the full meaning of the dream. He related the phallus to the alchemical god Mercurius, a trickster who plays at the threshold between life and death. "The spirit in Mercurius is male instinct, spirit corked up in the male body that wants expression through phallus. Uncorked, Mercurius 'becomes the one animating principle of all created things.'[9] Atum carries this dual sexuality necessary to bring all created things into manifestation. "Atum," says Hare, "is, in fact, defined as 'he who became, in coming lengthened, which he did in Aunu. He took his phallus in his fist and made sweet ejaculation from it, and the twins, Shu and Tefnut,

Figure 10.1. Mercurius.

were born.' (Pyramid Texts 1248a–d)." On close examination of the hieroglyphs that describe this scene, Hare reveals the essential meaning
of these sexual images, where phallus is masculine and the accommo-
dating fist feminine. At some point the two are indistinguishable: in
their broader meaning, the hieroglyphs signify expansion that involves
a "process of matter and a process of consciousness."[10] In typical trickster fashion, Mercurius, like Thoth before him, conjoins psyche and
matter into one principle from which all creation issues.

The importance of the phallus as a dominant image in Egyptian cosmology is enacted in the phallic worship at the Heb Sed festival in
the Middle Kingdom era. The masculine was always more prominent
throughout dynastic rule, while the feminine was a hidden force not
to be ignored. We see evidence of this in Hatshepsut adopting a masculine persona and Akhenaten's "natural inversion,"[11] both of which
underscore the prominence of male authority. While this masculine
persona was obvious in the court, women in everyday life were on a
fairly equal footing with men. In either case, we must look a bit more
closely to appreciate the special, less obvious way feminine power is
expressed within this cultural milieu.

The most obvious expression of feminine power is sexual. Throughout Egyptian myths, goddesses use cunning and beguiling magic to
acquire knowledge and influence among their male cohorts. Women
are principally shown adorning and adoring male gods. Less obvious is
their mutability, their power to change form—the ease with which the
feminine, like water,[12] accommodates even the most horrid situations
and the genius of women for identifying with power as a means to an
end. We see all these qualities exhibited par excellence in Isis. She is
everywhere as mercurial as Mercurius himself! If women are the power
behind the throne, perhaps more so than even priests, then their place
in the court may be more a matter of strategic positioning than feigned
subservience.

While we ordinarily associate the phallus with masculine symbol-ism, a closer look reveals hidden aspects of the feminine. Previously we observed how the alchemists exploited even the tiniest scintilla of gold buried deep in their original metal, lead, in order to grow that seed into gold. Likewise, the phallus possesses feminine traits that provide the source material allowing the adept to begin balanc-ing spirit (masculine) and soul (feminine) to create the lapis. The hermaphrodite symbolizes this amalgam in its crudest form. Mercury possesses these same bisexual attributes: the fluidity of the feminine and the energetic spirit of masculinity. How do these two seemingly opposite sexual aspects combine in the phallic symbolism of Mercu-rius, the patron god of alchemy? This same question can be asked of Osiris, since we've seen both his submissive side as well as the (verti-cal) strength symbolized in the djed column. In reviewing Jung's list of Mercurius's characteristics, Monick observes the beguiling inten-tions driving phallic behavior:

First, Mercurius is portrayed as male. He is understood to be male even in his dualistic aspect as male/female or when he appears as a female. . . . Sec-ond, Mercurius is quixotic—he comes and he goes, he rises and falls, as inexplicably as does phallus. Third, Mercurius disguises himself and hides, so that one is never quite sure where he is. He is a trickster, like phallus. He plays limp; he appears under the cover of foreskin; he hides between the legs and pretends he is not interested. Playing the gentleman, he lays the ground for seduction. Courting, he finds every kind of excuse to ma-neuver his prey into a favorable situation. "May I buy you dinner?" "How about a drink?" "Would you like to go for a drive?" I have a daughter. I hear the telephone conversations with their veiled proposals. I also have a son. The telephone calls to him from girls are not the same. They inquire about how he is and what he's doing, they may even manipulate, but they do not often imitate phallos.[13]

Hiding, coyness, passivity, and pretense are all aspects of the mythological feminine, here an integral part of the everyday life of the phallus.

Appreciating the feminine psyche also helps us understand Osiris's seemingly passive nature. He is not so much Seth's victim as he is a malleable substance in the hands of a god who takes pleasure in deconstruction. In its healthy form this process includes discrimination, a *separatio* that reduces nebulous ideas into meaningful sentences. At no point do we see Osiris put up a fight. And yet, his passivity is his strength, allowing all that is needed for individuation to occur—more for universal reasons than personal gain. Reflecting on some critical events, we recall Osiris's submission at Seth's party, his "being asleep" in the floating coffin, the embrace of the acacia tree, his dismemberment, and Isis's seduction. In every case, there is a remarkable sense of accommodation and acquiescence. We typically regard passivity as a weakness, but this is only true when it remains unconscious and is counterproductive to the individuation process. To embody this god we must take into account his "individuation" as he matures into a cosmic archetype. What he does is not for self-gain but for the benefit of all. Ultimately, the spirit of the dead arrives in the duat, the fitting place for him to reign as god of the dead and master of unconscious forces.

Despite our efforts to accurately describe how these early people dealt with this sexual complex, masculinity and femininity, we find that we really have no words to capture the essence of this syzygy that forms the world axis. While cultural, political, historical, and religious factors affect how these forces are expressed, this timeless monad does not change at all. Horus, the mythic representative of ego consciousness, strives to fit the complex within a frame of law and order, while Seth, whose primitive energies usher forth in undiluted form from nature, fights to preserve the instinctual basis of consciousness. There are two truths here, and our task is to bring them into a complementary relationship. We will see how this psychic struggle plays out as the myth draws to a conclusion, but, whatever the outcome, we will in the end be uncomfortably confronted with a mystery that defines the nature of human being and all that makes up the created world.

11

MA'A-KHERU

Seth is enraged by the reversal of the verdict, to say nothing of his hatred of Isis. He declares war on Horus, who is happy to oblige him. The contest turns into a number of bloody battles that last for eighty years, with both sides alternately claiming victory. In one of these confrontations, Seth attacks Horus but again Isis steps in and outwits Seth. The gods finally intercede and demand to know why Seth won't allow the court to settle the dispute. To their great surprise, Seth agrees to stop fighting and allow the verdict to go to Horus. Ptah is pleased that justice has been served but still feels that Seth has not been given his rightful share of power. Ra shrewdly sees how Seth's warlike nature might serve him. He has him sit by his side in the solar boat, where, when necessary, Seth is used to intimidate humans and enemies alike. Horus, declared the rightful heir to the throne, descends into the duat to awaken his sleeping father. With his newly sanctioned powers Horus revives Osiris's soul, and together they bring new order to the world above and the world below.

I n Armour's telling of the epic version of the conflict between Horus and Seth, a long and bloody battle is waged. The battle scenes are surreal, with each combatant variously shape-shifting into crocodiles and hippopotamuses. Horus transforms into a flaming winged disk to confuse Seth's armies by distorting their ability to recognize one another. At one point, Horus cuts a soldier into fourteen pieces, mistaking him for Seth. On another occasion, Horus captures Seth, binds his hands, and has Isis guard him while he goes after the enemy army. In a complete reversal of power, it is Seth this time who outwits Isis with clever words. An intelligent soldier learns to mimic his enemy's tactics!

Appealing to his sister's sense of fraternal duty, Seth convinces Isis to loosen the ropes that bind his hands, and he escapes. On learning what happened, Horus is so outraged that he cuts off his mother's head. At this point Horus is difficult to distinguish from Seth. Thoth rushes to the rescue, replacing Isis's head with one from a cow—an instance when Isis and Hathor are conjoined into a single goddess. In the final battle, Seth, in the form of a red hippopotamus, is struck by Horus's deadly harpoon. The blade pierces his skull, and he dies. This is the classic story of good triumphing over evil; the battle is won by the physically stronger of the two.

Despite the simplicity of this version, it raises important questions that point to a process of individuation. Clearly, we once more see Isis in her maternal role protecting her son, a role that in the end results in Horus cutting off her head. This action is certainly the separation— cutting the apron string—necessary for Horus to become his own man. Perhaps for the first time we see Isis weak, charmed by Seth. As a result of the decapitation, Isis's fierceness is replaced by the gentler maternity of Hathor, the cow-headed goddess. We also see a significant loss of body parts in both warriors. Horus loses an eye and some of his divine vision, while Seth loses some of his virility. When either spirit or soul becomes too extreme, one can expect an *enantiodromia* (a rapid reversal to the opposite that restores balance). We see here Horus and Seth being prepared to become one. Joseph Campbell explains: "Mythologically representing the inevitable dialectic of temporality, where all things appear in pairs, Horus and Seth are forever in conflict; whereas in the sphere of eternity, beyond the veil of time and space, where there is no duality, they are at one."[1]

While these epic battles are physically brutal, the war described in the satiric version is filled with irony, sarcasm, and caustic wit—all suggesting that the Great War is a parody, one better understood for its symbolic value. By far the most absurd scene in the satiric version takes place during an apparent truce. Seth invites Horus to lay down his arms, but we quickly learn this is only a trick. Horus agrees, and with uncharacteristic, inexplicable trust he accedes to Seth's invitation that they physically lie down together. Laying down arms is one thing but lying down next to each other transports the myth into a realm of symbolic farce. Certainly, these accommodations do not at all fit with the animosity shown by Horus throughout the myth. Rather, this is a literary device used to set up a scene in which Seth suffers his final defeat. Tom Hare summarizes what happens next:

> Setekh [Seth] invites Horus over to his house obligingly and Horus not only accepts, but also stays the night. And in the night, Setekh tries to rape Horus, inserting his penis between Horus' thighs, but Horus evades penetration and catches Setekh's semen in his hand. He runs away to his mother, Isis, to report: "Come see what Setekh did to me!" And when he opens his fist to show her, she shrieks, chops off his hand, and tosses it to the waters. Then she replaces his hand magically and lubricates his penis, masturbating him into a jar. The semen of Horus she takes, in turn, to Setekh's garden, to spread on the patch of lettuce from which he makes his salad every day. And when Setekh ate his lettuce that day, he was impregnated by the semen of Horus.[2]

These are the antics we typically see in vaudeville acts; the seed is tossed about as if this were a game of hot potato.

Humor aside, the attempted rape carries important implications. Sufficient evidence exists to show that homosexuality in ancient Egypt was regarded as a taboo. It comes, then, as no surprise that the gods react

179

with disgust. I should add that the charge of homosexuality was levied only on the recipient of the act, not on the instigator. Seth attempts to win the trial, in other words, by having Horus seen as a homosexual. Little did Seth know of Isis's trick until he unwittingly becomes pregnant with Horus's semen—a surreal image of how opposites sometimes join as a result of chaotic circumstances. Horus protests the charge, and Thoth demands that Horus's semen be called as a witness. By this time, Seth could no longer hide the fact that he had duped Horus and, in turn, been once more outwitted by Isis.

Before continuing with this bizarre story, we should recall that this is not the first incident in which Seth attempts to rape Horus. Early on we saw Seth, in the form of a scorpion, sting the child Horus. It is a curious fact that this particular arachnid is a favorite of none other than Isis![3] In any event, "we see that Seth," according to H. te Velde, "had discharged his seed into the body of Horus: 'The seed of Seth is in the belly of Horus since Seth has emitted it against him.'" Then, much later in the myth we learn that Seth gouges out Horus's eye, and in return, Horus tears out Seth's testicles. While many Egyptians believed that Seth had been castrated, closer examination reveals that Horus "intercepts the seed of Seth's testicles."[4] In this final encounter, Seth's seed is again "intercepted," and the ejaculate lands in Horus's hand. Putting aside moral and even sexual concerns, we might regard these attempts on Seth's part as a need to join with Horus. Earlier I commented that this was preparatory for the emergence of the two gods into a nondualistic afterlife.

In the strange, animistic world of ancient Egypt where we previously witnessed the autonomous, potentially mutinous heart, it should not surprise us to hear Thoth call the semen to the stand. "Come out, semen of Horus." To which, the semen responds, "Where shall I come out?" To everyone's amazement, the semen appears from Seth's crown as a celestial disk. Thoth quickly removes the disk and places it on his own forehead.[5] Following this incident, several letters are dispatched to the underworld. Osiris appears and "reminds the gods that he created barley and wheat and cattle, and that they would be without sustenance were it not for him, adding as well, that Horus is his rightful heir."[6]

With the judgment now going to Horus, Seth attempts one last time to challenge him to a fight. By now, the gods have had enough. Isis drags Seth, bound in chains, into the court. Atum-Ra, in a final plea, asks Seth why he won't honor the court's verdict. In a sudden reversal of everything we've seen in this fiery god, and after eighty years of battle, Seth agrees to stop fighting and recognize Horus as the rightful heir to Osiris's throne for all eternity.

What kind of ending is this? Why does Seth abruptly surrender? What does this attempted rape signify? What is the meaning of the seminal witness? Why was Seth's life spared? Unless we answer these questions, this grand myth would be little more than a crazy fantasy.

Horus is a grown man by the time he actively engages Seth in all-out warfare. His father is in the underworld, and we are not told of Horus's upbringing. Other than Thoth arming him with a magical disk and Isis adorning his battleship, we know nothing of the inner psychological preparation that transformed him into a warrior. (This is unusual since we have records detailing how certain pharaohs embodied the spirit of Seth and Neith to vanquish their enemies.) To be sure, Horus is untried in battle and ill prepared to take on Seth. This war between the Two Fellows is not only aimed at deciding who will be the rightful heir but serves as the psychological field on which Horus is tested— not as Osiris's rightful son, but as an independent adult man. I use the word "man" here rather than god because this battle appears more human than divine. Horus is being humanized and prepared to serve as a model for every pharaoh to come. Unlike his passive father, Horus is vigorously active; even though he is saved many times by his mother,

Isis, he is struggling to become his own person. We might say that as Osiris has descended to the underworld, Horus is establishing his authority on earth; henceforth he becomes the power of the pharaoh's throne. Osiris has activated the unconscious, and now Horus must take his place at the center of a newly formed position, namely, ego consciousness. "Osiris is yesterday; Horus is today." These actions show these archetypal gods are moving into place, creating the ecology of the modern psyche and civilized society.

To achieve his position, Horus proves himself as the legitimate son of Osiris by his unrelenting drive to avenge his father. As noted, he literally has some of Seth's sulfuric energy in him. But, lest he be no better than Seth, he must subdue his enemy for the *right* reason. Justice, not retaliation, must drive him to his goal. He must act as a mature warrior, not an angry boy. To accomplish this, he must separate from his mother and reestablish an adult relationship with his father. Without Seth's persistent challenges, however, Horus would be robbed of the possibility to achieve these ends. It is Seth's instigation that sets in motion a process of separation-individuation that eventually transforms Horus into the ideal pharaoh. This is Seth's particular function in the psyche. He brings us to the edge of insanity but in the process forces us to define ourselves. He is our shadow, representing chaos and challenge—confusion necessary in bringing forth order.

In describing the hero's journey, artist Dorothy Norman describes Seth as "the shadow of Horus; a god of bondage who sets the problems that the hero in man must solve. It is the very inert quality of Seth that stimulates Horus to develop: to become the ascending one: to follow the path of the hero."[7] It is tempting to hate Seth and dismiss him, but the separation-individuation process involves the dark as well as the light aspects of personality. Thus, Horus was always warned not to kill Seth, for in killing him, he would be destroying an essential part of himself, one without which he would never gain liberation.[8]

This battle for the Self is important on every level of reality, the intrapsychic structuring of the individual personality as well as integration of the forces of above and below. Again, Dorothy Norman reminds us that the "Pharaoh in Egypt was looked upon as *the embodiment of the two gods, Horus and Seth, in a single person*. Or, as Henri Frankfort has written, the Egyptian king was identified with the Two Lords, 'the perennial antagonists, Horus and Seth.' This was so, 'not in the sense that he was considered the incarnation of the one and also . . . of the other,' but rather that he embodied both as a pair, as opposites in equilibrium. Hence the ancient title of the king: 'The Two Lords.'"9

This scene loses some of its numinosity because the situation is something so familiar to anyone who's struggled to separate from the mother, be that one's personal mother or the many surrogates who play a similar role. The contention between Horus and Seth represents the emergence of the individual as distinct from one whose personality was virtually indistinguishable from his or her service to the collective or, most particularly, the pharaoh. The mock rape is not simply a literary device to turn the tables on Seth, but, more importantly, a ritual act in which Seth attempts to *inject masculinity* into the younger Horus. It also explains why Seth tries to join with Horus: psychologically, the shadow is attempting to reveal itself to the ego, but such an action cannot be forced; the ego must be ready to receive the shadow and its threatening contents.

We see this type of ritual rape carried out in rites of passage in which older tribesmen have sex with young boys being initiated into the mysteries. Circumcision is another integral part of rites aimed at separating a boy from his mother so that he gains the ferocity needed to stare down enemies and kill with impunity. In certain South African tribes, a newly crowned king is given a small totem of his mother to wear on his belt, and at the same time he is prohibited from having any further contact with her. He possesses "the bull of the mother" within him.

In telling the "Tale of Two Brothers," Hare describes the protagonist Bata: "He has a god's strength in him." Later, he says that Bata's wife possesses "the fluid of every god . . . in her," meaning that she is extremely beautiful. In the case of Hatshepsut, by adopting a man's persona she was sure to create a new myth in which Amun raped her: "He came up to her at once, and He was filled with passion for her, and He gave His heart into her, and He gave unto her His form as god to see. And when He had come before her, she rejoiced at His perfection. The love of Him penetrated her body."[10]

Empowerment, in concrete terms, requires embodiment of a god. Once Horus is touched by the royal seed of his divine shadow, he is enlivened and embodies the ideal model of power.[11] Henceforth, he becomes pharaoh and thereafter the patron of all pharaohs to follow. "The sun and the shadow" are integrated in his divine body. Now when he speaks to the court, it is not the young warrior seeking to avenge his father's murder, but a man who is "true of voice."

I have used this epithet *maʿa-kheru*, meaning "true of voice," previously to indicate consonance between one's words and one's heart. It comes in different ways. We saw it in the children who informed Queen Astarte of the strange woman on the beach (Isis). Thoth came often to give Isis assistance when hearing the truth in her voice. In the struggle between the Two Fellows, this same truth is evidenced when the instincts are exhausted and the hero speaks truth with heartfelt conviction. This act explains why Seth suddenly surrenders to the court and why the gods are resolute in their final decision. Seth returns to his former place as lord of storms, helping Atum-Ra in his nightly battle with Apopis, while Horus has one last task to perform before the myth comes to an end.

While the term *maʿa-kheru* is a legal term that justified Horus's claim to the throne, it persists throughout Egyptian history, where it has a much broader application. As with many Egyptian words, semiotic analysis yields deeper meanings that often lead to greater understanding and application. The first part of the phrase, for example, pertains to Ma'at, goddess of truth, justice, and cosmic order. But, more than this, she represents a principle and "a new vision of the ideal individual life" that served as an ethical standard for the development of consciousness throughout Egypt's long, tumultuous history.[12]

These many trials between Horus and Seth recall the ultimate trial each Egyptian faced at the end of life. The soul of the deceased was brought before Osiris and weighed against Ma'at's feather, symbol of spiritual justice. The outcome determined whether the individual possessed sufficient integrity and distinction—signs of the individuated Self—to gain entry into the everlasting land of the blessed dead. *Ma'a-kheru* describes the individual who has come to terms with his own heart rather than merely giving blind obedience to the state. The heart and now even semen have been integrated into the personality, indicating the individual is no longer simply a solitary unit who must blindly obey gods or pharaohs.

Without having to resort to either the nature spirits or the king, God is within reach of every individual. No longer are people defined in terms of functions, but rather a new degree of complexity defines each person, one that may or may not accord with the demands of the collective. Seth represents old world simplicity, in that one was either with him or against him. But Horus is a much more complex character representing the incorporation of inner values and with it, an individuation process that perfects the uncivilized shadow that dwells within each of us. He nobly embodies Ma'at and brings plentitude to the world where the rule of order is in place.

Horus's victory is humankind's triumph over nature and the collective, liberating free will and individuality. With Horus's defeat of Seth, every individual is now capable of transcending his or her own passions, the appetites of the flesh, as well as gaining everlasting life through one's own efforts. The reason Horus is born of a dead king is that he is "in the world, but not of it." Osiris's seed produced a model of masculinity that was fathered by spirit and mothered by the soul. Horus is the link between his ancestors and all future pharaohs. His numinous birth, his near-death experiences, his descent to the underworld, and his encounter with shadow portray the rite of passage required for producing a highly conscious, integrated human being. "One of the basic phenomena of totemism and of all initiation rites," says Erich Neumann in his classic *The Origins and History of Consciousness*, "is that the totem or ancestor is reincarnated in the initiate, finding in him a new dwelling place and at the same time constituting a higher self. This result can be traced all the way from the sonship of the Horus hero and its connection with the apotheosis of his father Osiris to the Christian Incarnation and the phenomenon of individuation in modern man."[13]

Individuation, in this myth, is achieved by sublimating nature and the world of instinct, while spiritualizing the father and incorporating his spirit within each person. "It is Osiris," writes Dorothy Norman, "whom Horus must resurrect: namely, that for which we live: the embodiment of fulfilled life. Osiris is the goal achieved, by way of struggle—the primary goal possessed of the power to lead toward meaningful rebirth."[14]

History, then, is the five-thousand-year-old story of individuation, an evolution and involution that continues to bring forth the complete individual. Horus's final task is to reunite with the father and embody his power and wisdom. "Every king," adds Neumann, "was once Horus and becomes Osiris; every Osiris was once Horus. Horus and Osiris are one."[15] Horus and Seth are one. Osiris and Isis are one—each a vital part of the integrated personality of the modern human being.

Embedded in the golden canon of alchemy we find this *mysterium coniunctionis* stated most eloquently by Hermes Trismegistus: "As

Above, So Below, for the Making of the One Thing." If one is true of voice, no obstacle stands in the way of becoming an indestructible part of the whole of creation. This is the unchanging truth of life and death. How we manage to go through life keeping hidden this most wondrous truth is a mystery.

12

EMBODYING GOD

Man, know thyself...and thou shalt know the god.
—Inscription from an inner temple wall

There where everything ends, all begins eternally.
—Hermes Trismegistus

The myth of Osiris prefigures the structure of the modern-day psyche and the process of individuation. It marks a critical transformation of consciousness that began in ancient Egypt some five thousand years ago. Emerging from the primitive Neolithic period, the earliest beginnings of an enduring civilization coalesced in a very inhospitable environment; not only did a country blossom in the desert, but the rudimentary structure of a conscious mind also formed. All this occurred in a dynamic ecology where strange tribal traditions migrated north from deep Africa to help establish a dynastic empire that would dominate the world for three millennia. Animal totems, nature spirits, magic, and the central importance of kingship were some elements that influenced the shaping of ancient Egyptian governance, religion, psychology, and cultural beliefs.

The pharaoh was the center of ancient Egyptian society. As we have seen throughout this book, his role was threefold: (1) he was in charge of temple building, divine offerings, and all that "made the gods and goddesses at home on earth"; (2) through devotion and prayer, he kept the cosmos moving in the right direction such that the sun rose in the east and set in the west, and the Nile inundated the parched land on a consistent basis; and (3) he "enacted the central myth that sustained the Egyptian state."[1] In each case, the pharaoh's chief duty was not only to commune with certain powerful deities but to be, in fact, the actual embodiment of the gods.

I have tried to illustrate a central myth, the story of Osiris, that describes the importance of the pharaoh in modern psychological terms since we are far better equipped to understand archetypes than ancient gods and kings. As I have pointed out, these mythic personages have long since taken residence in the psyche—their psychic presence is closer at hand than their historical reality. But for the ancient Egyptians the king was the living Self, and, having embodied Horus, he "held together the community of deities, humans, and transfigured dead."[2]

The mythology of ancient Egypt emerged from two very different cultures and a geography divided by a sacred river. Cultural differences divided the country north and south, and the Nile split the desert into east and west. These separations cried out for unity. The Nile and its annual flooding were vital to survival regardless of which shore one lived on. Beyond the rich, black land adjacent to the river was the un-inhabitable red desert. Farming communities were established along the banks of the Nile, but beyond this narrow margin of fertile land only nomadic tribes could survive. As we've seen, Osiris was credited with bringing life to these farming communities, while Seth dominated the wild desert lands.

The contrast between Upper and Lower Egypt was no less striking. To the north, Lower Egypt was nestled in the fertile Nile Delta where, owing to its proximity to the Mediterranean Sea, temperatures were milder than the hot winds that blew in the south. Memphis was the traditional capital of Lower Egypt. In the Memphite Theology, papyrus represented the flowering of the First Time. To the south, Upper Egypt stretched another seven hundred miles to the border of Nubia, home of the two lakes feeding the Nile. The modern city of Aswan is the traditional dividing point, with Thebes serving as both the capital and religious center of Upper Egypt. Replete with very different views of life, these were the Two Lands that every pharaoh, beginning with Narmer, strove to maintain as a single nation. We can therefore appreciate the superhuman task of the pharaoh—he was the yoke holding earthly and spiritual forces in place. The political and psychic fate of Egypt's future rested in his hands.

From this perspective, it is easy to appreciate the emphasis put on constancy; even small changes could easily upset the delicate balance and throw all of Egypt into chaos. Despite their efforts to remain steadfast to the demands facing them on every front, pharaohs still had to adapt to the uncontrollable forces of nature. In retrospect, we recognize the collective unconscious as one of the forces shaping events. At nearly the midpoint of Egypt's long dynastic rule, these forces became sufficiently strong to break the chain of tradition that had held Egypt intact for nearly 1500 years. More precisely, during the reign of Akhenaten in the years 1353–1336 BC, evolution and involution, history and tradition, came to loggerheads. His break with tradition was a radical departure from the long-held emphasis on constancy; by resisting change, many pharaohs before Akhenaten had kept Egyptian society from disintegrating.

In addition to having a bizarre, alien physical appearance, Akhenaten held a view of traditional religion that was strange, mysterious, and, most of all, threatening. He declared Aten, a sun deity, the supreme and only god. By concentrating power into a single god, the whole structure of the traditional Egyptian pantheon was thrown into disarray. For millennia the fragile bond unifying Upper and Lower Egypt was a common belief in a multiplicity of gods and the innumerable ways they figured into maintaining everyday life. It was the gods, the "community of deities," through direction by the pharaoh that kept the mills turning, the Nile flowing, and the winds blowing.

Figure 12.1. Akhenaten worshipping Aten.

All this changed with Akhenaten. Centralizing power in Aten meant not only diminishing the importance of the entire Egyptian pantheon, but in effect erasing much of its mythology. "The proscription of Osiris by Akhenaten," writes Egyptologist Cyril Aldred, "ensured that the gods of burial were banished together with the pantheon, and a new eschatology has to be invented." The emphasis put on this sun god displaced Osiris, a lunar deity, and his significance to life, both present and in the hereafter. "All mention of Osiris, together with the gods of his cycle [the Ennead], was suppressed in the funerary texts, and the Osirian epithet of 'justified' with the force of the 'deceased' was dropped from the titles of the defunct."[3] Henceforth, Aten, who has no female consort and is self-created, reigns supreme along with Akhenaten, his wife Nefertiti, and their children, who become the new holy family; in effect, Akhenaten supplants Osiris, Isis, and Horus. An apotheosis is occurring in that royal humans are embodying what had formerly been strictly the province of the gods. No longer did one see gods in animal forms or read the magic spells that activated their image. In symbolic terms, the moon is being eclipsed by the sun in broad daylight, a phenomenon that will reach its apogee with the dawning of Christianity.

The new mythology that sprang up with Akhenaten's reign maintained that both living and dead simply sank into sleep each night and awakened to the rays of the morning sun. In future, it was to be Aten, and sometimes Akhenaten, to whom the living and dead would turn in prayer and adulation, since the king and his god had become their eternal caretakers. This revolutionary change had a disquieting effect on the people, and, for the most part, Akhenaten's effort essentially failed. His failure was due in large part to the fact that his mythology was incomplete.

As we now know, individuation is a process founded upon integrating light and shadow, Self and ego, Osiris *and* Seth. "The concept of an all-encompassing God must necessarily include his opposite," writes

Jung. "The principle of the coincidence of opposites must therefore be completed by that of absolute opposition in order to attain full paradoxicality and hence psychological validity."[4] In this case, Self, in the form of Aten, was given sole authority. Had Akhenaten figured the dark gods, like Osiris, more prominently into his mythology it may have gained greater acceptance. Although Akhenaten's reign lasted only seventeen years and old traditions were quickly restored following his death, it had, I believe, a lasting effect on the Egyptian psyche.

In Aldred's view, Akhenaten's "creed reveals an attempt to rationalize beliefs that had developed accretions from prehistoric times. It sought to establish the relationship of the dead with the living, and mankind and all the natural world with a unique, invisible and self-created god."[5] Rationalized beliefs were a modern concept that not only contradicted the common belief in many gods, but now also called for individuals to think for themselves. Gone was the underworld where the weight of one's soul determined a person's fate. With Akhenaten we have the first stirrings of conscience and with it the need for redemption. This complexity came by proclamation, not through the gradual introduction of a new mythological narrative. Aten was singled out as the ultimate celestial authority, and all other gods were reduced in importance. Akhenaten took a bold step that theologians before him had avoided: he declared the existence of one true God. The Egyptians, says Siegfried Morenz, "avoided liquidating individual gods but did not remain content with building up a hierarchical pantheon; they boldly went on to advance the theory that behind the plurality of gods there was a basic unity."[6] Akhenaten named this unity Aten.

People were simply not prepared to make the leap, although surely some blindly accepted Akhenaten, while others tolerated him and still others feigned allegiance for monetary gain. Soon after the king's death came a flurry of rededications aimed at reviving the old order. But a process had begun that could not be changed. Today, we would refer to it as the individuation process, which holds that in every man, woman, and child is an instinctive urge toward the growth of individuality. No longer was assurance of physical survival and evolution enough, for henceforth an unconscious process of involution had seeded itself in the human psyche. A new dimension of personal, psychological depth was added to the ancient eschatology of the Old Kingdom. With Akhenaten, no longer was the world a mass of selfobjects,[7] but instead the possibility of an individual psyche emerged, one that was private and separate from the collective, consisting of a conscious and unconscious domain.

Comparing Old Kingdom tombs to those made during the Roman occupation, we find significant changes in form and decoration in exterior artwork. The anthropoid coffin shaped in the form of the human body began appearing during the Middle Kingdom. Some suggest that this design arose directly from the custom-tailored tomb in which Osiris was interred. Following further development of the individual psyche, coffins in the Roman era have accurately painted portraits of the deceased's face on the lid. Like earlier mummy masks, these Fayum portraits served to protect the face of the defunct. I offer this observation as partial evidence that a distinct change in coffin artwork emerges as the individual psyche distinguishes itself from collective consciousness.

I further contend that a critical evolution in cognitive development, a gradual shift from concrete to abstract thought, explains the emergence of an individual psyche. In alchemical language, abstract cognition is the separatio that allowed Akhenaten to isolate the one god from the many. This kind of sophisticated symbolic thinking was far more than the average Egyptian was used to. While the populous feared that many thousands of other gods would perish, the truth is that this radical change represented an introjection of the gods into the unconscious. In fact, they did not die; instead, a long process began in which external gods transformed into interior archetypes. In a sense, the old gods, like Osiris, had resurrected.

Many thousands of years would pass before the Osiris myth evolved to the point that people came to understand the gods of the Ennead as psychological entities rather than immortal deities. This shift in consciousness began, I believe, with the fall of Akhenaten. Thereafter, the Book of the Dead was no longer a guidebook meant strictly to serve the deceased but slowly became an instruction manual for the living. To be sure, the myth of Osiris was never a static document but rather changed according to political necessity and, over the course of many thousands of years, responded to the psychological exigencies of the collective unconscious. In the earliest times, Osiris was a common god, as were all the gods of the Ennead. He was the god of the dead; Horus the Elder, the herald of creation; Seth, god of storms and thunder; and Isis, an aspect of the Great Mother. But, since individuation involves movement from simplicity to forms of ever-greater complexity, these gods could no longer maintain their singular place in the Egyptian pantheon. The simple merging of gods was not sufficient symbolically to convey the complexity emerging in the development of consciousness. For now, a shift was occurring that required a calculus of change separating the individual from the body politic. This shift involved a gradual redefinition of the person from one viewed as a function of something other than him- or herself to someone having all the vicissitudes of an inner world.

We may recall that the original hieroglyph for god, Neter, indicates a numinous presence that serves more as a function than as a static divine being. As such, Osiris, lord of becoming, functions in much the same way as the process of individuation. While both function and process are unseen to the naked eye, they nonetheless have a powerful affect on the physical and psychological world. This development is immediately seen in contemporary life where depth psychology and cognitive science are penetrating matter as well as the interior mind, opening vast new mind-body dimensions of consciousness. Current research into the psychoid dimension has pried open the subatomic world. The place where mind and matter interface is becoming increasingly accessible.

We are beholding mysteries that Egyptian priests worshipped and alchemists intuited. We are embodying the kind of divine consciousness that was formally possessed exclusively by pharaohs. The difference is that divine consciousness today is not mediated by heka; rather, it is accomplished through a combination of empathic engagement with the gods (archetypes) and advanced psychological processes. A whole new philosophy of embodiment has spawned areas of research that are shaping today's world.[8]

Much of these contemporary advances stem from the history and mythology we have been studying in this book. A wise old saying makes this point: "Yesterday's magic is tomorrow's science." And, in fact, magic played a crucial role in the radical transition from an unconscious collective to the gradual awakening of individual consciousness. In chapter 4, I described how early Egyptians must have marveled at the transformations appearing in plain view when wheat and barley were changed into bread and the juice of the vine into a spiritual elixir. This magic depended less on a god's favor than on the knowledge one possessed in the kitchen. Channeling the Nile's floodwaters, irrigating the soil, stockpiling seed, and strategic harvesting, all seemingly simple tasks, were actions that replaced magical commands with a practical means of marshalling nature's power.

Osiris and Isis taught people how to use the Nile to cultivate their fields. This knowledge marked a significant advancement in the development of consciousness. For with the means of producing one's own food, the gods weren't something out there that came of their own will and in their own time to provide for the people. What had been a divine power was now, to some extent, in the hands of farmers, bakers, and cooks. With self-sufficiency, people were less dependent on the state; filled storehouses established a healthy market for trade and commerce. At the same time, one's spiritual destiny was no longer a function of the pharaoh, but rather every person had direct access to God (Aten)—a major change in how his or her fate in the afterlife would be determined.

As a result, the great gods became increasingly more abstract and their role in this alchemical process more important. Osiris had been a god of the dead, but he now represents the god of change and becoming—an alchemical god much in the likeness of Mercurius. Seth was no longer just the god of thunder and storms; he now becomes the nightly slayer of Apopis, the serpentine enemy of consciousness. Isis emerges not only as wife and sister, but also as mother and even as a creator goddess who re-members and animates her dead husband. Horus the Elder appears to merge with the younger Horus, together establishing a vital new order on earth. Horus comes to represent the new man who rules with an earthly authority founded upon his father's sovereignty in the underworld. It is possible that the idea of the new man, the second Adam, derives from Horus, for in him we find the seminal traits elaborated much later by other groups: the Cabbalists with their concept of Adam Kadmon, the Gnostics with their doctrine of the Anthropos, and the alchemists with their *filius philosophorum*, the first "man of light"—Mercurius. More generally, what I am describing is the formation of a psychological world where gods become archetypes and the dark underworld, the earliest beginning of a personal unconscious.

Had Jung pursued his research in this area further, he would not only have found evidence to support his theory of individuation but would certainly have discovered the earliest structuring of the human psyche. With his genius, he certainly might have provided encyclopedic evidence that Ra is the personification of the Self. No doubt he would have gone further and found Horus to be the prototype for the ego archetype and Seth, the shadow archetype. Osiris would prove to be the prima materia that transforms from a passive, undifferentiated state to a perfected image of the philosopher's stone. While Jung relied principally on medieval alchemy, I believe he might more profitably have turned to ancient Egypt where the Royal Art was born and cultivated. As I suggested early in this book, consciousness is a continuous process of unfolding, punctuated by dislocations and reunions; the Osiris myth marks many of the key points in this evolution. Indeed, it is a priceless alchemical myth of existence given to us by nature and sculpted by humankind.

"Evolution," observed spiritual teacher Ernest Holmes, "is the time and the process through which an idea unfolds to a higher state of manifestation."⁹ The idea in our case is the creation of the individual— be that a person or an independent nation—that conjoins the masculine consciousness of the spirit and the feminine consciousness of the soul. We saw this same concept prefigured in the *coniunctio* of the passive (yin/soul) Osiris and the active (yang/spirit) Horus, further perfected when this *heiros gamos* is unified with the Self, Ra. Obviously, this concept has not yet been fully realized, and it may take, as Jung said, some six hundred more years to complete. But, from where we stand now, the individuation process must necessarily include work with the psychoid sphere where psyche and matter converge in mysterious ways. In lieu of a mummy that transports the soul to another dimension, the immaterial world is present with us at this very moment. This immaterial world consists of a stratified unconscious that includes personal and collective realms of reality. The vessel is filled with dreams, synchronicities, memories, coincidences, intuitions, reveries, déjà vu, illusions—all of which borrow something of this world and something of other realities. Whereas in bygone days myths emerged from the unknown, today we live in a mythic reality where we daily encounter the seemingly impossible.

APOTHEOSIS

The two pillars of alchemical work are theory and practice. To this point, we have done a good deal of theoretical work by describing the circumstances that gave rise to the Osiris myth and studying the myth using a Jungian and phenomenological approach. But the obvious question confronting us as we draw the book to a close is, how might we actually embody Osiris? Answers to this question are contained in the myth itself.

At the outset of the myth we learned Osiris was born during the five extra days created by a trickster god, Thoth. Here is an important clue to how we can begin building an internal image of Osiris. We start our practice by moving out of ordinary time and into imaginal time. This isn't as difficult as it first appears, when we consider how much of our day is spent in the unconscious. In other words, we must first embody ourselves in order to build a temple that invites the spirit of Osiris to enter. Anchoring consciousness in the body enlivens our physical being. By aligning clock time with earth time (the natural movements of the sun and moon, seasons, the rise and fall of the tides, etc.) we are "in the moment." Time is very dynamic, but we can, with a little practice, stop our mind from wandering aimlessly and bring it home. Our goal is not to lessen or extend our experience of time, but simply to be present in the here and now. Ironically, I have found the best way to do this is to increase our awareness of those moments when we are *not* embodied! By noticing these intervals, a subtle shift brings attention back to the present moment, and we are in a better state of mind for entering the imaginal world.

Once Osiris is born he is nearly indistinguishable from the land—he is the spirit of the soil that causes it to regenerate. The thought that we are made of clay and that this clay originates from star dust is lost on us. The mind forgets, but our bodies remember. The body exists only in the present moment, and by setting an intention to recall its history beginning with our very first memory, we start to enliven our awareness of the body—the thousands of operations being carried out continually. The body is animated by spirit at the precise moment when consciousness enters it. By analogy the Egyptians celebrated this same moment when the morning sun broke the plane of the horizon at dawn.

Just as we must embody ourselves in time, we need also to do the same with physical space. All too often our bodies are merely objects carrying out the functions of the day. To embody space, we must attune our attention to the body's constant rhythms. Noticing the rise and fall of breath, the rhythm of digestion and elimination, the cadence of walking, the blinking of the eyes, etc., all remind us that the body is in a synchronistic relationship with the earth. One shamanic practice proposes that we can actually sense the earth rotating beneath our feet if we develop this kind of subtle awareness.

Aligning the body with universal rhythms causes the ego to shrink; it is humbled and made small. The ego must be sufficiently strong in this process to avoid disintegration. Ironically, humbly acknowledging what we may never know, as suggested at the beginning of this book, strengthens the ego. By making ourselves small, we create a space large enough to accommodate a god. And, when in complete sympathy with the god, we become a worthy vessel ready to receive divine spirit.

In the above two exercises we are more embodied—time and space are located within us. These exercises involve a slow, creative practice requiring intention, discipline, and determination. The result of such practice is described in Kabbalah: "To know the stages of the creative process is also to know the stages of one's own return to the root of all existence."[10] It is precisely at that point between the conscious, civilized world and the dark, unconscious world that we meet Osiris.

Another word that comes close in meaning to embodying is *ensouling*; the first situates time and space within the body, the second animates it with soul. Ensouling is a creative process that involves conceiving the interior body as if it were a community combining psychic and physical elements. "Soul begins," writes Jungian scholar Thomas Moore, "in the moist, solid earth, the realm of ordinary experience. Without this embodied world there could be no soul."[11] For this reason the Egyptians spoke of fluids, semen, and blood as physically carrying thoughts and emotions. Speaking of the creator god Ptah in *Ancient Egyptian Religion*, Frankfort writes, "He made their bodies (statues) resemble that which pleased their hearts (that is, the forms in which they desired to be manifest). And so the gods entered into their bodies of every kind of wood, of every kind of stone, of every kind of clay, of every kind of thing which grows upon him, in which they have taken form."[12]

By animating the body with consciousness, we are filled with *akh* soul, or what we call grace; the gods pour into us, and everything in our world is ensouled. We begin life with little self-awareness; the body carries out basic operations without much, if any, conscious thought, but as the mind matures it is capable of incrementally drawing consciousness into the body, not simply reacting to its basic physical needs but increasingly attending to its spiritual requirements.

In the *Corpus Hermeticum*, Thoth tells us how we prepare ourselves to embody a god: "Do not roam about searching for God; but sit calmly at home, and God, who is everywhere, and not confined to the smallest place like the daemons, will come to you. And, being calm in body, calm also your passions, desire and pleasure and anger and grief and the twelve portions of death. In this way, taking control of yourself, you will summon the divine [to come] to you, and truly it will come, that which is everywhere and nowhere."[13]

We must be sufficiently still in order for soul as well as the spirit of Osiris to be willing to enter the temple of our physical being. For this reason, it is quite possible that the alchemists chose the image of a stone to represent the goal of their work: a rock does not move—its duration is founded in immovable stillness. A stone appears lifeless, an apt metaphor for the part of us that is wholly devoid of soul, and, at the same time, a stone is a perfect vessel of receptivity. This explains an insightful recipe given by the sixteenth-century alchemist Gerhard Dorn: "Transmute yourselves from dead stones into living philosophical stones."[14] The lapis is a living embodiment of earth and heaven. The Field of Reeds was the quintessential image for producing this symbolism. This "field" of consciousness integrated the best of Egypt's beloved land with the eternity of heaven.

Stillness does not always come voluntarily. More often abuse, trauma, and crisis stop us dead in our tracks; some part of the psyche

Figure 12.2. The Field of Reeds.

automatically shuts down and appears dead, denied, paralyzed, and cut off from consciousness. Similarly, the myth informs us that Osiris is captured by Seth and sealed in a leaden coffin. To be suddenly and utterly cut off from family, friends, and the world would be frightening for us. The only comfort we might take in this situation would be in knowing we are not really alone in that coffin. All may seem lost, everything gone. But, as long as we are aware of our own *presence*, hope remains, and at our darkest hour, some mysterious force in the universe comes to our side. A god is there, perhaps unseen, but his presence is palpable. He is the light in the dark, and with that light comes hope that the journey we are on will take us to a better place.

Days and years may pass in this "dark night of the soul." The opening stanzas of the poem by St. John of the Cross describe the experience:

> In darkness, and secure,
> by the secret ladder, disguised,
> —ah, the sheer grace!—
> in darkness and concealment,
> my house being now all stilled.
>
> On that glad night,
> in secret, for no one saw me,
> nor did I look at anything,
> with no other light or guide
> than the one that burned in my heart.[15]

Eventually we reach a distant shore that portends new life. Osiris is taken to Byblos, far away from his home, and in this foreign land a beautiful acacia tree embraces him, infuses his body with strength, and essentially brings him back from the dead. He assumes an upright position and becomes a pillar of strength. We embody this same strength by not allowing the fear of death to overwhelm us. By acknowledging death each day, we discover its dark beauty and its transformative power. Such strength enables us to endure being separated from the security of our homeland. Although we remain in the jaws of darkness where depression, loneliness, and isolation dominate, we know that this isn't our natural place in life; we may be down, but not out.

This is a foreign place, but there is no land that is devoid of nature. She embraces us, renews our spirit, and empowers us. Instincts are the force that gives rise to archetypes. Eventually, we stand tall and find our "backbone" and the core strength that can support the weight of the world.

Isis takes her dead husband home; little does she know that the worst is yet to come. Not a moment is lost when we are cut to pieces and scattered about the world. For some it is a mental breakdown, for others a spiritual crisis that is a critical step in embodying a god. In our practice the body is being dismembered for a purpose. If it is not severed from the earth, it will die in it and never have a chance at resurrection. It will become a slave to habits, passions, routines . . . deteriorating in the field of time and space. Death is an implicit part of entering Osiris's eternal kingdom. "In Goethe's words, *stirb und werde*, die and become."[16] One must die to this world in order to become part of a greater reality. Submission to this ordeal must be neither suicide nor martyrdom, for both are a retreat from life, a constriction that cuts us off from existence, physical and divine.

Osiris is a model of submission. He allows all the terrors that befall him to occur, just as the prima materia endures the tortures of the laboratory. Such deliberate sacrifice is meant to serve as a model for personal individuation. It justifies all the pain we daily suffer in order to transcend this world and leave it wiser and more enlightened. Submission and trust in this process allow love to enter the vessel. We are then embraced by the Mother and taken into her arms. Her only aim is that we bring something new and unique into the world. The dead ask no less of us. In the *Red Book*, Jung reveals that the dead want us to take up their unresolved burdens. We are left to reassemble our lives by submitting to our ancestral destiny. In this way, individuation is shaped by the Mother (*Anima Mundi*) and the souls of the departed who want us to bring their purpose to its rightful conclusion. And so, in similar fashion, we die, but our relationships live on for a time equal to the contribution we've made while living.

Just as Osiris dies but is not nonexistent, we too live on beyond physical death. Having an active relationship with the unconscious, we are not surprised by death nor, as Jung suggests, are we ever alone! We have prepared ourselves for this transition—another point of constriction that we have faced before in so many different ways. With Osiris in the underworld, the unconscious becomes a safe place for death *during* our lifetime. Here it is a powerful resource and teacher. Death serves to remind us that physical life is limited and that we must enjoy every finite moment before entering a timeless place. This realization casts a special beauty over everything that occurs in life. Darkness enhances life's treasures; death tinges the light with softness. The melancholy of an Indian flute, the sound of a foghorn in the mist, tears at the cinema—these are subtle pleasures that emanate from the deepest places in our soul. Darkness adds mystery to the soul; it colors the personality. Even sad and depressing events are welcomed because they remind us that life oscillates between joy and sadness; each limits and expands the other. This is the dynamic order of life, what the Egyptians recognized in the rule of Ma'at—the constant rhythms found everywhere in the universe.

We die many deaths before we fully embody Osiris. The infant in us dies to allow the child to be born; the child dies so that the adolescent can further individuate; adolescence gives way to adulthood and, eventually, old age. At every turn there are forces that pull us back and more powerful ones that push us forward. It is the sting of Seth that causes us to shake off the idyllic world of childhood and adopt a mature orientation to life. Where we don't confront and change our childish ways, the world will do it for us. We may be fired from a job, or a wife leaves. In these instances, we feel as if cold water has been thrown in our face, but shock alone is not enough to make a shift to an adult life. The aim is not to destroy the innocence of childhood, but instead to transmute old energies into new ones. *Don't eliminate, transform!* Then, for example, what had been impulsivity transforms into spontaneity, doubt becomes curiosity, and chaos transforms into endless possibilities for creation.

Still one more battle must be fought: the shadow of everything that is unseen, every secret ambition and dark desire must be dragged into the light. We spend an inordinate amount of time keeping these things hidden. Shame prevents the shadow from being made conscious. The battle goes on for many years, and it never seems to end. For, on the one hand, the ego digs in its feet and resists all things that challenge its authority. The shadow, on the other hand, is insistent, for it is driven by the urge to individuate—to bring wholeness to the individual.

It is important to recognize that "grace can only descend on what is imperfect and willing to claim its own destitution, ugliness and inferiority." Psychologist Jerry Fjerkenstad, quoting an alchemical theologian, elaborates on this important point: "This is the ultimate mystery of us: that even our evil, even our tendency against wholeness, exposes us to the love of God. And it exposes us to that love in a way and at a depth to which even our desire for wholeness does not expose us."[17] Fearless humility is a necessary quality, along with stillness, to allow grace to enter the vessel we have prepared.

The secret agent that brings peace to these two noble warriors, shadow and ego, is a trickster. In the myth this battle is personified in the gods Seth and Horus, who are not able to find peace. It is Thoth, the ibis-headed trickster god, who calls upon Neith to prevent bloodshed.

When Osiris finally steps in and declares Horus his legitimate son and heir to the throne, it is Thoth who says that Osiris speaks "true of voice," and the matter is settled.

Thoth, like Hermes and Mercurius, is a servant of the Self. He possesses the wisdom that enables opposing factions to find a creative solution. If, for instance, we unwittingly battle with evil, we risk finding ourselves never able to disengage from it; thus, an intermediary is needed to intervene and transcend the opposites. While Thoth intercedes, it is the Self that brings resolution. The Self takes no sides, for it has so many sides that are all important to existence. In this way, the Self is, as the twelfth-century French theologian Alain de Lille described God, "an intelligent sphere whose center is everywhere and circumference is nowhere."[18]

In order to embody Osiris in an alchemical way, we need to learn how to apply the dictum "Descent of the Spirit, Ascent of the Soul." Simply put, this instruction calls for a constriction of spirit and an expansion of soul, a prescription that recalls the recipe solve et coagula. The dense body can only be made subtle by "rising up," being sublimated, so that every cell of our body, mind, and soul is as light as a feather. In other words, we must reverse the natural order—an *opus contra naturam*—to achieve alchemical transformation. The body resurrects while the earth becomes living spirit.

Osiris's death and resurrection is a religious act; perhaps the origin of the very word *religious*, meaning to "bind" and "tie back," derives from breaking down and renewing our dark thoughts and feelings. We've seen how this alchemical god becomes "spiritualized earth" through the many operations described throughout this book. His dismemberment is certainly the harshest example of this process. Osiris must give up the gross matter of mundane reality in order to be lifted up into the spiritual realm. The ordeal was referred to as the Mysteries because of the secrecy kept by every "religious tongue." In practice, this realm is most immediate in psychological experience because spirit is no longer "out there" but embodied in our being. The gods that dwelled in every cell are not gone, but they need loving attention to once again be a living part of our human process.

The psyche resides in a psychoid dimension where spirit and soul meet, marry, and transform the personality into one integrated and enlightened being. In the final scene, this integration is depicted when Horus, representing earthly time, embraces his father's soul; temporality is touched by eternity.[19] Our physical being is static, and what is needed is an energetic process of becoming that individuates consciousness. Again words from the *Corpus Hermeticum* beautifully describe this process:

> So thus Eternity is in God, the cosmos is in Eternity.
> Time is in the cosmos. Becoming is in time.
> And while Eternity stands still in God's presence,
> The cosmos is in motion in Eternity.
> Time passes in the cosmos and
> Becoming comes to be in Time.[20]

In other words, if we are sufficiently still—as still as a corpse—eternity enters us. Then a god may come into our being, bringing eternity to mind and the experience of continual creation. Becoming isn't something that begins and ends with our time on earth but rather is an emergent property of the universe.

Osiris is the name we use to signify this archetypal god of becoming as it is experienced in time in this world. This is the god we so desperately need in contemporary life where regenerative sciences are physically altering the human landscape. While there are many meditative practices that put us in touch with "becoming," we have focused on Osiris as an archetypal symbol that illuminates an ancient way of understanding the unconscious, its contractions and expansions, its suffering, and its immortality. We can now embrace Osiris as an alchemical figure representing eternity in time, the ceaseless process of becoming and individuating in which birth and death are only markers along the way.

The secret of alchemical transformation is revealed to us by "becoming Osiris" and unveiling the mysteries of regeneration. This ancient god, Osiris, born of earth and sky, is very much like us, and we, like him, die and resurrect. His myth is a formula for achieving the alchemist's dream of transmuting flesh and transforming spirit into an enduring, integrated being that transcends earthly existence. The Osiris mystery shows how this transformation occurs—how the very body that allows us to exist on earth is simultaneously the vehicle that enables us to embody a god.

ACKNOWLEDGMENTS

There are many people who helped in the writing of this book; some played an active role, others contributed without ever knowing the value of their gift. Among the former, I especially thank my beloved wife, Cynthia, who for years tolerated a possessed man. She is always my first editor and confidante. I am also grateful to the loving support of my family: Ananda, my daughter; my brother, Robert; and my sister, Dyan.

This book would not have been possible without the vision of my senior editor, Richard Smoley. He saw a book hidden in a paper I'd written on ancient Egypt. Later, he shaped my original manuscript into the book's present form. His friendship has been everywhere as important as his editorial prowess. I want also to thank Sharron Dorr, the publishing manager at Quest Books, for coalescing the pieces of this project and guiding it to completion. I very much appreciate Andrea Bronson for her enthusiasm and expert proofing of the manuscript; also Allen Page for reading and commenting on an early draft. I am especially grateful to Will Marsh for the meticulous, painstaking care he provided in editing my work.

I am also indebted to Jeremy Naydler for his wise counsel and insight into ancient Egypt. His books have inspired and informed my work. His personal guidance helped clarify the mercurial world of Egyptian cosmology. Dennis Hauck, a dear friend and accomplished alchemist, has supported my work in many ways. His endorsement of the original manuscript assured me that my book held promise and added something unique to the contemporary world of alchemical psychology. Among other writers in this field, I particularly want to acknowledge Drs. Jeff Raff and Stanton Marlan whose work and support is very much appreciated. I thank Professors Barrett and Dieleman for their advice regarding pronunciation of ancient names.

We come then to others who helped in other ways. My analyst and mentor Dr. Pan Coukoulis continues the arduous task of shaping me and, in turn, my work. I wish to acknowledge many patients who enlivened the myth by sharing their own stories, dreams, and details from their personal therapy. Two people who were important to the author died during the writing of this book: Veeriah Bulliah Chadalavada and Michele Roseman Cavalli. These vibrant souls helped in numinous ways.

Lastly, there are a host of authors—chief among them C. G. Jung and R. A. Schwaller de Lubicz—who ventured into the deepest mysteries of the psyche, struggled with the vagaries of alchemy and ancient Egypt. These are the masters who provide us with a vision of a future that marries spirit and matter, safely maintains the rhythms of life, and guides those who practice the regenerative arts. In this regard, I thank Osiris for embodying me in this life and, hopefully, allowing me to become one with him in the next.

Appendix 1

Egyptian Gods That Appear in This Book

The source for the material in this appendix is Richard Wilkinson, *The Complete Gods and Goddesses of Ancient Egypt* (New York: Thames and Hudson, 2003). The page numbers in parentheses refer to this source.

Amaunet: Consort of Amun and known as the female Hidden One. She and Amun together are known as a symbol of protection. She is typically shown in human form bearing the Red Crown of Lower Egypt and carrying a papyrus-headed staff.

Amun: Chief god of Thebes, first mentioned in the Pyramid Texts. His consort is Mut, and his son, Khonshu, was worshipped as the god of the moon. Known as "Amun rich in names," his epithets include concealed god (the Hidden One); creator god (believed to have created the world through his thoughts); solar god (combined with Ra); fertility god (Bull of the Mother, his ithyphallic form); warrior god (attributes retained from Montu, whom he replaced); king of the gods (later equated with Zeus in Ptolemaic times); universal god (he who "exists in all things"). He is typically shown in human form wearing a short kilt with a feather pattern. Sometimes he is depicted with the head of a ram adorned with a double plume of feathers that associates him with the wind.

Anubis: Prior to Osiris, the chief god of the dead, responsible for all matters involving funerary rituals and practices. Eventually, he was assimilated into the Osiris myth and became the sole offspring of Osiris and Nephthys. He is most often depicted in dog form, especially the jackal with its tall erect ears and long snout. His many epithets describe the range of his divine attributes: lord of the sacred land; he who is upon his sacred mountain (overseeing burials); ruler of the bows (enemies who might disturb the dead); he who is in the place of embalming; foremost of the divine booth (tomb or burial chamber).

Apopis (also Apophis): God of "dissolution, darkness, and nonbeing," and Ra's adversary. He is almost exclusively shown as a giant serpent. A number of deities in various books are credited with slaying this serpent god.

Aten: Solar god who rose to prominence during the reign of Akhenaten. Under his rule, Aten was depicted as a sun "disk with a uraeus at its base and with streaming light rays which terminated in hands which were either left open or shown holding ankh signs" (240). The supreme importance of this god is attested to by the fact that Akhenaten incorporated the god's name into his own; he was formally known as Amenhoptep IV.

Atum: "Self-engendered" god of Heliopolis mythology. The root of his name, *tum*, means "complete" or "finish," as is seen in his many manifestations: lord of totality, creator, father of the gods and the king; primal mound (which initially gave rise to the created world; the sun god Ra is often fused with Atum); chthonic god (punisher of enemies of the sun). He is often represented in a seated anthropomorphic form or in his more primeval forms as a ram, serpent, lion, bull, lizard, mongoose, or ape.

Benu: An avian deity who represents Atum, Ra, and Osiris. His name means "to rise." We find him flying over the primeval waters when

Atum initiates creation. He was also considered the ba of Ra, which eventually led to his association with the phoenix symbolism of immortality. In this connection he is also associated with Osiris. In his association with Atum his head is shown in the form of the yellow wagtail, which later changed to the two-feathered crested grey heron. Eventually in his association with Osiris, he became the famed *ben-ben* stone that capped some pyramids.

Bes: Protector god with qualities very similar to those of ten other gods and therefore difficult to understand. He may originate from Libya and the Near East. Nonetheless, he became popular as an apotropaic deity particularly known for his protection of children and pregnant women. He is "portrayed as dwarf-like with shortened legs and an enlarged head. . . . His mask-like and invariably bearded features frame large staring eyes and a protruding tongue, and he is often depicted with the mane of a lion and a lion's tail" (102).

Geb: God of earth, son of Shu and Tefnut, husband to Nut, and father of Osiris. Geb is most often seen "reclining on his side supporting himself with one arm beneath the personified sky" (106). His skin is usually colored green to indicate his fertile nature.

Hathor: Ancient goddess who may have originated in Predynastic Egypt. She is typically represented in a female anthropomorphic form adorned with cow horns. Often her image is confused with Isis, who assumed many of the goddess's attributes. Her bovine form is particularly associated with Thebes. Her epithets describe the breadth of her dominion: mother or wife of Horus; sky goddess (solar deity); wife or daughter and Eye of Ra (consort of Ra); cow goddess (the king's protector and nurse); goddess of women, female sexuality and motherhood (later emerging as the Greek Aphrodite); mother or wife of the king; goddess of foreign lands and their goods (inferring universality); goddess of the afterlife (nurturing the dead); goddess of joy, music, and happiness (including ample use of alcohol).

Hapy: Associated with the life-giving significance of the Nile flood and often thought of as the father of the gods. "Representations of Hapy usually show the god as a swollen-bellied man wearing an abbreviated belt or loincloth and with long hair and pendulous, female breasts" (107). Clearly, he is a god who brings fecundity to the land and thus is also considered a creator god.

Hauhet: Female consort of Heh (Hud). The couple are members of the Ogdoad, the original eight elements in the Hermopolitan cosmology. Heh and Hauhet represent Infinity as part of the initial elements of creation.

Heka: God who existed from the beginning and enabled the creation to occur. His name aptly means "power." His power is the magic that energizes the gods, and as a result they often fear him. For similar reasons, Heka is sometimes shown as a combination of all the gods. More typically, he is depicted as a man with the curved beard of a god.

Horus: Existed from Predynastic times; those who worshipped him during this period were called the "followers of Horus." His epithets include sky god ("the distant one," represented as a celestial falcon); sun god (three forms: Horakhty, "Horus of the two horizons"; Ra-Horakhty, when merged with the sun cult of Heliopolis; and the Great Sphinx of Giza, which represented the hawk-winged sun disk Hor-em-akhet [Harmachis]); son of Isis; god of kingship (includes the Golden Horus name). In his avian form, Horus is shown as a falcon in various positions. As son of Osiris and Isis, he is more typically depicted as the child Horakhty suckling at his mother's breast.

Hud (Heh): See Hauhet.

Imhotep: Known as the "overseer of works," Imhotep built the first Step Pyramid in Saqqara. Although of human birth, his skills and knowledge in architecture, writing, and medicine led him to be regarded as the son of Ptah. In Greece, his image was assimilated into the physician god Askeplios. He is typically shown in the garb of a scribe, donning a long kilt and skullcap with a papyrus roll across his lap.

Isis: Although first mentioned in the fifth dynasty, her origin is unknown. The span of this great protector goddess is great, extending beyond dynastic Egypt and into the Greco-Roman world. Her universality is attested to by the fact that she was venerated by virtually all Egyptians and had no special place of worship: she was everyone's goddess. She was the first daughter of Nut and Geb. Her epithets speak to her range of power as sister-wife of Osiris; mother and protector of Horus; mother of the king (who drank from her breasts); goddess of cosmic associations (affinity with Sirius, Isis-Sothis); great of magic; mourner, sustainer, and protector of the deceased (in her kite form she let out the mournful cry of mourners). She is shown in anthropomorphic form wearing a sheath dress with the hieroglyph "throne" above her head or, later, wearing horns embracing the solar disk. She holds the sistrum rattle and *menat* necklace, an ankh and papyrus staff. In her protector role she is shown with outstretched arms adorned with feathered wings. Her animal forms include the kite, scorpion, and sow. She also appears as a tree goddess, and on amulets she is symbolized as the *tyet* or Isis knot.

Kamutef: See Amun.

Kauket: As a consort to Kek, forms a pair of male and female deities that represent Darkness in the Hermopolitan cosmology of creation.

Khepri: One of the three forms of the sun, he was believed to be swallowed by Nut each evening and reborn every morning. He is also often shown as a scarab of a dung beetle with associations of "developing" and "coming into being," i.e., a symbol of rebirth. In this guise he is sometimes fused with the body of a man, ram, falcon, or vulture.

Khonshu: The god of the moon who figures prominently in the Theban triad as son of Amun and Mut. His temperament changes from a benign god to one who, in the Cannibal Hymn, is shown to be a bloodthirsty assistant to the king. This lunar deity, like Thoth, influences the gestation of animals and humans, as well as being the god responsible for deciding a person's lifespan. Often shown as a young man, he is distinguished from other gods by a "lunar disk resting in a crescent new moon upon his head" (113).

Khnum: Shown with the head of a ram and described as the "personification of creative force" (194), Khnum is particularly associated with the first cataract and believed to control the Nile's inundation. He is also portrayed as a potter on whose wheel he fashioned all living things. The word for ram has direct association with the ba soul, and Khnum was called the ba of Ra; thus, we sometimes see a ram-headed Ra or the god becomes Khnum-Ra. He is depicted as a man with the head of a ram, wearing a kilt and a wig separated by long undulating horns, atop which is the White Crown of Upper Egypt. In this guise he is often shown at his potter's wheel forming a child or infant king; such images often appear in the birth houses of the temple.

Kuk: See Kauket.

Ma'at: At the time of creation, Ma'at came into being to represent truth, order, and balance. The "two Ma'ats" describe her dual role in asserting the right of "deceased king to the throne of Geb" and the judging of souls in the Hall of the Two Truths that determined whether the deceased was sufficiently worthy to enter into the Field of Reeds. She is typically shown in anthropomorphic form wearing a tall feather, but sometimes the feather alone is all that is needed to represent the goddess. At other times, she is portrayed as the "plinth upon which statues of the gods were placed" (150). Like other goddesses, she is sometimes shown with winged arms outstretched, but always bearing the single feather atop her head.

Naunet: Consort of Nun (Nu) and with him forms a pair of male and female deities that represent Water in the Hermopolitan cosmology of creation.

Neith: The origin of this goddess goes back to prehistoric Egypt, making her one of the most important (and mysterious) deities in the Egyptian pantheon. Her epithets described the range of her divine attributes accumulated over the entire period of dynastic rule. These include warrior goddess ("ruler of arrow," "mistress of the bow"); creator goddess (as demiurge, created both Ra and Apopis); mother goddess (mother of the crocodile god Sobek); goddess of Lower Egypt; funerary goddess (together with Isis and Nephthys held vigil over Osiris, guardian of the stomach of the deceased, invented weaving). In the earliest times Neith was shown simply as two crossed arrows mounted on a pole. In her warrior image she is depicted in human form holding a bow and arrow or harpoon. More generally she bears an ankh and *was* (power) staff. Her animal forms include a kneeling cow, serpent, and Nile perch.

Nephthys: One of four deities born to Geb and Nut, she marries her brother Seth but bears a child, Anubis, with Osiris. Her name means "mistress of the mansion." Because of her marriage to her dark husband, Seth, she is known as a protector of the dead. She is usually shown in female form with her name above her head, but she is also depicted, like her sister, Isis, as a kite. Both sisters are typically portrayed together near or behind the throne of Osiris.

Nu/Nun: Part of the Ogdoad, who represents the primeval waters of creation. The water image extends beyond its cosmogonic significance to include all bodies of water and even those waters that continue beyond the world's end. In this role, Nu/Nun is shown in a male human form "as a large figure with the tripartite wig and curved beard of the gods whose upraised arms lift the sun . . . into the horizon from which it was reborn into a new day" (117). He was also shown in the undulating walls surrounding temples, a symbol that expressed the outer perimeter of the universe.

Nut: Part of the Ennead of Heliopolis and daughter of Shu and Tefnut. She represents the heavenly vault, the firmament, "whose 'laughter' was the thunder, and whose 'tears' were the rain. . . . She was also the 'mother' of the heavenly bodies who were believed to enter her mouth and emerge again from her womb each day. The sun was thus said to travel through the body of the goddess during the night hours and the stars travelled through her during the day" (161). As a funerary deity she plays an important role in the resurrection of the deceased king. She, like Isis, is often conflated with the image of Hathor. In her female human form, she is identified by a water pot atop her head. As a cosmic deity she is shown with her arched body forming the firmament with her fingers and feet touching the earth. Accordingly, her image often is painted on the inner top lids of coffins and sarcophagi. In animal form, Nut is portrayed as a sky cow with each of her four hooves touching the cardinal points. Following her cosmic image in which the sun travels through her body, she is also seen as a female pig who eats her piglets.

Osirapis: See Serapis.

Osiris: His name probably means "mighty one," indicating the importance he held throughout Egyptian rule. He is god of fertility, death, and resurrection. He is the first born of the Ennead, husband to Isis and father, with Isis, of Horus and, with Nephthys, of Anubis. His legendary birthplace is Rostau, located in the Memphis desert. Osiris was mostly regarded as a gentle, benign god who represented "physical salvation." His ba was believed to reside in either the sacred ram or Apis bull. Osiris had a close and complex relationship with Ra; together, they represent the body and soul of one great composite god. They also symbolize the powers of the moon and sun, respectively. Osiris is above all the gods of the underworld. He is exclusively shown in human form, usually wrapped in mummy bandages. His skin is colored black (death), green (fertility), and sometimes white (reflecting the color of his wrappings). He typically bears the crook and flail as part of his royal regalia. He is variously shown wearing the White Crown of Upper Egypt or the Atef Crown over a divine wig. He also wears the traditional curved beard of male deities. At times he is depicted symbolically as the djed column or pillar, which is variously shown having arms and bearing his traditional royal accoutrements.

Ptah: One of the oldest Egyptian gods, Ptah, together with his consort, Sekhmet, and their son, Nefertem, make up the Memphite triad. His major roles are reflected in his many epithets: lord of Memphis (his place of origin); craftsman (especially sculptor and smith); creator god (containing within him Nun and Naunet); chthonic and afterlife god (combined with Osiris and Sokar); hearer of prayers. He is consistently shown as a standing male form with "feet together and with his hands protruding from his tightly wrapped shroud to hold his characteristic scepter . . . wearing a skullcap" (125). Typically, he stands on a plinth that recalls Ma'at (truth) or a workman's measuring rod. His beard is straight and a large tassel usually hangs from the back of his garment.

Ra (also Re): Other than possibly Horus the Elder, Ra is the oldest Egyptian god. As a sun god he merged with many other deities. With Horakhty he was the morning sun and with Atum, the evening sun. His presence is seen in the heavens, as a creator god, on the earth, as king and divine ruler, and in the underworld, as carrier of the lamp of light and consciousness. Typically he is shown as a fiery solar disk, sometimes with outstretched wings. Less often he is depicted in anthropomorphic form as a man with the head of a falcon, ram, or scarab. When merged with Osiris, he is shown in mummified form with a ram's head. Rarely is he shown with a female consort. By the

Fifth Dynasty, Ra's consort is Raet or Raettawy. Other solar images, like winged sun disks, flying vultures, and golden bands, were used in architecture to depict the god. In this same dynasty Ra had become something of a state god. His center of worship was at Heliopolis, where a number of huge temples were built in his honor. He was, however, a perennial god, worshipped by kings and commoners alike throughout Egypt's long history.

Sekhmet: Leonine goddess with both destructive and protective attributes. She was known as the daughter of Ra, who, seeing her destructive nature, transformed her into a healing goddess (Hathor). As such, she protected the king and also warded off disease. She was consort to Ptah, with whom she bore a child, Nefertem. Sekhmet was also associated with the destructive aspects of Mut and other feline goddesses. Her name means "power."

Serapis: Egyptian-Hellenistic deity who combined many attributes of Osiris and the Apis bull needed for the new culture that emerged during the Ptolemaic period. Isis, who was embraced by the Greeks and Romans, was made consort to this composite god. When shown together, they are depicted as serpents, Serapis donning a beard. Otherwise, he is portrayed as a man in Greek garb holding a "corn modius or measure on his head" (128). Serapis is the Egyptian god of dreams.

Seth: The origins of this god go back to Predynastic times where evidence shows that his image or name appears in connection with the protodynastic ruler Scorpion. He was incorporated in the Heliopolitan Ennead as the dark son of Geb and Nut. Throughout his long history he remained mostly a desert deity, affiliated with foreign lands and the enemies of Egypt. Yet, there are times when he is seen in a more positive light, as is the case when, in the Middle Kingdom, he repels the evil Apopis serpent. He is god of violence, chaos, and confusion (as the "Red One" he is sometimes associated with Neith), god of strength, cunning, and protective power (his extraordinary strength was sometimes put to good use). Originally shown in animal form with a curved head, his image gained stature, especially in his relation to Horus. At times he is portrayed in a male body having both the head of Horus and his own canine head. Due to his malevolence his image was attached to any number of animals considered dangerous to the Egyptian people.

Shu: God of air and sunlight, he is part of the Heliopolios Ennead, born of Atum and husband to Tefnut (moisture). Like Ma'at, Shu wears a feather on his head, but he is sometimes seen as a lion. He is often depicted supporting Nut with his upstreched arms. The same posture is duplicated in a headrest found in the tomb of Tutankhamun.

Sobek: As a god of water, this crocodile deity offers both protection and fertility. He is the son of Neith and in this image is called the "raging one." His power made him a symbol of the king's strength and potency. He is shown either completely in his crocodile form or as a man with a crocodile head. In either case he is typically colored green. In his anthropomorphic form, his headdress bears the insignia of the sun disk with a horn and tall plumes.

Sokar: Initially, this god was closely associated with Ptah and even (as Ptah-Sokar) took Ptah's consorts as his own. Thus, he was originally associated with craftsmanship. As his image evolved, he became associated with Osiris, and eventually the three were merged into Ptah-Sokar-Osiris. In his original form he was shown as a falcon. "As a falcon-headed man Sokar is often represented as mummiform and sometimes wears a complex conical crown with sun disk horns and cobras" (210). In all his images, his strength over the nether regions is evidenced. In his trifold combined form he can also be seen as a "squat, pygmy-like male, sometimes with a scarab beetle on his head, and the amuletic deity Pataikos appears to have been derived from these particular . . . images" (210).

Sothis (Gk. Sopdet): Goddess who represents the bright Dog Star, Sirius. She is the "bringer of the New Year," since the first appearance of Sirius marked the beginning of the Nile's inundation. Thus, she was associated with Osiris, and her husband is Sah, or Orion, a neighboring star that represented Osiris. Their son is Soped or Sopdu, also an astral deity. Sothis is believed to have joined with Osiris to produce the morning star, Venus. Because of Isis's association with Osiris, the two goddesses were joined to form Isis-Sothis. Her earliest representation is that of a reclining cow with a plantlike emblem (perhaps representing the "year") between her horns.

Tefnut: Goddess of moisture, daughter of Atum, and husband to Shu. Her enigmatic nature is expressed in one myth that has her quarreling with Ra. She flies off to Libya and is only convinced to return by Thoth. She is depicted in a lion-headed female form, typically wearing a wig adorned with a large uraeus.

Thoth (Djehuty): God of knowledge, writing, and symbols, who plays an integral role in the Osiris myth. Although his origins are found in the Predynastic period, he is said to be the son of Horus, conceived through the semen of Seth. As the inventor of writing, he is the scribe of the Ennead who registered the judgments of the dead. Accordingly, he possesses great magic and secrets unknown to other gods. Although he is shown either as an ibis or a baboon, both lunar animals, the former is primary. As a lunar deity he is sometimes considered a "night sun" in relation to Ra. His chief consort is Nehemetawy, but he is also at times associated with Seshat, goddess of writing. He was eventually assimilated into Greek mythology, where he is shown as Hermes or Hermes Trismegistus.

APPENDIX 2

TIME LINE AND BRIEF DYNASTIC HISTORY

Years	Periods/ Dynasties	Main Events (Italics indicate events significant to Osiris myth)
3100–2950 BC	Late Predynastic Period	- Earliest known hieroglyphic writing - Foundation of Egyptian state - *First dynasty under Narmer founded*
2950–2575 BC	Early Dynastic Period (1st–3rd Dynasties)	- Creation of capital city of Memphis - First pyramid built: Step Pyramid at Saqqara - *First evidence of Pyramid Texts (2400 BC)*
2575–2160 BC	Old Kingdom (4th–8th Dynasties)	- Great Pyramids built at Dahshur and Giza - Pyramids and elite tombs include first extensive inscriptions
2160–2055 BC	1st Intermediate Period (9th–11th Dynasties)	- Egypt splits into two smaller states, ruled from Memphis in north and Thebes in south - *Evidence of Coffin Texts in which the Ogdoad is first mentioned*
2055–1650 BC	Middle Kingdom (11th–14th Dynasties)	- Mentuhotep II reunites Egypt - Amenemhat I founds new royal residence near Memphis - Egypt conquers Lower Nubia under Senwosret I and III - Classical period of art and literature
1650–1550 BC	2nd Intermediate Period (15th–17th Dynasties)	- Hyksos kings seize power in north - Theban 17th Dynasty in south

1550–1069 BC	New Kingdom (18th–20th Dynasties)	- Egyptian empire in Near East and Nubia - Elaborate tombs of Valley of Kings - Rameses II rules for 67 years - *Rule of woman pharaoh Hatshepsut (1479–1458 BC)* - *Akhenaten attempts to introduce a monotheistic religion* - *Brief reign of Tutankhamun*
1069–664 BC	3rd Intermediate Period (21st–25th Dynasties)	- Disunity and Libyan settlement in Egypt - Nubians conquer Egypt (late 8th century)
664–332 BC	Late Period (20th–30th Dynasties, 2nd Persian Period)	- Egypt conquered briefly by Assyrians - Cultural revival under kings from Sais - Persian conquest of Egypt (525 BC) - Egypt independent again (404–343 BC) - *Last use of hieroglyphic writing* (300 BC)
332 BC–AD 395	Greco–Roman Period (Macedonians, Ptolemies, and Romans)	- Alexander the Great occupies Egypt - Alexander's general, Ptolemy, becomes king and founds a dynasty - Egypt becomes province of Roman Empire (30 BC) - *Rosetta stone carved* (195 BC) (discovered AD 1799; translated 1822) - *Cleopatra VII reigns* (51–30 BC) - *First alchemical writings credited to Bolos of Mendes* (200 BC)

Other Important Dates

Neolithic period: 9500–1700 BC
Archaic period: 3100-2700 BC
Egypt unified: 3150 BC
Amarna period: 1352–1335 BC
Ptolemaic period: 332–30 BC

Pyramid Texts: 2400–2300 BC
Coffin Texts: 2181–2055 BC
Book of the Dead: 1650–1550 BC
Bible: 1513 BC–AD 96

Hesiod's histories: seventh century BC
Corpus Hermeticum: third century BC

Akhenaten: 1353–1336 BC or 1351–1334 BC
Plutarch: AD 46–120
Alexandrian Library: third century BC–AD 642
R. A. Schwaller de Lubicz: 1887–1961
C. G. Jung: 1875–1961

APPENDIX 3

MAP OF ANCIENT EGYPT

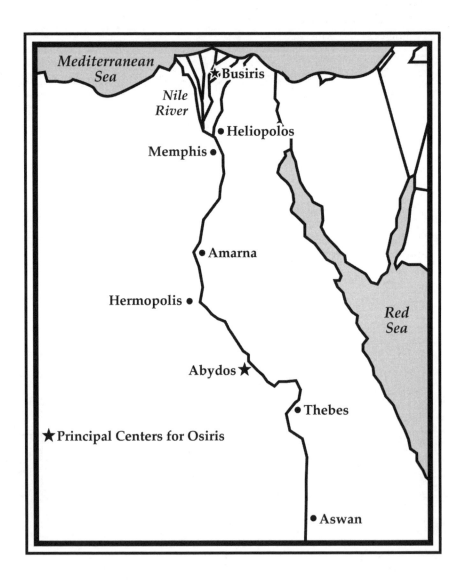

NOTES

FOREWORD

1. Rig Veda 10:168, in *The Rig Veda*, ed. and trans. Wendy Doniger O'Flaherty (London: Penguin, 1981), 176.

2. Plutarch, *On Isis and Osiris*, 65; in G. R. S. Mead, *Thrice-Greatest Hermes: Studies in Hellenistic Theosophy and Gnosis* ([London: Theosophical Society, 1906] York Beach, MN: Weiser, 1992), 1:240.

3. J. G. Frazer, *The Golden Bough* (New York: Macmillan, 1922), 438.

4. Plutarch, 45, 49; in Mead, 1:224, 228, 229. Bracketed and parenthetical insertions are Mead's.

5. Plutarch, 53, 55; in Mead, 1:231, 233.

INTRODUCTION

1. Jeremy Naydler, *The Future of the Ancient World* (Rochester, VT: Inner Traditions, 2009), 68.

2. For an excellent account of the phenomenological approach that emphasizes scholarship and empathic engagement, see Jeremy Naydler, *Shamanic Wisdom in the Pyramid Texts: The Mystical Tradition of Ancient Egypt* (Rochester, VT: Inner Traditions, 2005), 324. Here Dr. Naydler refers to van der Leeuw, who summarizes this approach: "The method is . . . an attempt to re-experience a certain entity as such, to transpose oneself into an object as an organic whole. . . . The criterion in all cases is the evidence . . . through which it is not so much we who discover the object, but the object that manifests itself to us" (126–27).

229

3. Stephen Mitchell, ed., *The Enlightened Mind: An Anthology of Sacred Prose* (New York: HarperCollins Publishers, 1991), 34. Dating the *Corpus Hermeticum* is difficult; its original material was redacted from the first to third centuries AD, indicating that much of the material stemmed from pharaonic Egypt. Others argue that the language is too new to support these dates. For more information on the *Corpus Hermeticum* see Clement Salaman and others, trans., *The Way of Hermes: New Translations of The Corpus Hermeticum and The Definitions of Hermes Trismegistus to Asclepius* (Rochester, VT: Inner Traditions, 2000), 57.

4. Bojana Mojsov, *Osiris: Death and Afterlife of a God* (Malden, Maine: Blackwell Publishing, 2005), 50.

5. While the Egyptian contribution to our understanding of the development of consciousness is invaluable, we must also recognize the vast insights of other major cultures. But we must acknowledge that Egypt was in its eighteenth or nineteenth dynasty by the time the Old Testament was probably written. The *Mahabharata*, the great Sanskrit epic of ancient India, was written about the eighth century BC, the period marking the end of some three thousand years of Egyptian rule. And, by the time the Koran was set to paper (AD 610–632), ancient Egypt was little more than a faded memory.

6. E. A. Wallis Budge, *Osiris and the Egyptian Resurrection* (New York: Dover Publications, 1973), 101.

7. Albert Einstein, from the memoir of William Miller, *Life*, May 2, 1955. See Alice Calaprice, *The New Quotable Einstein* (Princeton: Princeton University Press, 2005), for more quotes by Einstein.

8. Robert Thomas Rundle Clark, *Myth and Symbol in Ancient Egypt* (London: Thames and Hudson, 1959), 12.

9. Thomas Norton, in C. G. Jung, *Psychology and Alchemy*, trans. R. F. C. Hull (Princeton: Princeton University Press, 1968), 270. See

John Reidy, ed., *Thomas Norton's Ordinal of Alchemy* (London: Oxford University Press, 1975) for complete manuscript.

10. Albert Einstein, in "What Life Means to Einstein: An Interview by George Sylvester Viereck," *Saturday Evening Post*, October 26, 1929.

11. Dimitri Meeks and Christine Favard-Meeks, *Daily Life of the Egyptian Gods* (Ithaca, NY: Cornell University Press, 1996), 127.

12. Peter Kingsley, *In the Dark Places of Wisdom* (Inverness, CA: Golden Sufi Center, 1999), 171.

13. According to Jung's typology, the personality has two axes, a rational axis composed of thinking and feeling, and a nonrational axis consisting of the sensate and intuitive functions. See C. G. Jung, *Psychological Types*, trans. R. F. C. Hull (Princeton: Princeton University Press, 1971), for Jung's original research in this area.

14. Julian Jaynes, *The Origin of Consciousness in the Breakdown of the Bicameral Mind* (Boston: Houghton Mifflin, 1976), 186.

15. Naydler, *Shamanic Wisdom*, 316.

16. Marie-Louise von Franz, *The Golden Ass of Apuleius: The Liberation of the Feminine in Man* (Boston: Shambhala, 1992), 208.

17. The Egyptians had three systems of tracking time: the beginning year of the pharaoh's reign; the Nile's inundation (Inundation, June 21 to October 21; Emergence, October 21 to February 21; Summer, February 21 to June 21); and the Sothic year based on the Sirius star system and a modulus of 6 in which 1 hour = 60 minutes, 1 day = 24 hours, 1 month = 30 days, 1 year = 12 months, and a Sothic year = 365.25 days.

18. C. G. Jung, *The Structure and Dynamics of the Psyche*, trans. R. F. C. Hull (Princeton: Princeton University Press, 1960), 441.

19. The six characteristics commonly found in all alchemical systems are animism, oneness, transcending time and reason, transformation, facilitation, and creating new life. See Thom F. Cavalli,

Alchemical Psychology: Old Recipes for Living in a New World (New York: Tarcher/Putnam, 2002), 32–36.

20. Jung, *Structure and Dynamics of the Psyche*, 438.
21. The *ba* soul was the nonmaterial aspect of a person. It defines the unique qualities of an individual in his or her personality. While the concept of the ba comes close to our modern conception of personality, it is distinct in that it is very attached to the physical body. Thus, when an individual dies the ba, in the form of a bird with a human head, flies off to meet and ultimately join with the *ka*, the living soul, in order to make the deceased immortal *akh* and as such, an ancestor.
22. Naydler, *Shamanic Wisdom*, 84.
23. Mojsov, *Osiris*, 51.
24. Rosemary Clark, *The Sacred Magic of Ancient Egypt: The Spiritual Practice Restored* (St. Paul, MN: Llewellyn Publications, 2003), 55.
25. The Rosetta stone is an artifact that unlocked the key to deciphering hieroglyphic writing. It represents a decree announcing the repeal of taxes, written in three languages: hieroglyphic, demotic, and Greek. It was made in 196 BC during the Ptolemaic period and discovered in 1799. A momentous breakthrough came with the discovery made by Jean-François Champollion that the hieroglyphs were both pictoral and phonetic. Together with Thomas Young, Champollion unveiled the principles underlying the structure of hieroglyphic writing, and the actual words of the ancient Egyptians could at last be understood.

CHAPTER ONE

1. Two hypotheses are current regarding human evolution. The first posits a multiregional evolution in which *Homo erectus* evolved from Africa some one to two million years ago. The second theory contends that early humans evolved from Africa one hundred

thousand to two hundred thousand years ago and spread to the rest of the world. The latter theory is supported by mitochondrial DNA evidence and is more generally accepted by archeologists. Dating the earliest civilizations is even more problematic. Although there were dynasties as early as 2100 BC, it wasn't until Emperor Qin Shihuang at the end of the Warring States period (476–221 BC) that China first unified and the country derived its name from his dynasty. Dating the unification of India is more complicated. The Indus Valley civilization flourished on the Indian subcontinent as early as ca. 2600 BC, but it wasn't until the Portuguese settled in Bombay in 1498 and later when the British seized control that India became a unified country. By contrast, Narmer unified Egypt in 3000 BC.

2. The date when Osiris first appears in the Pyramid Texts, the oldest religious text in the world.

3. Egyptians referred to their enemies as the "nine bows." The term is a euphemism that collectively refers to anyone living outside the Nile Valley. These enemies included the Nubians, Libyans, Hykos (Asian kings), Mianni, Hattie and Assyrians, Sea People (Sherden, Sheklesh, Lukka, Tursha, and Akawasha), and Persians.

4. Mojsov, *Osiris*, 11 (see intro., n. 4).

5. John Anthony West, *Serpent in the Sky: The High Wisdom of Ancient Egypt* (Wheaton, IL: Quest Books, 1993), 127.

6. Naydler, *Shamanic Wisdom*, 284 (see intro., n. 2).

7. Theodor Abt and Erik Hornung, *Knowledge for the Afterlife: The Egyptian Amduat—A Quest for Immortality* (Zurich: Living Human Heritage Publications, 2003), 104.

8. Mojsov, *Osiris*, 39.

9. Cyril Aldred, *Akhenaten, King of Egypt* (London: Thames and Hudson, 1988), 114.

10. Recent DNA evidence indicates that the injury previously believed to have killed Tutankhamun was actually sustained after his death,

that he had a clubfoot and, unlike his father, did not have Marfan disease.

11. Edward F. Edinger, *Anatomy of the Psyche: Alchemical Symbolism in Psychotherapy* (La Salle, IL: Open Court, 1985), 72.
12. West, *Serpent in the Sky*, 83.
13. Rundle Clark, *Myth and Symbol in Ancient Egypt*, 119 (see intro., n. 8).
14. Jung, *Psychological Types*, 460 (see intro., n. 13).
15. This triple rulership may have given rise to Hermes Trismegistis (thrice greatest).
16. Henri Frankfort, *Ancient Egyptian Religion: An Interpretation* (Mineola, New York: Dover Publications, 2000), 89.
17. Mojsov, *Osiris*, 17.
18. Erik Hornung, *Conceptions of God in Ancient Egypt: The One and the Many*, trans. John Baines (Ithaca, NY: Cornell University Press, 1982), 213.
19. Edward F. Malkowski, a proponent of de Lubicz's work, extends this rule to the province of mind: "Thought always occurs beneath the thinker's essence. So, being below God's essence, man can think of God. On the other hand, since there can be nothing above God, then God can never think of Himself. Therefore, God thinks of Himself as being nothing else but what He thinks" (*The Spiritual Technology of Ancient Egypt: Sacred Science and the Mystery of Consciousness* [Rochester, VT: Inner Traditions, 2007], 290).
20. Hornung, *Conceptions of God in Ancient Egypt*, 160–61.
21. See ibid., 163.
22. Personal communication. For more information I highly recommend Dr. Naydler's books, *Shamanic Wisdom in the Pyramid Texts*, *Temple of the Cosmos*, and *The Future of the Ancient World*.
23. Hornung, *Conceptions of God in Ancient Egypt*, 179.

CHAPTER TWO

1. Bolos of Mendes, also known as Democritus, is credited with joining theory and experiment, isolating the four elements that lead to atomic structure and coining the well-known alchemical expression "One nature is charmed by another nature, one nature overcomes another nature, one nature dominates another nature." Before Bolos of Mendes, transmutation was no more than a change in appearance, not a true transformation of matter.

2. Garth Fowden, *The Egyptian Hermes: A Historical Approach to the Late Pagan Mind* (Princeton: Princeton University Press, 1986), 67–68. Fowden writes, "We have no records that the ancient Egyptians made astronomical observations; but some form of time-keeping was essential to the smooth functioning of the temples." He goes on to describe how the Egyptians divided the night into "hours" and later developed "decans" that make up the zodiac.

3. Alison Roberts, *My Heart My Mother: Death and Rebirth in Ancient Egypt* (East Sussex, England: Northgate Publishers, 2000), 216.

4. Fowden, *The Egyptian Hermes*, 24.

5. von Franz, *Golden Ass of Apuleius*, 189 (see intro., n. 16).

6. Zosimos's famous vision is important to us for a number of reasons. First, with the help of Jung's interpretation, we clearly see that this allegory is describing specific alchemical operations. Although Zosimos perfected gliding metals to an art form, he is also credited with the "formulae of the Crab," which supposedly provide the secret of transmutation. Secondly, Zosimos's dream contains many of the same themes (torture, dismemberment, embalming) that we find in the Osiris myth. Third, and most importantly, it speaks to the purpose of the current book, namely, in Jung's words: "We have to learn the psychological secrets of alchemy. . . . Only he who knows the secret of the stone understands their [alchemists'] words. It has long been asserted that this secret is sheer nonsense. . . . But this

frivolous attitude ill befits the psychologist, for any 'nonsense' that fascinated men's minds for close on two thousand years . . . must have something about it which it would be useful for the psychologist to know" (C. G. Jung, "The Visions of Zosimos," in *Alchemical Studies*, trans. R. F. C. Hull [Princeton: Princeton University Press, 1967], 69). Only by interpreting the Osiris myth might we begin to unveil its many alchemical secrets that aid us in the process of individuation.

7. In order to extend his concept of synchronicity so that it more broadly encompassed the region between psyche and soma, Jung used the term *psychoid archetype*, stating, "For just as a man has a body which is no different in principle from that of an animal, so also his psychology has whole series of lower storeys in which the spectres from humanity's past epochs still dwell, then the animal souls from the age of Pithecanthropus and the hominids, then the 'psyche' of the cold-blooded saurian, and, deepest down of all, the transcendental mystery and paradox of the sympathetic and parasympathetic psychoid processes" (C. G. Jung, *Mysterium Coniunctionis: An Inquiry into the Separation and Synthesis of Psychic Opposites in Alchemy*, trans. R. F. C. Hull [Princeton: Princeton University Press, 1970]), 212).

8. Jeremy Naydler, *Temple of the Cosmos: The Ancient Egyptian Experience of the Sacred* (Rochester, VT: Inner Traditions, 1996), 127.

9. Serge Sauneron, *The Priests of Ancient Egypt*, trans. David Lorton (Ithaca, NY: Cornell University Press, 2000), 158.

10. Ibid., 163.

11. David Rankine, "Heka, The Practices of Ancient Egyptian Ritual and Magic," excerpt from *Heka—The Practices of Ancient Egyptian Ritual and Magic*, http://www.heka.co.uk (accessed January 2009).

12. Frankfort, *Ancient Egyptian Religion*, 13 (see chap. 1, n. 16).
13. While heat and air are needed to create life, they are also responsible for killing it. By removing the humidity, alchemists sought to drain the corpse of these corrosive elements.
14. Naydler, *Shamanic Wisdom*, 320 (see intro., n. 2).
15. Rundle Clark, *Myth and Symbol in Ancient Egypt*, 165 (see intro., n. 8).
16. von Franz, *Golden Ass*, 204 (see intro., n. 16).
17. Hornung, *Conceptions of God in Ancient Egypt*, 213 (see chap. 1, n. 18).
18. See ibid., 157–165, for further discussion of the fate of the gods and the world.
19. von Franz, *Golden Ass*, 187.
20. The image is strikingly similar to the herm stones of ancient Greece, blocks of stones bearing the head of Hermes, the trickster god, and an erect phallus midway from the base. These statutes were placed at crossroads, a favorite dwelling place for chaos and change. See Norman O. Brown, *Hermes the Thief: The Evolution of a Myth* (Great Barrington, MA: Lindisfarne Press, 1990).
21. Naydler, *Shamanic Wisdom*, 320, 313.
22. See Hornung, *Conceptions of God in Ancient Egypt*, 177–178.
23. "Osiris," observes M. Esther Harding in *Woman's Mysteries, Ancient and Modern* (New York: Harper and Row, 1971), "is thought of primarily as Moonman, [who] having been raised from the dead by the power of Isis, becomes immortal. He remains the moon . . . even though he is eventually made one with Ra, the sun" (186). He "represented knowledge, . . . the Reason, the Logos, which is that organizing, comprehending capacity which can map out, and foresee. He is the Logos, the Moon who metered out the heavens, portioning them into areas by his movements through the zodiacal constellations, and by his cyclic changes dividing the eternal flow of

time into season and months, so teaching men law and order and justice" (184).

24. Mojsov, *Osiris*, 8 (see intro., n. 4). The quote is from the Coffin Texts.

CHAPTER THREE

1. Hornung, *Conceptions of God in Ancient Egypt*, 182, 173 (see chap. 1, n. 18).

2. Naydler, *Shamanic Wisdom*, 311 (see intro., n. 2).

3. West, *Serpent in the Sky*, 217 (see chap. 1., n. 5).

4. Heinrich Brugsch, quoted in E. A. Wallis Budge, *Egyptian Religion: Egyptian Ideas of the Future Life* (New York, NY: Citadel Press, 2000), 21.

5. Rundle Clark, *Myth and Symbol in Ancient Egypt*, 51 (see intro., n. 8).

6. Hornung, *Conceptions of God in Ancient Egypt*, 163.

7. In addition to knowledge of the earth's spherical form, the ancient Egyptians very likely derived complex data from astrological observation that they depicted in large, carefully arranged stone megaliths. After analysis of "Complex Structure A" at Nabta Playa, UC Berkeley biologist Thomas Brophy says, "Astonishing as it may be, the bedrock sculpture . . . appears to be an accurate depiction of our Milky Way, as it was oriented astronomically at a specific time: vernal equinox heliacal rising of the Galactic Center in 17,700 BC" (Thomas G. Brophy, *The Origin Map: Discovery of a Prehistoric, Megalithic, Astrophysical Map and Sculpture of the Universe* [New York: Writers Club Press, 2002]), 54.

8. With such heavy reliance on the ego to orient and protect us in earthly reality, we often mistakenly confuse these functions with executive decision making. While the ego is excellent at data collecting and even coalescing data into rational knowledge, it is neither wise

nor knows anything about the unconscious realms. For that we resort to the Self. Paradoxically, the ego makes us aware of the Self but at the same time can obfuscate its power when we most need it. The ideal person, through inner work, can discipline the ego and align it with the Self so that the two are in a harmonious relationship.

9. Rundle Clark, *Myth and Symbol in Ancient Egypt,* 93.

10. According to Jung, "The division into two was necessary in order to bring the 'one' world out of the state of potentiality into reality. Reality consists of a multiplicity of things. But one is not a number; the first number is two, and with it multiplicity and reality begin" (*Mysterium Coniunctionis*, 462 [see chap. 2, n. 7]). This multiplicity also shows up in alchemy in a now famous axiom of Maria: "One becomes two, two becomes three, and out of the third comes the one as the fourth."

11. Jan Assmann, *Death and Salvation in Ancient Egypt* (Ithaca, NY: Cornell University Press, 2001), 30.

12. Ruth Schuman Antelme and Stéphane Rossini, *Becoming Osiris: The Ancient Egyptian Death Experience* (Rochester, VT: Inner Traditions, 1998), 41–42.

CHAPTER FOUR

1. Kathryn Bard, "The Egyptian Predynastic: A review of the evidence," *Journal of Field Archaeology* 21, no. 3 (1994): 265–288.

2. Wendell Berry, "The Man Born to Farming," in *The Selected Poems of Wendell Berry* (Washington, DC: Counterpoint, 1998), 67.

3. Marie-Louise von Franz, *On Dreams and Death: A Jungian Interpretation* (La Salle, IL: Open Court, 1998), 13.

4. Jolande Jacobi, ed., *Paracelsus: Selected Writings* (Princeton: Princeton University Press, 1995), 93.

5. Schwaller de Lubicz believed that the merging of an animal head with a human body signified an incorporation or realization of the

specific animal's wisdom. Osiris, who is never shown in animal form, has realized the full wisdom of the animal kingdom.

6. Hornung, *Conceptions of God in Ancient Egypt*, 128 (see chap. 1, n. 18).

7. Rundle Clark, *Myth and Symbol in Ancient Egypt*, 114 (see intro., n. 8).

8. Ibid., 128.

9. John O'Donohue, *Anam Cara: A Book of Celtic Wisdom* (New York: Cliff Street Books, 1997), 92–93.

10. Ibid.

11. von Franz, *On Dreams and Death*, 10.

12. Naydler, *Temple of the Cosmos*, 125 (see chap. 2, n. 8).

13. C. G. Jung, *Modern Man in Search of a Soul* (New York: Harcourt Harvest, 1955), 49.

CHAPTER FIVE

1. Jung, *Mysterium Coniunctionis*, 335, n. 288 (see chap. 2, n. 7).

2. Jung, *Alchemical Studies*, 265–66 (see chap. 2, n. 6).

3. Liz Greene, *Saturn: A New Look at an Old Devil* (York Beach, ME: Samuel Weiser, 1976), 14.

4. Meeks, *Daily Life of the Egyptian Gods*, 118 (see intro., n. 11).

5. See Jules Cashford, *The Myth of Isis and Osiris* (Boston: Barefoot Books, 1993). The Osiris myth is scattered throughout the Pyramid Texts in the form of spells and exhortations. There is no narrative telling and, most significantly, no mention of Osiris's death. Nonetheless, reports have been made even in recent times of Osiris's grave being found.

6. Roberts, *My Heart My Mother*, 55 (see chap. 2, n. 3).

7. Jung, *The Practice of Psychotherapy*, trans. R. F. C. Hull (Princeton: Princeton University Press, 1954), 257.

8. Rundle Clark, *Myth and Symbol in Ancient Egypt*, 108 (see intro., n. 8).

9. Edinger, *Anatomy of the Psyche*, 47 (see chap. 1, n. 11).

10. Johannes Fabricius, *Alchemy: The Medieval Alchemists and Their Royal Art* (Copenhagen: International Booksellers and Publishers, 1976), 78.

11. Frankfort, *Ancient Egyptian Religion*, 96 (see chap 1, n. 16).

12. Raymond Faulkner, trans. *The Egyptian Book of the Dead: The Book of Going Forth by Day* (San Francisco: Chronicle Books, Inc., 1994), plate 32, #42.

13. Jung, *The Practice of Psychotherapy*, 257.

14. M. Esther Harding, *Psychic Energy* (Princeton: Princeton University Press, 1963), 431.

15. Edinger, *Anatomy of the Psyche*, 168–169 (see chap. 1, n. 11).

CHAPTER SIX

1. Papyrus was the symbol of Lower Egypt. Its hieroglyph is often accompanied by *sa*, meaning "protection." The concept of papyrus means "around" and "behind" as in "All life and protection are around."

2. The acacia is one of a number of possible trees mentioned in various versions of the myth. The tamarisk tree is often cited as the tree in question. Plutarch said it was the erica tree, but unlike the acacia both the tamarisk and erica are rather small, too thin to contain a coffin. By contrast the acacia is larger and heavily concentrated along the Nile (perhaps explaining why it became a leading candidate).

3. Richard H. Wilkinson, *Symbol and Magic in Egyptian Art* (New York: Thames and Hudson, 1994), 93.

4. While many scholars, including Plutarch, compare Dionysus with Osiris, there are differences in the myths. See Walter Otto, *Dionysus: Myth and Cult* (Bloomington, IN: Indiana University Press, 1965), 195, for a discussion of some significant differences. At the same time, neglecting the obvious similarities between Dionysus

and Seth would be a serious oversight; both drive men to madness. Indeed, Dionysus combines elements of both Osiris and Seth.

5. Herodotus, *The Landmark Herodotus: The Histories*, trans. Robert B. Strassler (New York: Pantheon Books, 2007), 2:146, 186.

6. Rundle Clark, *Myth and Symbol in Ancient Egypt*, 129 (see intro., n. 8).

7. Many associations can be drawn with this image of the phallic tree. In Peter Levenda's *Stairway to Heaven: Chinese Alchemists, Jewish Kabbalists, and the Art of Spiritual Transformation* (New York: The Continuum International Publishing Group Inc., 2008), 17, he points out some of these associations: the adze used in the Opening of the Mouth ritual, The Bull of Heaven or the Great Bear (the Big Dipper), wands and staffs, and the "Thigh of Set." Thus, he writes, "This instrument [the adze] is referred to as the Thigh of Set, and at times in other hieroglyphic panels we can see that the thigh of a bull is also presented during the Opening of the Mouth ceremony. . . . The word 'thigh' has often been used as a euphemism for phallus, such as in the term 'wounded in the thigh. . . .' In each of these myths there is a clear link with fertility and birth."

8. Stanislav Klossowski De Rola, *The Secret Art of Alchemy* (New York: Avon Books, 1973), plate 39.

9. Fabricius, *Alchemy*, 86 (see chap. 5, n. 10).

10. Denise Dersin, *What Life Was Like on the Banks of the Nile* (Alexandria, VA: Time-Life Books, 1997), 38.

11. Roberts, *My Heart My Mother*, 136 (see chap. 2, n. 3).

12. Malkowski, *The Spiritual Technology of Ancient Egypt*, 191 (see chap. 1, n. 19).

13. Manly P. Hall, *Paracelsus: His Mystical and Medical Philosophy* (Los Angeles: The Philosophical Research Society, Inc., 1964), 41.

14. Jill Purce, *The Mystic Spiral* (New York: Thames and Hudson, 1974), plate 18.

15. Ananda K. Coomaraswamy, quoted in Joseph Campbell, *The Hero with a Thousand Faces*, 3rd ed. (Novato, CA: New World Library, 2008), 92.
16. Meeks, *Daily Life of the Egyptian Gods*, 116 (see intro., n. 11).
17. Lyall Watson, *Lifetide* (New York: Bantam Books, 1979), 272.
18. Ibid., 273.
19. Loren Eiseley, quoted in Watson, *Lifetide*, 169.
20. Frankfort, *Ancient Egyptian Religion*, 4 (see chap. 1, n. 16).
21. While orientation is important in understanding Egyptian art and writing, other factors play an equally critical role. In his research, Richard Wilkinson includes form, size, location, materials, color, actions, and gestures to arrive at a fuller understanding of Egyptian artifacts. His book on the subject, *Symbol and Magic in Egyptian Art*, is well worth reading.
22. Hall, *Paracelsus*, 63.
23. The term *Divine Self* is used to indicate a very high level of consciousness that equates with the rubedo stage of alchemy. For more information, see Cavalli, *Alchemical Psychology* (see intro., n. 19).
24. According to Peter Levenda, this stairway is the polestar, true north. It "can be found in many of the world's religions; in the religions of the ancients, such ideas were fundamental to their ideas of macrocosm and microcosm. The Pole was situated in the north, but also in the human body. If the Pole in the human body could be aligned with the Pole in the northern sky, then celestial ascent was possible" (*Stairway to Heaven*, 216).

CHAPTER SEVEN

1. W. Brede Kristensen, quoted in Naydler, *Shamanic Wisdom*, 131 (see intro., n. 2).
2. Jan Assmann, *The Search for God in Ancient Egypt* (Ithaca, NY: Cornell University Press, 1984), 4.

3. Naydler, *Temple of the Cosmos*, 147 (see chap. 2, n. 8).

4. Sir James Frazer, *The Golden Bough* (New York: Macmillan Co., 1953), 14.

5. According to Henri Frankfort, "If there is water to cross [in the underworld], there must be a ferryman. If one imagines a closed Hereafter there must be a gate with a porter. But the ferryman or the porter may be a bully, or may insist on payment, or on a password, and so on. One arms oneself as best one can with magical spells; one pretends to be an important person, for whom the gods are waiting; or one pretends that one is a god oneself" (*Ancient Egyptian Religion*, 116 [see chap. 1, n. 16]).

6. Assmann, *The Search for God in Ancient Egypt*, 156.

7. Naydler, *Temple of the Cosmos*, 148.

8. Emma Jung, *Animus and Anima* (Zurich: Spring Publications, 1978), 29.

9. Ibid.

10. For a more complete rendering of "The Great Hymn to the Aten," see Aldred, *Akhenaten*, 241–43 (see chap. 1, n. 9).

11. Paracelsus, quoted in Edinger, *Anatomy of the Psyche*, 32 (see chap. 1, n. 11).

12. Ibid., 40.

13. Marie-Louise von Franz, *Alchemy: An Introduction to the Symbolism and the Psychology* (Toronto: Inner City Books, 1980), 87.

14. von Franz, *Golden Ass of Apuleius*, 146 (see intro., n. 16).

CHAPTER EIGHT

1. Tom Hare, *ReMembering Osiris: Number, Gender, and the Word in Ancient Egyptian Representational Systems* (Stanford, CA: Stanford University Press, 1999), 251.

2. Jung, quoted in Edinger, *Anatomy of the Psyche*, 166 (see chap. 1, n. 11).

3. If the body were divided along the thighs instead of the waist, there would be fifteen body parts. Some versions of the myth cite fifteen sections. In this case, we might conjecture that the lost penis is not counted in the total number of body parts (see note 11 below).

4. Joseph L. Henderson and Dyane N. Sherwood, *Transformation of the Psyche: The Symbolic Alchemy of the Splendor Solis* (Hove, England: Brunner-Routledge, 2003), 95.

5. Ibid.

6. Ibid.

7. Ibid., 96.

8. Ibid., 95.

9. See Cavalli, *Alchemical Psychology* (intro., n. 19), for discussion of the Real and the False Self.

10. Hare, *ReMembering Osiris*, 108. See chapter 3 in Hare for a full discussion of this subject.

11. In some versions of the myth, Isis fashions an artificial penis and the actual member is never retrieved.

12. According to Mojsov's telling of the myth, these fish are "the lepidotus, phagrus, and oxyrynchus" (*Osiris*, xx [see intro., n. 4]).

13. Rundle Clark, *Myth and Symbol in Ancient Egypt*, 106 (see intro., n. 8).

14. Edinger, *Anatomy of the Psyche*, 47 (see chap. 1, n. 11).

15. Heraclitus, quoted in Bertrand Russell, *History of Western Philosophy*, 2nd ed. (New York: Routledge, 2004), 51.

16. Assmann, *Death and Salvation in Ancient Egypt*, 31 (see chap. 3, n. 11).

17. Refer to the work of Margaret Mahler for discussion of the phases of the separation-individuation process from a developmental psychological perspective. See Margaret Mahler, Fred Pine, and Anni Bergman, *The Psychological Birth of The Human Infant: Symbiosis and Individuation* (New York: Basic Books, 2000).

18. Origen, quoted in Marie-Louise von Franz, *Psyche and Matter* (Boston: Shambhala Publications, 1988), 150.

19. Gerhard Dorn, quoted in Jung, *Mysterium Conunictionus*, 221, n. 555 (see chap. 2, n. 7).
20. Robert A. Armour, *Gods and Myths of Ancient Egypt*, 2nd ed. (Cairo: The American University Press, 2001), 73.
21. Antelme and Rossini, *Becoming Osiris*, 23 (see chap. 3, n. 12). The authors give a complete description of the rites involved in "becoming Osiris."

CHAPTER NINE

1. Rundle Clark, quoted in Armour, *Gods and Myths of Ancient Egypt*, 69 (see chap. 8, n. 20).
2. The *ib* heart represents our general expression of emotional energy and the *haty* heart the immediate attitude we have toward events at different moments in time. The heart represents an intuitive, noncognitive type of intelligence, something more akin to the soul than the mind. Thus, Wheeler points out: "Ib is also the Egyptian determinative for 'imagination' and 'to imagine,' for other words relating to the expression of life through non-rational experience. 'Sailing To Heart's Center-point' was a metaphor for the transition of death, and the soul itself is referred to as 'The Great Thing within the Heart's Centerpoint'" (Ramona Louise Wheeler, *Walk Like an Egyptian: A Guide to Ancient Egyptian Religion and Philosophy* [Mount Shasta, CA: Allisone Press, 2000], 34–35).
3. Wheeler, *Walk Like an Egyptian*, 36. There are exceptions. A narcissist, for example, often behaves like the *puer aeternus*, the archetype of the eternal youth. In this case, the puer denies the shadow and blindly "flies off" into endless, wild adventures. He or she takes no notice of consequences and often acts childish. Peter Pan is a good literary example of this character who can't acknowledge his shadow and as a result relies on others to pin it to his back.

4. C. G. Jung, quoted in James Hollis, *The Middle Passage: From Misery to Meaning in Midlife* (Toronto: Inner City Books, 1993), 97.

5. Kingsley, *In the Dark Places of Wisdom*, 68 (see intro., n. 12).

6. H. te Velde, *Seth, God of Confusion: A Study of His Role in Egyptian Mythology and Religion* (Leiden: E. J. Brill, 1967), 38.

7. Rundle Clark, *Myth and Symbol in Ancient Egypt*, 217 (see intro., n. 8).

8. This ash is an essential carrier of life forms according to de Lubicz's "pharaonic evolutionary theory." "Within this ash," explains Malkowski, "is an alkaline salt [fixed salt], which, if sown into the earth, promotes the generation of form by its absorption into other life-forms . . . These fixed salts, which are never destroyed and are recycled through the food chain, provide the physical framework through the influence of cosmic energy (consciousness) for a new form" (Malkowski, *The Spiritual Technology of Ancient Egypt*, 367–368 [see chap. 1, n. 19]).

9. Dennis William Hauck, *The Emerald Tablet: Alchemy for Personal Transformation* (New York: Penguin/Arkana, 1999), 400.

CHAPTER TEN

1. An epic is a long poetic composition that typically involves a hero and is constructed in a coherent, sophisticated form. Technically, Frankfort is correct in asserting that "the epic . . . was practically unknown in Egypt" (*Ancient Egyptian Religion*, 124 [see chap. 1, n. 16]). In fact, the Egyptian literature is mostly disjointed allusions that do not tell a cohesive tale from beginning to end. "The best proof," Frankfort writes, "that this anti-epical attitude towards mythological subjects was typical of Egyptian literature is the absence of a coherent account of creation. This is truly astonishing, for creation was . . . the only nonrecurrent event which the Egyptians

acknowledged as significant. . . . But, the Egyptians were so little prepared to dwell on any change, that they did not even describe in orderly and continuous fashion the supreme change which took place at what they called 'the first time.' We are obliged to reconstruct the creation story from allusions which are frequent and from certain learned commentaries" (131). Apparently Professor Armour does not take these technicalities into account but rather is more interested, as are we, in the Osiris myth as it has been "reconstructed" over millennia. By its nature the psyche seeks order and completion, so the unconscious steps in where the Egyptians left lacunae in their mythmaking. Given our modern love of epics, it is unsurprising that at least one version of the Osiris myth should emerge in this form.

2. Seth, like his brother and sisters, is born fully formed, while Horus develops along human lines from child to man. The fact that Isis and Thoth continue to support him in maturity suggests that he, representing the ego, is still not completely self-reliant. We are not born with a fully realized ego and must therefore rely on others. Even Osiris, symbolizing the *prima materia*, is not as developed as Seth right from the beginning. We can see Seth's strength, which is more closely tied to nature than humans. Thus, the battle between Seth and Horus can also be framed as a struggle between humans and nature.

3. Armour, *Gods and Myths of Ancient Egypt*, 81 (see chap. 8, n. 20).

4. William Kelly Simpson and Robert W. Reiter, trans., *The Literature of Ancient Egypt: An Anthology of Stories, Instructions, Stelae, Autobiographies, and Poetry*, 3rd ed. (New Haven: Yale University Press, 2003), 93–94.

5. In keeping with the idea that this myth may contain hidden recipes, it is interesting to speculate that these three gods represent the basic trinity of alchemical principles wherein Salt possesses the qualities personified in Ra; Sulfur, fiery qualities of Seth; and Mercury, the transmutational qualities of Osiris.

6. Hare, *ReMembering Osiris*, 148 (see chap. 8, n. 1).
7. Ibid., 125.
8. Ibid., 153, 116. With the term *androcentrism*, Hare suggests that the centrality of emphasis on the phallus is "not merely an abstract preference for male power [but rather] marks the discourses of theology, royal legitimacy, and social cohesiveness with seminal trace" (153). "Can we," he asks, "gain some epistemological perspective that does not depend on our necessarily gendered embodiment?" He concludes his argument by stating, "This leads to the problem that has bedeviled modern reconsiderations of Egyptian culture as well as, apparently, Egyptian culture itself" (154).
9. Eugene Monick, *Phallos: Sacred Image of the Masculine* (Toronto: Inner City Books, 1987), 50, 82.
10. Hare, *ReMembering Osiris*, 111, 113 (see chap. 8, n. 1).
11. See ibid., 148–154, for a highly lucid discussion of what he means by applying this term and its implications.
12. In this context it is interesting that the court should turn to Neith, whose name means "water." She was viewed as the personification of the primeval waters of creation.
13. Monick, *Phallos*, 82.

CHAPTER ELEVEN

1. Joseph Campbell, *The Masks of God: Oriental Mythology* (New York: Viking Press, 1962), 81.
2. Hare, *ReMembering Osiris*, 126 (see chap. 8, n. 1).
3. Some evidence indicates that a King Scorpion may have lived at the end of the Predynastic period. A mace head has been found that shows the image of a scorpion engraved near the face of the king. King Scorpion, the argument goes, may have been a contemporary of Narmer, or possibly they were one and the same person.
4. Velde, *Seth, God of Confusion*, 38–39, 40 (see chap. 9, n. 6).

5. For this reason Thoth is called "the cutter" and says to Osiris, "I am the son of your son, the seed of your seed, he who separated the two brothers" (ibid., 44). It is very curious that Thoth should put the seed to his forehead. Semen carries life, and, as we have seen, in the Egyptians' cosmology the origins of life begin with the masculine. At the same time the sun disk also represents life. In Hindu religion the forehead is the *Ajna* chakra, associated with divine intuition. It is the place dualism collapses into a nonmaterial, spiritual realm. In alchemy, the *monoculus* expresses this same type of singularity.

6. Hare, *ReMembering Osiris*, 126 (see chap. 8, n. 1).

7. Dorothy Norman, *The Hero: Myth, Image, Symbol* (New York: World Publishing Co., 1969), 38.

8. It is important to note that Isis spares Seth's life, for in her role as Mother Nature she allows all things, whether they stimulate growth or bring decay, to exist. See Harding, *Woman's Mysteries*, 183–84 (see chap. 2, n. 23). Additionally, Seth continues to serve the king, especially in times of war, when the king embodies this violent god's energies to vanquish his enemies. We should also recall that Horus and Seth alternately kill the serpent Apopis as the sun god makes his way through the *duat*.

9. Norman, *The Hero*, 38.

10. Hare, *ReMembering Osiris*, 128, 135.

11. In Egyptian iconography, de Lubicz suggests that a human head attached to an animal body signifies the integration or embodiment of that animal's power. When Isis, for example, shape-shifts by taking the form of a kite, she assumes the bird's ability to fly while being depicted as a kite with a human head.

12. See Richard H. Wilkinson, *The Complete Gods and Goddesses of Ancient Egypt* (New York: Thames and Hudson, 1994), 150, for further discussion of Ma'at in ancient Egypt.

13. Erich Neumann, *The Origins and History of Consciousness*, trans. R. F. C. Hull (Princeton: Princeton University Press, 1995), 247.
14. Norman, *The Hero*, 41.
15. Neumann, *The Origins and History of Consciousness*, 248.

CHAPTER TWELVE

1. Assmann, *The Search for God in Ancient Egypt*, 159 (see chap. 7, n. 2).
2. Ibid.
3. Aldred, *Akhenaten*, 246 (see chap. 1, n. 9).
4. Jung, *Alchemical Studies*, 210 (see chap. 2, n. 6).
5. Aldred, *Akhenaten*, 248.
6. Quoted in Hare, *ReMembering Osiris*, 164 (see chap. 8, n. 1).
7. The term *selfobject* derives from Heinz Kohut's Self Psychology. The selfobject is anything that functions to add to the development of the Self. The Egyptian gods were selfobjects in that they served to enhance that part of people's Self that is divine, transcendent, maintains a relationship with a deity, etc. For more information on selfobjects refer to Kohut's book, *Self Psychology and Humanities* (New York: W. W. Norton and Co., Inc., 1980).
8. The philosophies of embodiment began with the work of Kant, Husserl, and Merleau-Ponty. In recent years there has been a burgeoning growth of this philosophy into new areas of research, including embodied cognition, neurophenomenology, embodied epistemology, and situated cognition. While these studies appear to be quite esoteric, their applications are pragmatic, as for example, in artificial intelligence and robotics. We are already seeing these programs used in medicine, neuropsychology, and space science.
9. Ernest Holmes, *The Science of Mind* (New York: Tarcher/Putnam, 1998), 591.
10. Gershom Scholem quoted in Fowden, *The Egyptian Hermes*, 105 (see chap. 2, n. 2).

11. Thomas Moore, *The Planets Within: The Astrological Psychology of Marsilio Ficino* (Great Barrington, MA: Lindisfarne Press, 1990), 71.

12. Frankfort, *Ancient Egyptian Religion*, 24 (see chap. 1, n. 16).

13. Tobias Churton, *The Golden Builders: Alchemists, Rosicrucians, and the First Freemasons* (Boston: Weiser Books, 2002), 24.

14. Hauck, *The Emerald Tablet*, 127 (see chap. 9, n. 9).

15. St. John of the Cross, *The Essential St. John of the Cross: Ascent of Mount Carmel, Dark Night of the Soul, A Spiritual Canticle of the Soul, and Twenty Poems* (San Francisco: Wilder Publications, 2008), 646.

16. Edinger, *Anatomy of the Psyche*, 177 (see chap. 1, n. 11).

17. Sebastian Moore, quoted in Jerry Fjerkenstad, "Alchemy in a Nutshell," in *Meeting the Shadow: The Hidden Power of the Dark Side of Human Nature*, ed. Connie Zweig and Jeremiah Abrams (New York: Tarcher, 1998), 227.

18. G. R. Evans, *Alain of Lille: The Frontiers of Theology in the Later Twelfth Century* (Cambridge, England: Cambridge University Press, 2009), 77.

19. The integration of Ra and Osiris is one of the greatest mysteries in Egyptian religion. Ra, in this aspect, represents constancy (victory of the Sun at its zenith) and Osiris, the variable or cyclic rhythms of time; Ra-Osiris merges these two seemingly opposite orders of time, what the alchemists called the "fixed-volatile."

20. Brian Copenhaver. *Hermetica: The Greek Corpus Hermeticum and the Latin Asclepius* (Cambridge, England: Cambridge University Press, 1995), 37.

Bibliography

Abt, Theodor, and Erik Hornung. *Knowledge for the Afterlife: The Egyptian Amduat—A Quest for Immortality*. Zurich: Living Human Heritage Publications, 2003.

Aldred, Cyril. *Akhenaten, King of Egypt*. London: Thames and Hudson, 1988.

Antelme, Ruth Schumann, and Stéphane Rossini. *Becoming Osiris: The Ancient Egyptian Death Experience*. Rochester, VT: Inner Traditions, 1998.

Armour, Robert A. *Gods and Myths of Ancient Egypt*. 2nd ed. Cairo: The American University Press in Cairo, 2001.

Assmann, Jan. *Death and Salvation in Ancient Egypt*. Ithaca, NY: Cornell University Press, 2001.

———. *The Search for God in Ancient Egypt*. Ithaca, NY: Cornell University Press, 1984.

Bard, Kathryn. "The Egyptian Predynastic: A review of the evidence." *Journal of Field Archaeology* 21, no. 3 (1994): 265–288.

Barker, Kenneth, ed. *The Holy Bible*. New International Version. Grand Rapids, MI: Zondervan, 2002.

Berendt, Joachim-Ernst. *The World Is Sound: Nada Brahma*. Rochester, VT: Destiny Books, 1983.

Berry, Wendell. *The Selected Poems of Wendell Berry*. Washington, DC: Counterpoint, 1998.

Brier, Bob. *Ancient Egyptian Magic*. New York: Morrow, 1980.

Brophy, Thomas G. *The Origin Map: Discovery of a Prehistoric, Megalithic, Astrophysical Map and Sculpture of the Universe*. New York: Writers Club Press, 2002.

Brown, Norman O. *Hermes the Thief: The Evolution of a Myth.* Great Barrington, MA: Lindisfarne Press, 1990.

Budge, E. A. Wallis. *Egyptian Religion: Egyptian Ideas of the Future Life.* New York: Citadel Press, 2000.

——. *Osiris and the Egyptian Resurrection.* New York: Dover Publications, 1973.

Calaprice, Alice. *The New Quotable Einstein.* Princeton: Princeton University Press, 2005.

Campbell, Joseph. *The Hero with a Thousand Faces.* 3rd ed. Novato, CA: New World Library, 2008.

——. *The Masks of God: Oriental Mythology.* New York: Viking Press, 1962.

Cashford, Jules. *The Moon: Myth and Image.* New York: Four Walls Eight Windows, 2003.

——. *The Myth of Isis and Osiris.* Boston: Barefoot Books, 1993.

Cavalli, Thom F. *Alchemical Psychology: Old Recipes for Living in a New World.* New York: Tarcher/Putnam, 2002.

Churton, Tobias. *The Golden Builders: Alchemists, Rosicrucians, and the First Freemasons.* Boston: Weiser Books 2002.

Clark, Robert Thomas Rundle. *Myth and Symbol in Ancient Egypt.* London: Thames and Hudson, 1959.

Clark, Rosemary. *The Sacred Magic of Ancient Egypt: The Spiritual Practice Restored.* St. Paul, MN: Llewellyn Publications, 2003.

Copenhaver, Brian. *Hermetica: The Greek Corpus Hermeticum and the Latin Asclepius.* Cambridge, England: Cambridge University Press, 1995.

de Lubicz, R. A. Schwaller. *The Egyptian Miracle, An Introduction to the Wisdom of the Temple.* Rochester, VT: Inner Traditons, 1985.

——. *The Temple in Man.* Rochester, VT: Inner Traditions, 1977.

Dersin, Denise. *What Life Was Like on the Banks of the Nile.* Alexandria, VA: Time-Life Books, 1997.

De Rola, Stanislas Klossowski. *Alchemy: The Secret Art.* New York: Avon Books, 1973.

———. *The Golden Game: Alchemical Engravings of the Seventeenth Century.* London: Thames and Hudson, 1988.

Doniger O'Flaherty, Wendy, ed. and trans. *The Rig Veda.* London: Penguin, 1981.

Edinger, Edward F. *Anatomy of the Psyche: Alchemical Symbolism in Psychotherapy.* La Salle, IL: Open Court, 1985.

Einstein, Albert. "What Life Means to Einstein: An Interview by George Sylvester Viereck." *Saturday Evening Post*, October 26, 1929.

Evans, G. R. *Alan of Lille: The Frontiers of Theology in the Later Twelfth Century.* Cambridge, England: Cambridge University Press, 2009.

Fabricius, Johannes. *Alchemy: The Medieval Alchemists and Their Royal Art.* Copenhagen: International Booksellers and Publishers, 1976.

Faulkner, Raymond, trans. *The Egyptian Book of the Dead, The Book of Going Forth by Day.* San Francisco: Chronicle Books, Inc., 1994.

Fowden, Garth. *The Egyptian Hermes: A Historical Approach to the Late Pagan Mind.* Princeton: Princeton University Press, 1986.

Frankfort, Henri. *Ancient Egyptian Religion: An Interpretation.* Mineola, NY: Dover Publications, 2000.

———. *Kingship and the Gods: A Study of Ancient Near Eastern Religion as the Integration of Society and Nature.* Phoenix ed. Chicago: University of Chicago Press, 1978.

Frazer, Sir James. *The Golden Bough.* New York: Macmillan, 1953.

Fulcanelli. *Fulcanelli, Master Alchemist: Le Mystère des Cathédrales, Esoteric Interpretation of the Hermetic Symbols of the Great Work.* Translated by Mary Sworder. Suffolk, England: Spearman, 1971.

———. *The Dwellings of the Philosophers: Les Demeures Philosophales.* Boulder, CO: Archive Press & Communications, 1998.

Greene, Liz. *Saturn: A New Look at an Old Devil.* York Beach, ME: Samuel Weiser, 1976.

Hall, Manly P. *Paracelsus: His Mystical and Medical Philosophy*. Los Angeles: The Philosophical Research Society, Inc., 1964.

Harding, M. Esther. *Psychic Energy*. Princeton: Princeton University Press, 1963.

———. *Woman's Mysteries, Ancient and Modern*. C. G. Jung Foundation of Analytical Psychology. New York: Harper and Row, 1971.

Hare, Tom. *ReMembering Osiris: Number, Gender, and the Word in Ancient Egyptian Representational Systems*. Stanford, CA.: Stanford University Press, 1999.

Hauck, Dennis William. *The Emerald Tablet: Alchemy For Personal Transformation*. New York: Penguin/Arkana, 1999.

Hawass, Zahi. *The Royal Tombs of Egypt*. London: Thames and Hudson, 2006.

Henderson, Joseph L., and Dyane N. Sherwood. *Transformation of the Psyche: The Symbolic Alchemy of the Splendor Solis*. Hove, England: Brunner-Routledge, 2003.

Herodotus. *The Landmark Herodous: The Histories*. Translated by Robert B. Strassler. New York: Pantheon Books, 2007.

Hollis, James. *The Middle Passage: From Misery to Meaning in Midlife*. Toronto: Inner City Books, 1993.

Holmes, Ernest. *The Science of Mind*. New York: Tarcher/Putnam, 1998.

Hornung, Erik. *Conceptions of God in Ancient Egypt: The One and the Many*. Translated by John Baines. Ithaca, NY: Cornell University Press, 1982.

Jacobi, Jolande, ed. *Paracelsus: Selected Writings*. Princeton: Princeton University Press, 1995.

Jaynes, Julian. *The Origin of Consciousness in the Breakdown of the Bicameral Mind*. Boston: Houghton Mifflin, 1976.

Johnson, Robert A., and Jerry M. Ruhl. *Balancing Heaven and Earth: A Memoir*. San Francisco: HarperSanFrancisco, 1998.

Jung, C. G. *Alchemical Studies*. Translated by R. F. C. Hull. Princeton: Princeton University Press, 1967.

———. *Memories, Dreams, Reflections.* Edited by Aniela Jaffe. New York: Vintage Books, 1989.

———. *Modern Man in Search of a Soul.* New York: Houghton Mifflin Harcourt, 1955.

———. *Mysterium Coniunctionis: An Inquiry into the Separation and Synthesis of Psychic Opposites in Alchemy.* Translated by R. F. C. Hull. Princeton: Princeton University Press, 1970.

———. *The Practice of Psychotherapy.* Translated by R. F. C. Hull. Princeton: Princeton University Press, 1954.

———. *Psychological Types.* Translated by R. F. C. Hull. Princeton: Princeton University Press, 1971.

———. *Psychology and Alchemy.* Translated by R. F. C. Hull. Princeton: Princeton University Press, 1968.

———. *The Red Book, Liber Novus.* Edited by Sonu Shamdasani, translated by Mark Kyburz, John Peck, Sonu Shamdasani. New York: W. W. Norton & Co., 2009.

———. *The Structure and Dynamics of the Psyche.* Translated by R. F. C. Hull. Princeton: Princeton University Press, 1960.

Jung, Emma. *Animus and Anima.* Zurich: Spring Publications, 1978.

Kabat-Zinn, Jon. *Wherever You Go, There You Are: Mindfulness Meditation in Everyday Life.* New York: Hyperion, 1995.

Kelly, Edward. *The Alchemical Writings of Edward Kelly.* London: James Elliot, 1893.

Kingsley, Peter. *In the Dark Places of Wisdom.* Inverness, CA: Golden Sufi Center, 1999.

Kohut, Heinz. *Self Psychology and Humanities.* New York: W. W. Norton and Company, Inc., 1980.

Levenda, Peter. *Stairway to Heaven: Chinese Alchemists, Jewish Kabbalists, and the Art of Spiritual Transformation.* New York: The Continuum International Publishing Group Inc., 2008.

Lindsay, Jack. *The Origins of Alchemy in Graeco-Roman Egypt.* New York: Barnes & Noble, 1970.

Mahler, Margaret, Fred Pine, and Anni Bergman. *The Psychological Birth of the Human Infant: Symbiosis and Individuation.* New York: Basic Books, 2000.

Malkowski, Edward F. *The Spiritual Technology of Ancient Egypt: Sacred Science and the Mystery of Consciousness.* Rochester, VT: Inner Traditions, 2007.

Mead, G. R. S. *Corpus Hermeticum.* Charleston, SC: BiblioLife, 2009.

———. *Thrice-Greatest Hermes: Studies in Hellenistic Theosophy and Gnosis.* York Beach, MN: Samuel Weiser, 1992.

Meeks, Dimitri, and Christine Favard-Meeks. *Daily Life of the Egyptian Gods.* Ithaca, NY: Cornell University Press, 1996.

Mitchell, Stephen, ed. *The Enlightened Mind: An Anthology of Sacred Prose.* New York: HarperCollins Publishers, 1991.

Mojsov, Bojana. *Osiris: Death and Afterlife of a God.* Malden, ME: Blackwell Publishing, 2005.

Monick, Eugene. *Phallos: Sacred Image of the Masculine.* Toronto: Inner City Books, 1987.

Moore, Thomas. *The Planets Within: The Astrological Psychology of Marsilio Ficino.* Great Barrington, MA: Lindisfarne Press, 1990.

Naydler, Jeremy. *The Future of the Ancient World.* Rochester, VT: Inner Traditions, 2009.

———. *Shamanic Wisdom in the Pyramid Texts: The Mystical Tradition of Ancient Egypt.* Rochester, VT: Inner Traditions, 2005.

———. *Temple of the Cosmos: The Ancient Egyptian Experience of the Sacred.* Rochester, VT: Inner Traditions, 1996.

Neumann, Erich. *The Origins and History of Consciousness.* Translated by R. F. C. Hull. Princeton: Princeton University Press, 1995.

Norman, Dorothy. *The Hero: Myth, Image, Symbol.* New York: World Publication, Co., 1969.

O'Donohue, John. *Anam Cara: A Book of Celtic Wisdom*. New York: Cliff Street Books, 1997.

Otto, Walter. *Dionysus: Myth and Cult*. Bloomington, IN: Indiana University Press, 1965.

Purce, Jill. *The Mystic Spiral*. New York: Thames and Hudson, 1974.

Rankind, Dan. *Heka: The Practices of Ancient Egyptian Ritual and Magic*. London: Avalonia, 2006.

Reidy, John, ed. *Thomas Norton's Ordinal of Alchemy*. London: Oxford University Press, 1975.

Roberts, Alison. *My Heart My Mother: Death and Rebirth in Ancient Egypt*. East Sussex, England: Northgate Publishers, 2000.

Russell, Bertrand. *History of Western Philosophy*. 2nd ed. New York: Routledge, 2004.

Salaman, Clement, Dorine van Oyen, and William Wharton, trans. *The Way of Hermes: New Translations of The Corpus Hermeticum and The Definitions of Hermes Trismegistus to Asclepius*. Rochester, VT: Inner Traditions, 2000.

Sauneron, Serge. *The Priests of Ancient Egypt*. New ed. Translated by David Lorton. Ithaca, NY: Cornell University Press, 2000.

Schimmel, Annemarie. *The Mystery of Numbers*. Oxford: Oxford University Press, 1993.

Simpson, William Kelly, and Robert W. Reiter, trans. *The Literature of Ancient Egypt: An Anthology of Stories, Instructions, Stelae, Autobiographies, and Poetry*. 3rd ed. New Haven, CT: Yale University Press, 2003.

St. John of the Cross. *The Essential St. John of the Cross: Ascent of Mount Carmel, Dark Night of the Soul, A Spiritual Canticle of the Soul, and Twenty Poems*. San Francisco: Wilder Publications: 2008.

Stevenson, Robert Louis. *Dr. Jekyll and Mr. Hyde*. New York: Grosset & Dunlap, 1981.

Velde, H. te. *Seth, God of Confusion: A Study of His Role in Egyptian Mythology and Religion*. Leiden: E.J. Brill, 1967.

von Franz, Marie-Louise. *Alchemy: An Introduction to the Symbolism and the Psychology.* Toronto: Inner City Books, 1980.

———. *The Golden Ass of Apuleius: The Liberation of the Feminine in Man.* Boston: Shambhala Publications, 1972.

———. *On Dreams and Death: A Jungian Interpretation.* New ed. La Salle, IL: Open Court, 1998.

———. *Psyche and Matter.* Boston: Shambhala Publications, 1988.

Watson, Lyall. *Lifetide.* New York: Bantam Books, 1979.

West, John Anthony. *Serpent in the Sky: The High Wisdom of Ancient Egypt.* 1st Quest ed. Wheaton, IL: Quest Books, 1993.

Wheeler, Ramona Louise. *Walk Like an Egyptian: A Guide to Ancient Egyptian Religion and Philosophy.* Rockville, MD: Wildside Press, 2005.

Wilkinson, Richard H. *The Complete Gods and Goddesses of Ancient Egypt.* New York: Thames & Hudson, 2003.

———. *Symbol and Magic in Egyptian Art.* New York: Thames and Hudson, 1994.

Zweig, Connie, and Jeremiah Abrams. *Meeting the Shadow: The Hidden Power of the Dark Side of Human Nature,* New York: Tarcher, 1998.

ILLUSTRATION CREDITS

Frontispiece. Djed Pillar and Osiris (Zahi Hawass, *The Royal Tombs of Egypt* [London: Thames and Hudson, 2006], 80; photograph by Sandro Vannini).

Page 33   Figure 1.1. Ra in the Solar Boat (Zahi Hawass, *The Royal Tombs of Egypt* [London: Thames and Hudson, 2006], 98; photograph by Sandro Vannini).

Page 34   Figure 1.2. Apis Bull (Zahi Hawass, *The Royal Tombs of Egypt* [London: Thames and Hudson, 2006], 137; photograph by Sandro Vannini).

Page 73   Figure 3.1. Nun supporting the Solar Boat (British Museum, Papyrus of Anhai).

Page 76   Figure 3.2. Nut, Geb, and Shu (Louvre, Paris).

Page 84   Figure 4.1. Osiris with wheat growing from his body (reprinted in Marie-Louise von Franz, *On Dreams and Death: A Jungian Interpretation* [La Salle, IL: Open Court, 1998] 11, fig. 2).

Page 94   Figure 5.1. Entombed King (Stanislas Klossowski De Rola, *The Golden Game: Alchemical Engravings of the Seventeenth Century* [London: Thames and Hudson, 1988], 93, #73; reprinted from Michael Maier, *Atalanta fugiens*).

Page 98   Figure 5.2. Dissolving King (Stanislas Klossowski De Rola, *The Golden Game: Alchemical Engravings of the Seventeenth Century* [London: Thames and Hudson, 1988], 86, #60; reprinted from Michael Maier, *Atalanta fugiens*).

Page 110   Figure 6.1. Phallic Tree (Stanislas Klossowski De Rola, *Alchemy: The Secret Art* [New York: Avon Books, 1973], image 39; reprinted from *Miscellanea d'alchemia*, [Ashburnham 1166], Bibliotheca Medic-Laurenziana, Florence).

Page 113   Figure 6.2. Spiral Pschent Crown, detail (Zahi Hawass, *The Royal Tombs of Egypt* [London: Thames and Hudson, 2006] 296; photograph by Sandro Vannini).

Page 115   Figure 6.3. Raising the Djed Pillar (photograph from author's personal collection).

Page 137   Figure 8.1. The Golden Head (The British Library, MS Harley 3469).

Page 172   Figure 10.1. Mercurius (Johannes Fabricius, *Alchemy: The Medieval Alchemists and their Royal Art* [Copenhagen: International Booksellers and Publishers, 1976], 83, fig. 141; reprinted from *Mutus Libra*, France).

Page 192   Figure 12.1. Akhenaten worshipping Aten (Egyptian Museum, Cairo).

Page 203   Figure 12.2. The Field of Reeds (British Museum, London).

Index

in ancient Egypt, 50, 191, 196
archetypes and, 35, 71–72
Jung and, 47, 48, 52
in modern science, 2
Osiris and, 52, 71, 102, 155
Coming Forth by Day, The, 59
coniunctio, 199
consciousness. *See also* collective consciousness
  body and, 200–201
  development of, 2, 83, 96, 116–18,
    167, 196–98
  differentiation and, 77
  divine, 197
  Eastern thoughts on, 66
  expansion and contraction of, 36–37
  great civilizations and, 25
  modern science and, 197
  myths and, 48, 74, 77
  Osiris and, 65
Coomaraswamy, Ananda, 113
Corbin, Henry, 5
Corpus Hermeticum, 1, 4, 202, 209,
  230n.3 (4)
creation
  by autofellatio, 74
  Egyptians' view of, 43–44, 72–80, 162,
    247–48n.1 (166)
  gods and, 122, 123, 154, 173, 196,
    215–19
  of individual, 199, 207
  power of, 5
  story of, 6, 16, 21, 72–80
creatrix, 75

de Lille, Alain, 208
de Lubicz, R. A. Schwaller, 21, 28–29,
  239–240n.5 (85)
death
  Akhenaten and, 38, 194
  of consciousness, 41

creation and, 44
dealing with, 16, 97, 204–7
Egyptians' view of, 2, 3, 16–17, 41–44,
  96, 99, 101, 103, 144–46, 160, 185
excess and, 102
fear of, 5, 204–6
Hornung on, 43
of Horus, 160
individuation and, 2, 4, 103
of Jesus, 143
Jung on, 96
kings and, 32, 36
Osiris and, 4, 17, 21, 32, 37, 40, 49,
  58–59, 63–66, 95, 96, 105, 154,
  208, 220–21, xii
Saturn and, 92
Seth and, 60
decapitation. *See* dismemberment
*Definitions of Hermes Trismegistus to
  Asclepius, The*, (Salaman, trans.)
  230n.3 (4)
Demeter, 63, 129
Dersin, Denise, 111
differentiation, 77
Dionysus, 109, 241–42n.4 (109)
dismemberment
  alchemy and, 137–38, 148
  Golden Head, 137–40, 137 fig. 8.1
  individuation and, 23
  Osiris and, 10, 22, 134–38, 143, 145,
    160, 175, 208, 245n.3 (136)
  views of, 135, 136, 138–40, 151
  Zosimos and, 235–36n.6 (53)
Divine Mind, 141
Divine Self, 49, 118, 243n.23 (118)
djed pillar/column
  figure of, ii, 115 fig. 6.3
  numbers and, 136
  Osiris and, 64–65, 174, 221
  as spinal column, 114, 119
Dorn, Gerhard, 147, 203

ABOUT THE AUTHOR

Thom F. Cavalli, PhD, is a licensed clinical psychologist in private practice in Santa Ana, California. His first book, *Alchemical Psychology: Old Recipes for Living in a New World,* is a popular text used by students and teachers of psychological alchemy as well as psychotherapists in the United States and abroad. Thom is a favorite in the speaking circuit, where for the past several years he has given seminars at the annual International Alchemy Conference. Other scholarly seminars and workshops include presentations at Esalen Institute, the Philosophical Research Society, the C. G. Jung Institute of Los Angeles, and the Bowers Museum. He has appeared on national television and recorded on radio at the University of California, Irvine. For more information about Dr. Cavalli's work, visit his Web sites at www.AlchemicalPsychology.com and Cavallibooks.com, or email illavac@hotmail.com.

Contact Information
Thom F. Cavalli, PhD
2030 East Fourth Street
Suite 134
Santa Ana, CA 92705
714.972.0056

Quest Books

encourages open-minded inquiry into
world religions, philosophy, science, and the arts
in order to understand the wisdom of the ages,
respect the unity of all life, and help people explore
individual spiritual self-transformation.

Its publications are generously supported by
The Kern Foundation,
a trust committed to Theosophical education.

Quest Books is the imprint of
the Theosophical Publishing House,
a division of the Theosophical Society in America.
For information about programs, literature,
on-line study, membership benefits, and international centers,
see www.theosophical.org
or call 800-669-1571 or (outside the U.S.) 630-668-1571.

Related Quest Titles

Dreams of Isis, by Normandi Ellis

*Feasts of Light: Celebrations for the Seasons of Life
Based on the Egyptian Goddess Mysteries,*
by Normandi Ellis

Serpent in the Sky: The High Wisdom of Ancient Egypt,
by John Anthony West

The Traveler's Key to Ancient Egypt, by John Anthony West

To order books or a complete Quest catalog,
call 800-669-9425 or (outside the U.S.) 630-665-0130.

Praise for Thom F. Cavalli's
EMBODYING OSIRIS

"A refreshingly humane and insightful exploration of the interrelationships between depth psychology, alchemy, and the religion of ancient Egypt. Thom Cavalli shows that depth psychology has much to gain from opening itself to the rich and fecund world of the ancient Egyptian religious imagination."

—**Jeremy Naydler, Ph.D.,** author of *Temple of the Cosmos:*
The Ancient Egyptian Experience of the Sacred

"Brilliant! Thom Cavalli's interpretations of the Osiris myth have the power to reawaken our own capacity for imaginal apprehension. We are helped to recognize that the gods, and particularly this god, continue to live in our souls long after they have apparently died."

—**Christine Downing,** Professor of Mythological Studies,
Pacifica Graduate Institute, author of *The Goddess:*
Mythological Images of the Feminine and *Gods in Our Midst*

"Dr. Cavalli brings a brilliant new interpretation to the Osiris myth that connects with its deep archetypal power and proves its continuing relevance to our times. He reveals the secret alchemical operations hidden in it and describes ways to implement them in the step-by-step process of "Becoming Osiris." His groundbreaking research shows the myth to be a central archetype of transformation in alchemy, religion, psychology, and many other traditions."

—**Dennis Hauck,** Alchemist, author of
The Emerald Tablet: Alchemy for Personal Transformation

"A groundbreaking and much needed study of the connection between alchemy and the mysteries of ancient Egypt. Cavalli interweaves history, myth, and the evolution of human consciousness in a remarkable way. By taking us on a journey through the trials of Osiris, Cavalli not only illuminates the transformation that lies at the heart of alchemy but touches the very depths of the human soul."

—**Cherry Gilchrist**, author of
Explore Alchemy and *Everyday Alchemy*

"Thom Cavalli penetrates to the heart of the Osiris myth with a fresh eye, discovering an archetypal prefiguration of the modern soul and a foundational root of both depth psychology and alchemy. With his keen understanding of Jungian psychology and sensitivity to symbolic meaning, he takes us on a journey through the sacred history of the gods and into the consulting room of a master psychologist. I believe C. G. Jung would have welcomed this work as a creative continuation of his own discoveries".

—**Stanton Marlan, Ph.D.**, Jungian analyst, president of the
Pittsburgh Society of Jungian Analysts, author of
The Black Sun: The Alchemy and Art of Darkness

"In this fascinating study of Egypt and the myth of Osiris, Thom Cavalli brings to bear not only scholarship but imaginative insight to uncover a wide range of meanings. He reveals not only how the image of Osiris influenced the development of alchemy but also how it contains truths still of profound importance for those seeking wholeness and spiritual fulfillment."

—**Jeffrey Raff, Ph.D.**, Jungian analyst, author of
Jung and the Alchemical Imagination